THE HOLY TRINITY
IN THE LIFE
OF THE CHURCH

HOLY CROSS STUDIES
IN PATRISTIC THEOLOGY AND HISTORY

Previously published in the series

Wealth and Poverty in Early Church and Society
edited by Susan R. Holman

Apocalyptic Thought in Early Christianity
edited by Robert J. Daly, SJ

THE HOLY TRINITY
IN THE LIFE
OF THE CHURCH

EDITED BY
KHALED ANATOLIOS

Baker Academic
a division of Baker Publishing Group
Grand Rapids, Michigan

ORTHODOX
PRESS

© 2014 by Holy Cross Greek Orthodox School of Theology

Published by Baker Academic
a division of Baker Publishing Group
P.O. Box 6287, Grand Rapids, MI 49516-6287
www.bakeracademic.com

Printed and bound by CPI Group (UK) Ltd, Croydon, CR0 4YY

Library of Congress Cataloging-in-Publication Data
The holy trinity in the life of the church / edited by Khaled Anatolios.
        pages cm. — (Holy Cross studies in patristic theology and history)
    Includes bibliographical references and index.
    ISBN 978-0-8010-4897-5 (pbk. : alk. paper)
    1. Trinity—History of doctrines. I. Anatolios, Khaled, 1962–
BT111.3.H65 2014
231'.044—dc23   2014017530

Unless noted otherwise, translations of ancient writings are those of the authors.

Scripture quotations labeled KJV are from the King James Version of the Bible.

Scripture quotations labeled NRSV are from the New Revised Standard Version of the Bible, copyright © 1989, by the Division of Christian Education of the National Council of the Churches of Christ in the United States of America. Used by permission. All rights reserved.

Scripture quotations labeled RSV are from the Revised Standard Version of the Bible, copyright 1952 [2nd edition, 1971] by the Division of Christian Education of the National Council of the Churches of Christ in the United States of America. Used by permission. All rights reserved.

14 15 16 17 18 19 20   7 6 5 4 3 2 1

CONTENTS

v

Part 3. The Trinity and Ecclesial Being

FOREWORD

FATHER NICK TRIANTAFILOU
*President of Holy Cross Greek Orthodox School
of Theology and Hellenic College*

Holy Cross Studies in Patristic Theology and History is the first publication project of the Pappas Patristic Institute of Holy Cross Greek Orthodox School of Theology in Brookline, Massachusetts. This institute, founded in 2003 with a generous gift from Stephen and Catherine Pappas, has as its goal the advancement of patristic studies in the service of the academy and of the church. It does this by supporting ecumenically sensitive and academically open research and study in the Greek patristic tradition in conversation with other ancient Christian traditions. The Institute carries forward its mission through the leadership of its board of directors composed of scholars from the Orthodox, Roman Catholic, and Protestant traditions and headed by the Rev. Dr. Robert Daly, SJ, and its director, Dr. Bruce Beck.

One of the primary ways in which the Institute works toward this goal is through a series of annual fall conferences focusing on patristic themes that have the power to shed light on contemporary concerns. Each year, in collaboration with Baker Academic, the Institute invites established scholars to contribute papers on the theme of the conference. In order to disseminate to a broad readership the insights achieved by scholars participating in these conferences, the Institute invited Baker Academic, in cooperation with Holy Cross Orthodox Press, to publish the fruits of these annual conferences in a series of attractive volumes.

A prominent characteristic of the Orthodox tradition is its understanding that patristic theology is integral to all of Christian thought and life. It is our hope that the volumes published in this series will effectively mediate the rich legacy of the early church to our contemporary world—including Christians of all traditions—which is thirsting and hungering for such food.

PREFACE

The self-proclaimed renaissance of trinitarian theology has been going on for some time now, and we are arguably past the point of reveling in its mere promise and at a juncture where we can ask for an account of its tangible results. Unfortunately, it is by no means self-evident that these results amount to a resounding success. This hesitation is all the more warranted if we decline to regard as the only criterion of success the circulation of certain "trinitarian concepts," such as the primacy of relationality, among the guild of academic theologians and if we insist, rather, as Rahner put it in one of the pioneering texts calling for this renewal, that such success depends also on "understand[ing] and present[ing] the doctrine of the Trinity in such a way that it may become a reality in the concrete life of the faithful."[1] To what extent is trinitarian doctrine today a vital reality in the concrete life of the faithful?

Behind this question, now as much as when Rahner raised the issue, lurks the unsettling perception of a disproportion between the primacy and centrality of trinitarian doctrine, on the one hand, and its seemingly vague and dim presence in the consciousness of ordinary Christians, on the other. Of course, theologians can protest that they are not wholly responsible for the wide dissemination of their insights among the faithful. It is enough that they have sowed the seeds of elucidating the significance of trinitarian doctrine; it is for other laborers in the field to nurture these seeds to germination and fruition among the Christian laity. The partial justness of that rejoinder can be readily conceded, and yet it is still advisable to consider whether the prevailing strategies of approaching trinitarian theology, even within its modern "renewal," are somehow deficient, and indeed whether the whole "lost and found" narrative

---

1. Karl Rahner, *The Trinity*, trans. Joseph Donceel (New York: Crossroad, 2004), 10.

that is often implied in the self-proclamation of this "renewal" is somehow distorted. As to the latter, Bruce Marshall has astutely shown that it is highly problematic to presume that the most essential foundation of Christian faith has been simply missing from the practice of that faith for many centuries and needs to be reinserted by modern renovations of trinitarian theology. Marshall argues:

> But the idea that such a profound deformation of Christianity has occurred at all seems implausible. . . . If this doctrine really is the most essential Christian teaching, and articulates the most basic Christian beliefs about who God is, how could Christians be generally ignorant of it or indifferent to it? If there actually are communities whose identity turns on [trinitarian faith], then their members must generally know *how* to be trinitarian in their identification of God and their everyday religious life, even if they lack much explicit knowledge *about* the doctrine of the Trinity. Of course it is almost always worthwhile to try to make implicit knowledge more explicit, not least to head off possible distortions of communal belief and practice. But this should not be confused with restoring trinitarian conviction to the church, as though it were not even implicit, and to be put there by theologians.[2]

Marshall's distinction between "explicit knowledge *about*" trinitarian doctrine and the way that that doctrine operates in Christian life helps not only to resolve the conundrum posed by the "lost and found" narrative of trinitarian renewal but also to point the way to just how this renewal may bear the kind of tangible fruit that Rahner desired. The fundamental task for the renewal of trinitarian theology must be not to divine a hitherto unknown insight into the mystery of trinitarian being, but rather to draw attention to the ways in which that mystery is signified through all the aspects of Christian faith and practice. As the biblical Jacob woke from his vision of a ladder to heaven with the angels of God ascending and descending on it and declared, "Surely the LORD is in this place—and I did not know it!" (Gen. 28:16 NRSV), so must the renewal of trinitarian theology provide the resources to enable ordinary Christians to see how the inner contents of Christian faith and its outward vision of all reality are entirely permeated by the self-manifestation of the trinitarian God: "Surely the Trinity is in all this place, and I did not know it."

In my *Retrieving Nicaea*, I argued that the development of the formulation of trinitarian doctrine itself was constituted by a comprehensive interpretation of all aspects of Christian faith and practice as signifying the presence and

---

2. Bruce Marshall, "The Trinity," in *The Blackwell Companion to Modern Theology*, ed. Gareth Jones (Oxford: Blackwell, 2004), 193.

activity of Father, Son, and Spirit, each fully God, together one God.[3] Correspondingly, it has been one of the fundamental tenets of the modern renewal of trinitarian theology that trinitarian doctrine must inform the entirety of Christian faith. It was Karl Rahner again who complained of the "isolation of Trinitarian doctrine in piety and textbook theology,"[4] yet it is hard to escape the conclusion that this isolation persisted in Rahner's own work and still significantly characterizes too many of our modern treatments of trinitarian theology. This judgment should not be distorted into an assertion that modern theology utterly fails to draw connections between trinitarian doctrine and Christian faith and practice, as a whole, but should be recognized as indicating only an impatience that there are still not enough theological resources to provide the Christian faithful with the means of seeing how trinitarian theology is *already there* in all authentic Christian faith and practice—in certain ways of reading Scripture, celebrating the sacraments, understanding human nature, and so on. The renewal of trinitarian theology has not by any means been an abject failure, but perhaps the momentum that will carry it to a decisive success lies in just this direction.

The Pappas Patristic Institute, sponsored by the Holy Cross Greek Orthodox School of Theology, gathered together a number of notable scholars in 2008 for a conference entitled "The Trinity in the Life of the Church." Without any further elaboration, the very title of the conference witnessed to a vision consistent with my remarks above. The conference participants were to speak not simply of the Trinity as such but of the manifestation of the Trinity in the concrete life of the church. This volume consists of the essays originally presented at that conference, supplemented with some others that I, as editor, in consultation with the Pappas Patristic Institute and Baker Academic, deemed to be constructive to the fuller development of the theme of the conference. The collection does not purport to bring the renewal of trinitarian doctrine to its complete fulfillment, but our hope is that it provides some resources for an increased attentiveness to the pervasively trinitarian matrix of Christian faith and practice.

In his contribution, John Behr warns us of the distorting effect of the modern tendency to separate the integral mystery of the Christian economy into isolated compartments. This caution being heeded, it remains possible and indeed unavoidable to contemplate the one mystery as refracted from different perspectives. In this volume, it just so happened that a threefold framework

---

3. Khaled Anatolios, *Retrieving Nicaea: The Development and Meaning of Trinitarian Doctrine* (Grand Rapids: Baker Academic, 2011), esp. 7–13.

4. Rahner, *The Trinity*, 10.

suggested itself as a useful way to organize the essays it comprises (I leave it to the reader to judge whether this framework suggests a valid trinitarian *vestigium*): the Trinity in Christian Worship; Jesus Christ, the Trinity, and Christian Salvation; and the Trinity and Ecclesial Being.

In part 1, our initiatory essay is Joseph Lienhard's "The Baptismal Command (Matthew 28:19–20) and the Doctrine of the Trinity." As an exemplary illustration of how the church's trinitarian doctrine developed out of and as interpretation of the sacramental life of the church, Lienhard identifies some key points along the path whereby the baptismal rite gave rise to the church's trinitarian creed. He demonstrates how the retreading of this path impresses upon us the necessary unity of Scripture, liturgy, doctrine, and theology, which is indispensable for an authentic appropriation of trinitarian doctrine as it is for an appropriation of Christian faith in general.

Robert Daly's "Eucharist and Trinity in the Liturgies of the Early Church" also traces the dialectic of the church's rule of prayer (*lex orandi*) and rule of faith (*lex credendi*), this time from the perspective of the manifestation of trinitarian faith in the early church's celebration of the Eucharist. Daly shows how the eucharistic prayers of the early church gradually developed, reaching maturity in the fourth and fifth centuries. In the fourth century, we find eucharistic prayers expressing both Nicene and anti-Nicene theologies, despite common ground on the understanding of the transforming presence of Christ in the Eucharist. As Lienhard's essay provides resources for an increased attentiveness to the trinitarian structure and meaning of baptism, so Daly's article helps us to see the Eucharist as a privileged disclosure of the trinitarian mystery.

The theme of the role of worship in trinitarian faith is continued by Paul Hartog's "The Nascent 'Trinitarian' Worship of *Martyrdom of Polycarp* 14 and Ephesians 1." Hartog analyzes the trinitarian form of the hagiographical material that purports to be the martyr Polycarp's final dying prayer, and he finds that the text reflects early liturgical material. He identifies Ephesians 1:3–14 as a background to the trinitarian form of thanksgiving and praise in this prayer and thus places it within a trajectory that runs from the New Testament to the standardized trinitarian doxologies of the fourth century.

Nonna Harrison concludes this section with her essay, "Gregory of Nyssa on Knowing the Trinity." Harrison's essay presupposes that the church's prayer already identifies each of the divine persons distinctly and glorifies them together as one God. Her concern is not with the sources and developments of the church's trinitarian prayer, as are the essays that precede hers. Rather, she looks to Gregory of Nyssa for a theological exposition that can support the church's practice of trinitarian prayers. She finds this support in Nyssen's account of how the structure of origination of the trinitarian persons—the Father as source, the Son begotten immediately from the Father, the Spirit proceeding from the Father through the mediation of the Son—is manifest in all the divine activity toward creation. Nyssen's theology of trinitarian self-disclosure can help us to be attentive to the glorious mystery of God's trinitarian being that is disclosed through his creative and salvific beneficence toward us.

Part 2, which focuses on the disclosure of the Trinity in Jesus Christ and his salvific work, is inaugurated by John McGuckin's "The Holy Trinity as the Dynamic of the World's Salvation in the Greek Fathers," which also provides a bridge between this section and our opening contemplation of the Trinity in the church's worship. McGuckin insists emphatically that the proper matrix for trinitarian doctrine is doxological; the ultimate warrant of a doctrinal approach is its demonstrable consistency with the church's liturgy. The church's worship is permeated by the power of the trinitarian name, which refers not only to the unfathomable and ineffable glory of divine being but also to the perfect articulation of that glory in the crucified and risen Jesus. McGuckin encourages us to reencounter patristic trinitarian theology from this vital liturgical and existential perspective, which was the ambience of patristic theology itself.

The fruits of heeding such an exhortation are in full evidence in the succeeding essay, Brian Daley's "Maximus the Confessor and John of Damascus on the Trinity." Transcending the common recognition of how the "nature-person" language of trinitarian doctrine was foundational for the development of christological doctrine, Daley shows how, in turn, christological doctrine and language were employed to contemplate the trinitarian mystery. He presents two of the great synthesizers of patristic theology, Maximus the Confessor and John of Damascus, as exemplars of this approach. Daley's first concern is with how both Maximus and the Damascene considered trinitarian contemplation as the summit of liturgical and mystical experience. Within this contemplation, the christological mystery of the divine-human unity without confusion and of the divine-human distinction without separation finds its ultimate foundation in the unity within distinction of the trinitarian persons. Daley also analyzes the interplay of christological and trinitarian language and concepts in Maximus's understanding of deification and the Damascene's conception of trinitarian mutual indwelling (*perichōrēsis*). The existential and practical application of this interplay of trinitarian and christological doctrine is ultimately the conviction that the way to the Trinity is Christ: conformity to Christ's way of love enables us to be enfolded in the Spirit-filled community of the church as sons and daughters of the Father.

The way to the Trinity through Christ is also the subject of Matthew Drever's "Deification in Augustine: Plotinian or Trinitarian?" In this essay, Drever joins the growing chorus of scholars who have recently rushed to the defense of Augustine against accusations that he represents a Western essentialist and solipsistic trinitarian doctrine that is incompatible with an Eastern personalist and existential approach. Drever analyzes Augustine's presentation of the human ascent to God as substantively amounting to a doctrine of deification. Moreover, our path to God does not come about through introverted contemplation, as in the Plotinian tradition, but rather through our assimilation to Christ's humility and through sacramental participation in Christ's body, the church, whose unity is effected by the Spirit.

Patristic trinitarian theology was closely bound with a soteriological doctrine of deification. In Athanasius and the Cappadocians, we often encounter the argument that Christ and the Spirit must be fully divine because they divinize human beings and only true and unmitigated divinity can divinize. But the subsequent reception of the doctrine of deification was considerably complicated, especially in the Protestant traditions, by later disagreements about grace and justification. In view of this consideration, the patristic studies presented at the original conference that gave rise to this book are here supplemented by a magisterial article by Bruce Marshall, "Justification as Declaration and Deification." In this article, Marshall wrestles with the seeming contradiction in Luther's work between the conception of justification as a deifying personal union with Christ that transforms the believer such that she becomes "one person" with Christ and the equally emphatic understanding of justification as a forensic declaration whereby we are merely "reckoned" righteous through God's overlooking our sinfulness. Marshall concludes that the resolution to this conundrum can be found only in a properly trinitarian conception of salvation and justification. We are "reckoned" righteous not merely by God's turning a blind eye, as it were, to our sins and pretending that we are righteous when we are not really so, but rather because the Father loves us and judges us entirely within his love for his only begotten Son and his judgment on the Son's salvific work on our behalf. Christ's identification with our condition also wins for us the reception of the Spirit, which frees us from the law and the wrath of God. Marshall originally wrote this piece as a Lutheran and has since joined the Catholic Church. As a Catholic, he is still convinced that the integration of forensic and transformational elements must follow this trinitarian pattern, even if he now concedes that this integration was not fully realized by Luther himself. Regardless of adjustments to his estimation of Luther's success in realizing this integration, Marshall's essay stands as a profound meditation on the trinitarian content of salvation and deification.

Part 3 of this volume turns to the subject of the church's imaging of and participation in the life of the divine Trinity. Fundamental to this theme is the question of the analogical correspondence between human and divine personhood and communion. In the introductory essay of this section, "Personhood, Communion, and the Trinity in Some Patristic Texts," I acknowledge the truism that notions of personhood and communion in patristic theology have a different content than is signified by modern conceptions of these terms, but I argue against a facile extension of this truism to the blanket assertion that there is simply no continuity between modern and patristic versions of these conceptions. There are patristic resources for contemplating the divine persons as intentional, active, speaking agents who enjoy relationships of mutual delight and glorification. Such a contemplation can ground and motivate the human vocation to participate in the trinitarian life of God, a vocation fulfilled in the church.

John Behr's essay, "The Trinitarian Being of the Church," takes issue with a conception of the church as trinitarian image in which the church and the divine Trinity remain juxtaposed as parallel realities, as if the church is called to merely imitate trinitarian being. Rather, scriptural images of the church as "the people of God," "the body of Christ," and "the temple of the Spirit" should lead us to see the proper being of the church as located within the trinitarian relations. The church is called into being by the Father as the body of Christ animated by the Spirit; conversely, the church is enabled by its incorporation into Christ and its anointing by the Spirit to call upon God as Abba, in thanksgiving and praise. Behr also draws our attention to the necessity of distinguishing between the eschatological fulfillment of the church's calling to the fullness of trinitarian indwelling and the church's historical pilgrimage. This distinction should lead even those who profess to constitute the true church from overreaching toward the claim that they are also thereby the perfect church.

Thomas Cattoi furthers the reflection of the trinitarian being of the church in his essay, "The Relevance of Gregory of Nyssa's *Ad Ablabium* for Catholic-Orthodox Ecumenical Dialogue on the Trinity and the Church." In 2007, the Joint International Commission for the Theological Dialogue between the Roman Catholic and the Orthodox Church produced a document entitled "Ecclesiological and Canonical Consequences of the Sacramental Life of the Church: Ecclesial Communion, Conciliarity, and Authority," often cited as the "Ravenna Document." Cattoi notes that this document likens the ideal relation between the different local churches, manifesting a unity without inequality, to the communion of persons within the divine Trinity, in which there is no subordination. Expressing a critique from a Roman Catholic perspective, he finds the document lacking in a theological rationale for the primacy of the Roman Church and endeavors to find this rationale in Gregory of Nyssa's conception of the Father as the source of the other two divine persons. Within this trinitarian framework, the Roman Church would be considered as "ontologically equal" to the other churches but also as "the foundation of inner ecclesial order" and "invested with authority over all other ecclesial communities." Of the various rejoinders to this proposal that can be anticipated, one is whether such a model would correspond too much to Behr's evocation of the conception of the church extrinsically mimicking trinitarian being (If a certain church holds the place of the Father, is there another church or group of churches that holds the place of Christ and that of the Spirit, respectively?), while departing from the reality of the church's participation in trinitarian life precisely as the body of Christ who calls to the Father in the Spirit. Be that as it may, surely the way forward must be to keep the dialogue on the true nature of the church anchored in the contemplation of the trinitarian life that indwells the church, as both Behr and Cattoi aspire to do.

The final essay of this section, Kathleen McVey's "Syriac Christian Tradition and Gender in Trinitarian Theology," deals with the troubling fact that the trinitarian name, which is the warp and woof of the church's liturgical life, brings discomfort to many Christians, who interpret it as signifying the maleness of God and the ontological inferiority of human females. McVey recommends Ephrem the Syrian as a valuable resource for responding to this modern problem. Ephrem asserted both the utter transcendence of God and God's benevolent willingness to be clothed with human speech. He distinguished the "exact" names of God, which include "Father," and the "borrowed" names by which the plenitude of the riches of divine being can be appropriately imaged through creaturely likenesses. Among the latter, Ephrem applied maternal imagery to God, speaking of God as a nursing mother and of Christ as "the Living Breast" at which all of creation is suckled. McVey recommends following Ephrem's example by a greater use of female imagery in speaking of God, coupled with an awareness of the limits of applying creaturely categories and language to refer to God's transcendent being.

To conclude this volume, Brian Daley's "A God in Whom We Live: Ministering the Trinitarian God" contrasts the modern reluctance to speak of the mystery of the Trinity, painfully evident in the studied evasions of many a preacher on "Trinity Sunday," with the trinitarian fluency of the patristic proclamation and contemplation of the church's faith. What enabled this patristic fluency was an integral focus not reducible to the devising of logical categories to describe divine being but rather centered on the Trinity as the place in which all of Christian life happens. This is not to say that the trinitarian God has no self-sustaining objective reality, but rather that we have doxological access to this reality precisely through our sharing in it: the Trinity *in whom* we live. It is to be hoped that the contents of this volume will contribute to the church's ongoing quest to be doxologically attentive to the trinitarian life that grounds and animates its being.

Khaled Anatolios

PART 1

THE TRINITY IN CHRISTIAN WORSHIP

1

The Baptismal Command (Matthew 28:19–20) and the Doctrine of the Trinity

Joseph T. Lienhard, SJ

When I first read Gregory of Nyssa's *Great Catechetical Oration*, or, as it is sometimes called, the *Address on Religious Instruction*, one paragraph caught my attention, and it has held it ever since. Toward the end of the treatise Gregory writes:

> We are taught in the gospel that there are three Persons and Names through whom believers come to be born. He who is born of the Trinity is born equally of Father, Son, and Holy Spirit. For this is how the gospel speaks about the Spirit: "That which is born of the Spirit is spirit" [John 3:6]. Paul, moreover, gives birth "in Christ" [1 Cor. 4:15], and the Father is the "Father of all" [cf. Eph. 4:6]. And here I ask the reader to judge soberly, lest he make himself the offspring of an unstable nature, when he could have that which is unchangeable as the source of his life. For what happens in the sacrament of baptism depends upon the disposition of the heart of him who approaches it. If he confesses that the holy Trinity is uncreated, then he enters on the life which is unchanging. But if, on a false supposition, he sees a created nature in the Trinity and then is baptized into *that*, he is born once more to a life which is subject to change. For offspring and parents necessarily share the same nature. Which, then, is more

advantageous: to enter upon the life which is unchanging or to be tossed about once more in a life of instability and fluctuation?[1]

The words spoken at baptism are powerful words, Gregory says; they can incorporate us into the true God or into a false god, depending on what words are used and what meaning is intended. So, be careful of what God you are baptized into. Baptism is a form of paternity, and offspring share the nature of their parents. If you are baptized into an Arian or Anomoean god,[2] then you are the offspring of a mutable god, and you are baptized into a life that is subject to change, a life of instability and fluctuation. If you are baptized into the Trinity who is three Persons and three Names, the Three who are equal, then you enter into a life that is unchanging; so, know who your Father is before you are baptized into him.

There is far more than a rhetorical conceit here. Gregory is drawing a close connection between the words spoken at baptism and the reality of God himself. The passage raises an important topic: the relation between baptism in the Triple Name, on the one hand, and Christian faith in the Trinity and the theology of the Trinity in the early church, on the other.

The fathers of the church often used Matthew 28:19 in their doctrinal and theological argumentation. In some significant passages in their writings, they cited the baptismal command (Matt. 28:19) more or less verbatim and drew doctrinal or theological conclusions from it. The texts that meet these criteria are not numerous, but the ones that do are quite interesting. They fall roughly into three groups. The first group consists of passages relating the baptismal command to the development of the creed and, later, to the explication of the creed. The second group includes passages dealing with a specific, single word in the baptismal command and drawing a conclusion from the sense of that single word. The third group comprises passages that make more general theological points when quoting the baptismal command.

The Baptismal Command and the Creed

The baptismal command appears to be the origin of the creed, or at least the point from which baptismal creeds grew.[3] But there is no consensus about

1. Gregory of Nyssa, *Address on Religious Instruction* 38, in *Christology of the Later Fathers*, ed. Edward R. Hardy, trans. Cyril C. Richardson, Library of Christian Classics (Philadelphia: Westminster, 1954), 322.
2. The Arians taught that the Son is a creature and hence mutable; Neo-Arians systematized Arian teaching and said that the Son, as a creature, is "unlike" (in Greek, *anomoios*) the Father.
3. "Creed" and "baptismal creed" are used here to mean any of several local creeds that candidates for baptism were asked to profess. Creeds from Caesarea, Jerusalem, Rome,

the precise origin of the creeds. One reads sometimes that creeds developed when phrases and clauses were added to the Triple Name of baptism to refute heresies. There is some evidence for this claim, but not enough to reach certainty.[4]

A few highlights that trace the development of the creeds can be pointed out. The baptismal command in Matthew 28:18–20 is one of the most familiar texts in the New Testament. In the translation of the Revised Standard Version, it reads:

> And Jesus came and said to them, "All authority in heaven and on earth has been given to me. Go therefore and make disciples of all nations, baptizing them in the name of the Father and of the Son and of the Holy Spirit, teaching them to observe all that I have commanded you; and lo, I am with you always, to the close of the age."

The Greek has one imperative, "make disciples," and three participles parallel to that imperative, so that Jesus's words are equivalent to four commands: "go," "make disciples," "baptize," and "teach." One of the commands is to travel, one is to administer the sacrament, and two are to teach. The roots of Christianity as a doctrinal religion and a religion that has a creed, truths that must be accepted, are in this passage.

To mention just a few highlights in the development of the teaching and practice of baptism, we might begin with the *Didache*. In this famous document, which probably dates from the first half of the second century, baptism is a liturgical rite that is already developed. There is an almost rubrical concern about how the sacrament should be administered. But also, the Matthean formula with the Triple Name is clearly invoked:

> The procedure for baptizing is as follows. . . . Immerse in running water, "In the Name of the Father, and of the Son, and of the Holy Spirit." If no running water is available, immerse in ordinary water. This should be cold if possible; otherwise warm. If neither is practicable, then pour water three times on the head "In the Name of the Father, and of the Son, and of the Holy Spirit." Both baptizer and baptized ought to fast before the baptism, as well as any others who can do so; but the candidate himself should be told to keep a fast for a day or two beforehand.[5]

---

and other churches survive. The conciliar creed of the Council of Nicaea was not used liturgically.

4. See J. N. D. Kelly, *Early Christian Creeds*, 3rd ed. (London: Longman, 1972), 30–52.

5. *Didache* 7, in *Early Christian Writings: The Apostolic Fathers*, trans. Maxwell Staniforth (Harmondsworth: Penguin, 1968), 194.

In the *Didache*, the emphasis is on moral rather than doctrinal instruction; the first six chapters of this work treat "the two ways": the way of life and the way of death. The *Didache* gives little evidence of doctrinal norms, except perhaps in regard to the Eucharist: the Eucharist may be given only to those who have been baptized.[6]

Justin Martyr, in his *First Apology*, mentions some points that the *Didache* already made. Those who accept the truth of what the Christians say and teach pledge themselves to live according to Christian norms. They pray and fast to seek forgiveness. Then they are brought to water and baptized. The next sentence in Justin's work shows what is probably the beginning of a creedal development—that is, the addition of some further phrases to the Triple Name of Father, Son, and Holy Spirit: "In the name of God, the Father and Lord of all, and of our Savior, Jesus Christ, and of the Holy Spirit, they then receive the washing with water."[7]

Further evidence is found in Tertullian's treatise *On Baptism*, the only treatise on any sacrament preserved from the pre-Nicene period. Tertullian makes a clearer connection between the profession of right faith and the sealing of baptism. He writes of "faith signed and sealed in the Father and the Son and the Holy Spirit."[8] Tertullian interprets the Triple Name in light of the three witnesses of Matthew 18:16. "It is," he continues, "under the charge of the three that profession of faith and promise of salvation are in pledge"; "there is a necessary addition, the mention of the Church: because where there are the three, the Father and the Son and the Holy Spirit, there is the Church, which is a body of three."[9] Tertullian appears to be alluding to a primitive creed, in which the names of Father, Son, and Holy Spirit and the church are mentioned.[10] In a later development, mention of the church was incorporated into the third article of the creed.

An early witness to the use of a baptismal creed at the moment the sacrament is administered may be the *Apostolic Tradition*, a work traditionally

---

6. Ibid., 9.

7. Justin Martyr, *1 Apol.* 61, in *Saint Justin Martyr: The First Apology; The Second Apology; Dialogue with Trypho; Exhortation to the Greeks; Discourse to the Greeks; The Monarchy, or The Rule of God*, trans. Thomas B. Falls, FC 6 (New York: Christian Heritage, 1948), 99.

8. This and the following quotations are from Tertullian, *On Baptism* 6, in *Tertullian's Homily on Baptism*, trans. Ernest Evans (London: SPCK, 1964), 14–16.

9. Cf. Matt. 18:20; 1 John 5:7–8.

10. Later in the treatise Tertullian quotes Matt. 28:19 verbatim: "For there has been imposed a law of baptizing, and its form prescribed: 'Go,' he says, 'teach the nations, baptizing them in the Name of the Father and the Son and the Holy Ghost.' When this law was associated with that <well-known> pronouncement, 'Except a man have been born again of water and the Holy Spirit, he shall not enter into the kingdom of heaven,' faith was put under obligation to the necessity of baptism" (Tertullian, *On Baptism* 13, in *Homily on Baptism*, 31).

attributed to Hippolytus of Rome. This text's portrayal of the rite of baptism as it may have been administered at Rome early in the third century (or even earlier, since its purpose was to preserve authentic tradition, which it says is being corrupted) includes the profession of the creed, in interrogatory form, as the candidate is being baptized. The rite takes place at cockcrow. Prayers are offered over the water. If possible, the water should be flowing; but, if necessary, one may use still water. Candidates should undress. Children should be baptized first. Those who can speak for themselves should speak; otherwise their parents should speak for them. Then the men are baptized, and finally the women, after they have loosened their hair and put aside their jewelry. No one should take a foreign object into the font. At the moment of baptism, the bishop gives thanks over the oil; this oil is called the oil of thanksgiving (*eucharistia*). One deacon places the oil of exorcism at the left of the bishop; another deacon takes the oil of thanksgiving and places it at the right of the bishop. The bishop orders the candidates to renounce Satan and all his pomps and works. Then the baptism itself takes place:

> A deacon will descend with him in this manner. When he who is being baptized will have descended into the water, he who baptizes will say to him, while imposing his hand on him: "Do you believe in God the Father almighty?" And he who is being baptized will say in turn, "I believe." And immediately, he (who is baptizing), holding his hand placed on his head, will baptize him one time. And then he will say, "Do you believe in Christ Jesus, Son of God, who was born by the Holy Spirit of the Virgin Mary, was crucified under Pontius Pilate, died, was raised on the third day alive from among the dead, went up to heaven, and is seated at the right of the Father; and who will come to judge the living and the dead?" And when he shall have said, "I believe," he will be baptized a second time. Again he (who is baptizing) will say, "Do you believe in the Holy Spirit in the holy Church?" He who is being baptized will say, "I believe," and again he will be baptized a third time.[11]

Finally, an intriguing use of the baptismal command in association with the creed is found in Gregory Nazianzen's *Oration on Holy Baptism*. Near the end of this long oration, Gregory quotes the baptismal command—or

---

11. Hippolytus, *Apostolic Tradition* 21, in *La Tradition Apostolique de saint Hippolyte: Essai de reconstitution*, ed. Bernard Botte, Liturgiewissenschaftliche Quellen and Forschungen 39 (Münster: Aschendorff, 1963), 45–51. I translate Botte's French text, which he believes is the closest to the original. The traditional ascription of this text to Hippolytus has been challenged recently, and the final form of the text may date from as late as the mid-fourth century. See Everett Ferguson, *Baptism in the Early Church: History, Theology, and Liturgy in the First Five Centuries* (Grand Rapids: Eerdmans, 2009), 327–28.

rather, he tells the catechumens, "I will baptize you and make you a disciple in the name of the Father and of the Son and of the Holy Spirit."[12] He then adds an extended paraphrase of the creed, communicating the content of the creed, with the articles fleshed out and expanded, but without using the exact words of the creed. At the end of the section he alludes to the *disciplina arcani* when he says, "This is all that may be divulged of the sacrament, and that is not forbidden to the ear of the many."[13] To give just a sample of the phrases with which Gregory paraphrases the creed: "Believe that all that is in the world, both all that is seen and all that is unseen, was made out of nothing by God. . . . Believe that the Son of God, the Eternal Word, who was begotten of the Father before all time and without body, was in these latter days for your sake made also Son of Man, born of the Virgin Mary. . . . Believe that for us sinners he was led to death."[14] Curiously, Gregory does not summarize the third article, on the Holy Spirit.

Thus a dual development took place. As early as the *Didache*, baptism had become a rite. Catechesis must precede it, and rules for the rite are established: fasting, concern for the sort of water used. The catechesis in the *Didache* is moral. Justin, too, suggests a catechesis that is mostly moral. Tertullian, by contrast, stresses right belief and faith, with emphasis on the Trinity. Hippolytus preserves the oldest interrogatory creed that has survived. It is not unlikely that behind Tertullian and the *Apostolic Tradition* was a tradition of doctrinal catechesis, one built around the Triple Name of the Father, Son, and Holy Spirit. Much later, Gregory Nazianzen presents a fascinating picture of the bishop explaining to catechumens the content of the creed and explaining at length how the creed conveys the essential Christian outlook on reality, the true Christian philosophy, so to speak, without quoting the words of the creed verbatim. Candidates for baptism needed to profess faith in the Trinity, and they came to that faith through catechetical instruction. Thus the deepest roots of trinitarian theology are in the church's primitive sacramental life.

The Words of the Baptismal Command as Authoritative

One great difference between the fathers' approach to the Sacred Scriptures and modern readers' approach is the unit of understanding. For most modern readers, the unit of understanding is the narrative block, the "story" as it is

---

12. Gregory Nazianzen, *Oration 40: On Holy Baptism* 45, trans. Charles Gordon Browne and James Edward Swallow (*NPNF*[2] 7:376).

13. Ibid. (*NPNF*[2] 7:377).

14. Ibid.

often called. "What the story in today's gospel teaches . . . ," one often hears. But in antiquity, the unit of understanding was very different: it was the single word. Schoolboys were taught to analyze a classical text, literally, word by word. This sort of training is clear, for example, in Origen, who seems to have had a concordance in his mind, explaining one word in the Bible by instances of the same word elsewhere. Even in his simple catechesis, Cyril of Jerusalem exhibits the concordance mentality, or interest in word study, and can point out, for example, that the first time the word *ekklēsia* (church) occurs in the Scriptures is in Leviticus.[15]

Following this principle, the fathers and their opponents press single words in the baptismal command and draw significant doctrinal points from them. Three key instances are the word "name" itself, the three names "Father," "Son," and "Holy Spirit," and the conjunction "and," which joins the three names.

For example, the fathers draw doctrinal conclusions from the fact that the word "name," in "baptizing them in the name," is singular, not plural. Basil of Caesarea, in his letter 210 written in the summer of 375, defends himself against slanders directed toward him by some notable men in Neocaesarea. He reports that these men were returning to a form of Sabellianism. They called Father, Son, and Holy Spirit one thing with a plurality of faces and claimed that the singular noun "name" in the baptismal command pointed to a singular reality: God was one nature and one person, not three. Basil answered that, when one says "Father and Son and Holy Spirit," three names are joined by one conjunction, "and," and each name has its own signification. The nature of the three is the same, and the Godhead is one. Hence "baptize in the name" does not mean that only one name has been handed down to us.[16] Thus it is illegitimate, Basil says, to appeal to the singular noun "name" to support Sabellianism or modalism.

The fathers also appeal to the Triple Name, "Father, Son, and Holy Spirit," with the basic assumption that names must designate existents. Eusebius of Caesarea provides an early instance of this principle. When Eusebius was readmitted to communion at the Council of Nicaea, he was admitted on the basis of the baptismal creed of his church.[17] His formulation is cautious: "believing

---

15. "We should note that this is the first time that this word for 'assemble' (*ekklēsiason*) occurs in Scripture, at the point where the Lord places Aaron in the office of high priest [Lev 8:3]" (Cyril of Jerusalem, *Catecheses* 18.24, in *Documents in Early Christian Thought*, trans. Maurice Wiles and Mark Santer [Cambridge: Cambridge University Press, 1975], 166).

16. Basil of Caesarea, Letter 210.4.

17. See Eusebius of Caesarea's letter to his church (*A New Eusebius: Documents Illustrative of the History of the Church to A.D. 337*, ed. J. Stevenson [London: SPCK, 1968], 364–65).

each of these [three persons] to be and to exist, the Father truly Father, and the Son truly Son, and the Holy Spirit truly Holy Spirit, as also our Lord, sending forth his disciples for the preaching, said, *Go, teach all nations, baptizing them in the name of the Father and of the Son and of the Holy Spirit.*"[18] Thus Eusebius argues from the three names in the baptismal command to the distinct existence of the three persons and their distinct properties.

The Second Creed of the Dedication Council of Antioch, held in 341, develops the phrases in Eusebius's confession aggressively and adds a coda that is subordinationist and nearly tritheist:

> Our Lord Jesus Christ enjoined his disciples, saying, "Go, teach all nations, baptizing them in the name of the Father and of the Son and of the Holy Spirit," that is, of a Father who is truly Father, and a Son who is truly Son, and of the Holy Spirit who is truly Holy Spirit, the names not being given without meaning or effect, but denoting accurately the peculiar subsistence, rank, and glory [*hypostasis, taxis, doxa*] of each that is named, so that they are three in subsistence, and one in agreement [*tēi men hypostasei tria, tēi de symphōniai hen*].[19]

Another appeal to the names "Father," "Son," and "Holy Spirit" takes the form of insisting that these precise names are the names by which God is to be addressed and catechumens are to be baptized. No other names may be substituted for them. Several examples can be found.

In the first of his *Orations against the Arians*,[20] Athanasius argues that God is better called "Father," in relation to the Son, and not "Unoriginate," in relation to creatures. Moreover, Athanasius writes sharply, the Lord did not teach his followers, "When you pray, say 'God Unoriginate,' but rather 'Our Father, who art in heaven.'" He concludes:

> He commanded us to be baptized not into the name of unoriginate and originate, not into the name of creator and creature, but "into the name of Father, Son, and Holy Spirit." In this initiation, creatures though we are, we are made adopted sons. We use the word "Father"; and by our use of that word we acknowledge not only the Father but also him who is in the Father himself—the Word.[21]

Basil the Great, too, in his work *Against Eunomius*, insists that Matthew 28:19 has "Father" and not "Unbegotten." Near the beginning of the first

---

18. Ibid., 365.

19. Kelly, *Early Christian Creeds*, 269.

20. Athanasius, *Orations against the Arians* 1.34.

21. Ibid., in *Documents in Early Christian Thought*, trans. Maurice Wiles and Mark Santer (Cambridge: Cambridge University Press, 1975), 31.

book he writes, "We should not call him 'Unbegotten' rather than 'Father,' unless we wish to be wiser than the teachings of the Savior, who said, 'Go forth, baptize in the name of the Father.'"[22]

Gregory of Nyssa, likewise, in his work *Against Eunomius*, insists that the baptismal formula contains an exact expression of the true faith:

> We believe, then, even as the Lord set forth the faith to his disciples, when he said, "Go, teach all nations, baptizing them in the name of the Father, and of the Son, and of the Holy Spirit." This is the word of the mystery whereby through the new birth from above our nature is transformed from the corruptible to the incorruptible, being renewed from "the old man," "according to the image of him who created"[23] at the beginning the likeness of the Godhead.[24]

This faith, Gregory insists, was delivered by God to the apostles; it admits neither of subtraction, nor of alteration, nor of addition; whoever perverts this divine utterance by dishonest quibbling is of his father, the devil. Gregory does not say that the Eunomians baptized in names other than Father, Son, and Holy Spirit; but the fact that they elsewhere substitute other names for the three biblical names is reprehensible in itself. The inventors of this pestilential heresy call the Father "Maker" and "Creator" of the Son, rather than "Father" of the Son; they call the Son a "result," a "product," rather than "Son"; and they call the Holy Spirit the "creature of a creature" and the "product of a product" rather than his proper title, "Spirit."[25] Thus the Triple Name of the baptismal command becomes also a Rule of Faith.

Besides "name" as singular, and the three names "Father," "Son," and "Holy Spirit," the fathers also appeal to the simple conjunction "and." The Lord himself joined the three names by this conjunction. In a famous passage in his equally famous work *On the Holy Spirit*, Basil of Caesarea dealt with this point. Basil, as is well known, sometimes used the doxology "Glory to the Father through the Son in the Holy Spirit" and sometimes "Glory to the Father with the Son together with the Holy Spirit."[26] Toward the end of the treatise, he argues that the preposition "with" has precisely the same meaning as the conjunction "and." If the baptismal command had read, "the Father *and* the Son *with* the Holy Spirit," its meaning would not have been changed. The meaning is the same, he writes, "unless someone by cold grammar prefers the

22. Basil of Caesarea, *Adversus Eunomium* 1.5 (PG 29b:517a).
23. Cf. Col. 3:10.
24. Gregory of Nyssa, *Against Eunomius* 2.1, trans. H. C. Ogle (*NPNF*[2] 5:101).
25. Ibid., 2.2 (*NPNF*[2] 5:101).
26. Basil of Caesarea, *On the Holy Spirit* 1.3.

conjunction as copulative and making more of a union while he dismisses the preposition as lacking the same force."[27] The conjunction "and," Basil finally argues, brings us to confess the full divinity of the Holy Spirit.

These few examples should make the point clearly enough. These fathers used the precise words of the baptismal command as a norm for orthodoxy, or right belief. Sometimes the words were to be taken in their full literal sense, as with "Father" and "Son." Sometimes they needed right interpretation; a word like "name" cannot be invoked to support Sabellianism. Finally, the word "and" can be interpreted by means of synonyms. Here the Rule of Faith guides the interpretation of a scriptural text, for the Bible is the church's book.

The Baptismal Formula in Fourth-Century Greek Theology

Finally, in a few instances the baptismal command is used directly as the source of trinitarian theology.

One such use is found in Hilary of Poitiers, whose work *On the Trinity* is the only patristic source Augustine cites by name in his own work *On the Trinity*.[28] At the beginning of book 2, Hilary quotes the baptismal command and comments: "What is there pertaining to the mystery of man's salvation that [this command] does not contain? Or is there anything that is omitted or obscure? Everything is full as from fullness and perfect as from perfection. It includes the meaning of the words, the efficacy of the action, the order of procedure, and the concept of the nature."[29]

In his sixteenth catechesis, on the Holy Spirit, Cyril of Jerusalem invokes the baptismal command to affirm the place of the Holy Spirit within the Trinity. It would be an error, he writes, to separate the Old Testament from the New Testament and to find two Spirits, one in the Old Testament and one in the New. Rather, on the occasion of holy baptism, the Holy Spirit is included

27. Ibid., 25.59, in *St. Basil the Great: On the Holy Spirit*, trans. Stephen Hildebrand (Crestwood, NY: St. Vladimir's Seminary Press, 2011), 97.

28. Augustine himself makes little use of Matt. 28:19 in his work *On the Trinity*, although in other works he cites the passage often. In *On the Trinity* 15.36.46 he calls Matt. 28:19 "a passage in which the Trinity is especially commended." In 15.28.51, the prayers that conclude *On the Trinity*, Augustine begins: "O Lord, our God, we believe in You, the Father, and the Son and the Holy Spirit. For the Truth would not say: 'Go baptize all nations in the name of the Father, and of the Son, and of the Holy Spirit,' unless you were a Trinity. Nor would you command us, O Lord God, to be baptized in the name of him who is not the Lord God" (in *Saint Augustine: The Trinity*, trans. Stephen McKenna, FC 45 [Washington, DC: Catholic University of America Press, 1953], 523).

29. Hilary of Poitiers, *On the Trinity* 2.1.1, in *Saint Hilary of Poitiers: The Trinity*, trans. Stephen McKenna, FC 25 (New York: Fathers of the Church, 1954), 35.

with the Father and the Son in the Holy Trinity; and here Cyril quotes the baptismal command.[30]

Basil of Caesarea makes a similar argument in his letter 52 to the *kanoni-kai*, who were unmarried women living common life and devoted to works of charity. He wrote the letter around 370, just after he became a bishop. These women seem to have asserted, in a rather confused way, that the Spirit is before the Son, or older than the Father. Basil argues that "the Holy Spirit is reckoned along with the Father and Son, wherefore he also is above creation; and the place assigned to him is in accordance with the doctrine which we have derived from the words of the Lord in the Gospel: 'Going, baptize in the name of the Father, and of the Son, and of the Holy Ghost.'" To change the order of the divine names "involves the abolition of his very existence, and is equivalent to a denial of the whole faith."[31]

In *On the Holy Spirit* 10.24, Basil quotes Matthew 28:19 against those who say that the Holy Spirit should not be ranked with the Father and the Son. The obvious meaning of the words, Basil writes, is that the Holy Spirit is one with the Father and the Son. Further, the Father, the Son, and the Holy Spirit are "one" in baptism—that is, they are united in causing the effects of baptism.

A little further on, in *On the Holy Spirit* 18.44, Basil writes that Christ did not make arithmetic a part of this gift. He did not say, "In the first, second, and third," nor did he say, "Into one, two, and three." We are saved by faith, not by numbers. As Basil says at the end of the paragraph, first, second, and third or one, two, and three lead in fact to polytheism.

Gregory of Nyssa develops the same thought more positively in his sermon on the baptism of Christ, delivered on the feast of the Epiphany. In a passage directed against the Macedonians, Gregory writes:

> What says the Lord's command? "Baptizing them in the name of the Father and of the Son and of the Holy Spirit." How in the name of the Father? Because he is the primal cause of all things. How in the name of the Son? Because he is the maker of creation. How in the name of the Holy Spirit? Because he is the power perfecting all. We bow ourselves before the Father, that we may be sanctified; before the Son we also bow, that the same end may be fulfilled; we bow also before the Holy Spirit, that we may be made what he is in fact and in name. There is not a distinction in the sanctification, in the sense that the Father sanctifies more, the Son less, the Holy Spirit in a less degree than the other two. Why then dost thou divide the three Persons into fragments of different natures,

---

30. Cyril of Jerusalem, *Catecheses* 16.4, in *Documents in Early Christian Thought*, 82.
31. Basil of Caesarea, Ep. 52.4, in *Basil: The Letters*, trans. Roy J. Deferrari, LCL (Cambridge, MA: Harvard University Press, 1926), 1:335–37.

and make three gods, unlike one to another, whilst from all thou dost receive one and the same grace?[32]

The few examples supplied here suggest the uses to which the baptismal command was put in theology. Cyril of Jerusalem invokes it against any tendency to Marcionism, and also to teach the full divinity of the Holy Spirit. The Cappadocian fathers often invoke it against the Macedonians or Pneumatomachi, as they work together to elaborate formulas that would represent the church's true and right faith.

Conclusion

When the fathers of the church invoke Matthew 28:19, they demonstrate the unity of Holy Scripture, the liturgy, doctrine, and theology. They quoted the Gospel and insisted that each word they quoted revealed truth about God. One name implied divine unity. "Father," "Son," and "Holy Spirit" were the revealed names of the one true God. When these names were coordinated with the conjunction "and," the equality of the three persons was affirmed. And then, this baptismal command was used in one of the most solemn moments of the liturgy, the baptism of catechumens. By the fourth century, baptism took place preeminently at the Easter vigil. The sacramental words of baptism were mirrored in the creed, which grew out of the Triple Name. Candidates professed the truth of the Christian faith at the moment of their baptism, for their catechists had followed the Lord's command, "make disciples" and "teach." The creed soon became the focal point of Christian doctrine, which is—to quote Jaroslav Pelikan's excellent definition—"what the church of Jesus Christ believes, teaches, and confesses on the basis of the word of God."[33] And when the church speculates on doctrine in light of philosophy—which is simply clear thinking—and culture, the result is theology.

To isolate any one of these four elements—Scripture, the liturgy, doctrine, theology—from the others is to do violence to Christian faith and life. Scripture lives in the church's worship; Christianity teaches God's true revelation in its creeds and councils; theology is clear thinking about the church's doctrine.

32. Gregory of Nyssa, *On the Baptism of Christ*, trans. H. A. Wilson (*NPNF*[2] 5:520).

33. Jaroslav Pelikan, *The Emergence of the Catholic Tradition (100–600)*, The Christian Tradition 1 (Chicago: University of Chicago Press, 1971), 1.

2

EUCHARIST AND TRINITY
IN THE LITURGIES OF THE EARLY CHURCH

ROBERT J. DALY, SJ

Assuming, as not needing to be argued here, that the Holy Trinity is the central, overarching doctrine of Christianity and the Eucharist its central mystery, this chapter will explore one special way in which this central doctrine and central mystery actually play out in the life of the church. I will focus primarily on the eucharistic prayer, that "moment" within the ritual actualization of the central mystery that constitutes the most intimate and intense contact that is possible between the body of Christ, which is the church, and her Divine Partner.[1] It will be a *lex orandi/lex credendi* type of study, attending most specifically not only to the ways in which doctrine influences prayer, a relatively straightforward task, but also to the ways in which prayer influences doctrine, a much more difficult and methodologically challenging task. Although most of the data that I will analyze will be from the early church, the questions that I bring to those data and the conclusions I try to draw from them are those that have been taking shape in the ecumenically charged flowering of contemporary liturgical theology. What

1. See Edward J. Kilmartin, *The Eucharist in the West: History and Theology* (Collegeville, MN: Liturgical Press, 1998), 324.

I am attempting is a far cry from the traditional so-called positive theology of earlier generations, which often contented itself with extracting from the tradition whatever support it could find for its already-formed doctrinal positions. My task here is the much more humbling one not only of trying to discover what is actually there in the early data—not just what we hope to find there—but also of trying to bring a historical-critical appropriation of those data to bear on our often too-comfortably-formed doctrinal positions.[2]

To jump right into the middle of this quest, as well as to be open about the bias that I bring to it, I point out that foremost in my mind is the mature trinitarian theology of the Eucharist that contemporary liturgical theologians have been finding expressed not only in the classical anaphoras of the patristic golden age, especially those associated with the names of Chrysostom and Basil, but also in the rich progeny of today's eucharistic prayers that consciously descend from them. This central ecclesial event/mystery can be summed up, if I may paraphrase what I have written elsewhere, as follows:

> The Eucharist . . . is the high point of both the expression of and the inchoative realization of the Church's marital covenant relationship with God. The center of this Eucharist is the Church's ritual action and prayer in which *the assembly, led by its duly appointed minister, addresses God the Father, through the Son, and in the Holy Spirit, praising and thanking God for the salvation-historical gifts of creation, covenant, and redemption, especially redemption in Jesus Christ, and asking God to send the Holy Spirit in order, by means of the transformation of the Eucharistic gifts, to continue the transformation of the community and its individuals toward their eschatological destiny as the true Body of Christ.* The ritual celebration culminates in the Assembly coming forward to receive, as Augustine put it, "what you are," the Body of Christ. But this, of course, is still just the beginning. The full realization of the ritual celebration continues beyond what takes place in a church building. It continues as the Assembly is sent forth in the Spirit to live out this Eucharistic mystery in the world of everyday life, and it will finally be completed only at the *eschaton* when the universalistic hope expressed in the prophetic proclamation—"Blessed are those who have been invited to the marriage supper of the Lamb" (see Rev 19:9)—has been fulfilled.[3]

2. Although written specifically for inclusion in this volume, this chapter also borrows from or extensively adapts material that has appeared in a number of previous publications, most notably Robert Daly, SJ, "Trinitarian Theology in Early Christian Anaphoras," in *God in Early Christian Thought: Essays in Memory of Lloyd G. Patterson*, ed. Andrew B. McGowan, Brian E. Daley, SJ, and Timothy J. Gaden, VCSup 94 (Leiden/Boston: Brill, 2009), 39–69.

3. Robert J. Daly, SJ, "Eucharistic Origins: From the New Testament to the Liturgies of the Golden Age," *TS* 66 (2005): 1–2.

The Eucharistic Prayer

Since my primary focus is on the anaphora, the eucharistic prayer, I must explain here what I have in mind when I use the term "eucharistic prayer." It is, first of all, that part of the church's eucharistic celebration that is italicized in the above summation. This prayer has a basic content and structure that, even with what are at times significant variations, can be verified not only in the historical "classical" anaphoras of the East and the West but also in practically all the officially recognized eucharistic prayers now in use in mainstream Christianity, and even in the worship books of some of our contemporary free churches. Liturgical scholars commonly recognize that these prayers have ten elements (1–10) in five groups (A–E):[4]

A 1 introductory dialogue
   2 preface
   3 *sanctus*
B 4 post-*sanctus*
   5 preliminary epiclesis (alternative or additional post-*sanctus*)
C 6 narrative of institution
D 7 anamnesis
   8 epiclesis
   9 diptychs or intercessions, which may be divided
E 10 concluding trinitarian doxology

Despite possible variations in the order, and despite the occasional absence of this or that element or group, this content and structure is verifiable in all authentic eucharistic prayers. But in addition to this content and structure, there is also in these trinitarian eucharistic prayers, at least implicitly, a specifically trinitarian understanding of Christian sacrifice that can be summarized as follows:

> Christian sacrifice has three interconnected "moments." It begins not with us, but with the self-offering of God the Father in the gift-sending of the Son. The second "moment" is the totally free, totally loving response of the Son in his humanity, and in the power of the Holy Spirit, to the Father and for us. The third "moment"—and only here does Christian sacrifice begin to become real in us—takes place when human beings, in the Spirit, the same Spirit that was in

---

4. Typical of and highly representative of scholarly consensus on this is W. Jardine Grisbrooke's article "Anaphora," in *The New Westminster Dictionary of Liturgy and Worship*, ed. J. G. Davies (Philadelphia: Westminster, 1986), 13–21.

the human Jesus, begin to enter into that self-offering, self-giving relationship that is the very life and being of the Father and the Son.[5]

This, quite obviously, is not what was going on in the minds of anyone in attendance at the historical Last Supper. Indeed, it is overly optimistic to think that it is going on consciously in the minds of most people as they now participate in the Eucharist. For, in actual reality, and as guided by the Holy Spirit, it took the body of Christ several centuries to come, even implicitly, to that rich understanding of the Eucharist I have just outlined. And in actual fact, only in recent decades have liturgical theologians been able to articulate it more or less as I just have. How this came about and what we might learn from it is a fascinating story, part of which I will now try to tell.

But first, a caveat. We do not have enough data from the early Christian centuries to sketch out a continuous line of development from the Last Supper of Jesus to the theologically mature eucharistic prayers of the fifth century that we now understand to be the models for our proper and authentic contemporary eucharistic prayers. In fact, the data that we do have suggest that such a line of development does not even exist, or at least does not exist in a way that is now, or in any foreseeable future, accessible to us. For, as we move back from the theologically mature anaphoras of late patristic antiquity, into the earliest eucharistic celebrations, the more we move back the more we seem to encounter a plurality of practices, a plurality that only a ruthlessly applied procrustean methodology could bring into an ordered line of development. This would be a damning, debilitating admission for some theological positions, for example, for a position that, ignoring critical history, would naively assume that today's Eucharist is doing precisely what Christ did at the Last Supper.[6]

But those who believe that the Holy Spirit both was and is present in the church, actively guiding it, are invited to enter into an exciting search. For if, taking the Johannine Jesus at his word, we affirm that the Holy Spirit really is behind what has been happening, behind what is happening, and behind what will be happening, we don't have to worry if we are unable to identify every step along the path of this search. We don't have to worry if we cannot

5. Paraphrased from Robert J. Daly, SJ, "Sacrifice: The Way to Enter the Paschal Mystery," *America* 188, no. 16 (May 12, 2003): 14–15. See also Daly, "Sacrifice Unveiled or Sacrifice Revisited: Trinitarian and Liturgical Perspectives," *TS* 64 (2003): 26–32; Daly, *Sacrifice Unveiled: The True Meaning of Christian Sacrifice* (London: T&T Clark; New York: Continuum, 2009), 5–15.

6. See John Meier's helpful treatment of this issue in "The Eucharist and the Last Supper: Did It Happen?" *TD* 42 (Winter 1995): 335–51, esp. 347, where he sums up his exposition: "We must appreciate that the Last Supper and eucharist are not the same thing pure and simple."

establish that one thing has led to another and if so, how, or even that they are actually interconnected in historically verifiable ways. In other words, contrary to some popular thinking, as well as to a superficial reading of the encyclical of Pope John Paul II titled *Ecclesia de Eucharistia*, if one is thinking historically rather than existentially, it is not so much the Eucharist that makes the church, but rather the church that makes the Eucharist. In this sense, the Christ who instituted the Eucharist was not just the historical Christ who was responsible for its originating moment(s) but also the mystical body of Christ that was responsible for the basic shaping of the Eucharist that we now celebrate. It was a Spirit-guided process (that, because Spirit-guided, is still ongoing) that took several hundred years to bring to the kind of maturity that we find in the great anaphoras of the patristic golden age.[7] With all this in mind, let us now go back to the beginning.

The Eucharists in the New Testament

In the title of this subdivision, I have consciously written "Eucharists" in the plural rather than in the singular. For in the New Testament one can find witness to at least six different ways of celebrating what Christians have come to call the Eucharist. I will list them here in approximate "chronological" order, from what seems to be the most "primitive" to the most "developed."[8]

First, as we see throughout the Synoptic Gospels, there was Jesus's somewhat revolutionary practice of table fellowship, not restricted by the traditional purity rules but apparently open to anyone willing to associate with him or accept forgiveness (e.g., Matt. 11:18–19; Luke 7:33–34). Second, there was the "last" supper itself. It is not possible for us to recreate this event with historical precision, for the theology that is explicit and implicit in Mark 14:12–25, Matthew 26:17–29, Luke 22:7–38, and John 13–17 seems to reflect much more the Eucharists of the fifth and sixth types than what was probably taking place in the minds of those sharing with Jesus at the historical Last Supper. We cannot even be sure that it was just one event rather than simply the way Jesus began to share table fellowship with his closest disciples just before his death. But it is fairly clear that here we have something radically new, the obvious

---

7. This is an attempt not to deny but to understand and properly interpret the meaning of Trent's 1547 definition that each of the seven sacraments was "instituted by Jesus Christ our Lord" (Henrici Denzinger, *Enchiridion symbolorum definitionum et declarationum de rebus fidei et morum*, ed. Peter Hünermann [Freiburg: Herder, 1991], no. 1601).

8. For the highly detailed exegetical background for these "six different ways," see Bruce Chilton, *A Feast of Meanings: Eucharistic Theologies from Jesus through Johannine Circles* (Leiden/New York: Brill, 1994), 13–142, and summarized in my "Eucharistic Origins," 9–13.

originating moment in the institution of the Eucharist in which the shared wine is (at least) the equivalent of the blood of an animal shed in sacrifice, and the shared bread has the value of sacrificial flesh.

Third, we find, in the first three chapters of the Acts of the Apostles, that very early stage when, under the leadership of Peter, James, and John, in addition to (and apparently not in tension with) traditional prayer in the temple, the *berakah* prayer of Judaism was apparently becoming a principal model of the Eucharist, celebrated repetitively in the home and apparently only with bread, or at least with bread taking precedence over wine.[9] Fourth, there seems to have been a Christian Passover celebration in the circle of James, in Jerusalem, and also just once a year. Fifth, we find in the eucharistic texts of Paul and the Synoptic Gospels what can be called a "Hellenistic refinement of the Petrine type."[10] This presented the Eucharist as (also) a martyrological sacrifice for sin, and that, in an at least de facto counterpoint to the exclusivism of the circle of James, was open to non-Jews and Jews alike. And sixth, in chapter 6 of the Gospel of John, Jesus identifies himself as the manna and sacramentally offers/gives, profoundly more explicitly than in Paul and the Synoptics, his own personal body and blood in the Eucharist.

These are distinctly different ways of celebrating what are commonly called Eucharists, or practices that developed into Eucharists. But they can neither be reduced to each other nor accurately be seen (or projected back) as proceeding from or developing from each other in an orderly line of progression. Plurality of practice is what characterizes the New Testament witness to eucharistic origins.[11]

The *Didache*

But what about the origins of the eucharistic prayer—that is, that carefully structured prayer of (possibly) ten elements in five groups outlined above? When we ask that question, our earliest witness is the *Didache* whose chapters 9 and 10 contain prayers that are not only our earliest examples of texts of eucharistic praying but also quite possibly earlier than even the Gospels themselves:

9. Chilton, *Feast of Meanings*, 81–92, characterizes this as a Eucharist of the "Petrine circle."

10. See Chilton, *Feast of Meanings*, 109–30. But see also my suggestion that the emphasis on forgiveness and sin offering makes it just as much a Jewish as a Hellenistic refinement (Daly, "Eucharistic Origins," 12n26).

11. For a fuller exposition of the points outlined in the previous few paragraphs, see Daly, "Eucharistic Origins," 3–22.

(And) concerning the eucharist [*eucharistias*], eucharistize
[*eucharistēsate*] thus:

First, concerning the cup:
    We give you thanks, our Father,
    for the holy vine of your servant David
    which you revealed to us through your servant Jesus.

And concerning the broken [loaf]:
    We give you thanks, our Father,
    for the life and the knowledge
    which you revealed to us through your servant Jesus.
    To you [is] the glory forever.

Just as this broken [loaf] was scattered
    over the hills [as grain]
    and, having_been_gathered_together, became one
    in_like_fashion, may your church be_gathered_together
    from the ends of the earth into your kingdom.
    Because yours is the glory and the power
    through Jesus Christ forever.

(And) let no one eat or drink from your eucharist [*eucharistias*]
    except those baptized in the name of [the] Lord,
    for the Lord has likewise said concerning this:
    "Do not give what is holy to the dogs."

And after being filled [by the meal], eucharistize [*eucharistēsate*] thus:

We give you thanks, holy Father,
    for your holy name,
    which you tabernacle in our hearts,
    and for the knowledge and faith and immortality
    which you revealed to us through your servant Jesus.
    To you [is] the glory forever.

You, almighty Master, created all things
    for the sake of your name,
    both food and drink you have given to people for enjoyment
    in order that they might give thanks;
    to us, on the other hand, you have graciously bestowed
    Spirit-sent food and drink for life forever through your servant
        [Jesus].

Before all [these] things, we give you thanks
    because you are powerful [on our behalf].
    To you [is] the glory forever.

[10.5] Remember, Lord, your church,
to save [her] from every evil
and to protect [her] in your love
and to gather [her] together from the four winds
[as] the sanctified into your kingdom
which you have prepared for her,
because yours is the power and the glory forever.
[10.6] [A] Come, grace [of the kingdom]!
and pass_away, [O] this world!
  [B] Hosanna to the God of David!
  [C] If anyone is holy, come!
  If anyone is not, convert.
  [D] Come Lord [*marana tha*]! Amen!
(And) turn towards the prophets [allowing them]
to eucharistize [*eucharistein*] as much as they wish.[12]

When, in 1883, the (just recently discovered) *Didache* was first published, most scholars assumed that these obviously eucharistic prayers could not have been the prayers of an authentic eucharistic celebration. They contain no institution narrative or words of consecration, no idea of a transformation of the eucharistic elements, nor any clear evidence of a trinitarian theology. In addition, the Christology they do contain is so primitive that, even in comparison with the earliest gospels, these prayers can be described theologically as prechristological. Jesus is spoken of as servant (*pais*), but definitely not as God, nor as Son of God, nor even as Messiah. On the two occasions when the Lord (*Kyrios*) is mentioned (9.4 and 10.6), it is not at all clear that it is Jesus rather than the Lord God that the prayer has in mind.

On the other hand, and apart from the fact that the authors of the *Didache* obviously thought of these prayers as the centerpiece of a eucharistic celebration—and contemporary liturgical scholars increasingly concede that that is, likely enough, precisely what they are[13]—they are in fact also filled with elements that eventually became integral to the mature eucharistic prayers of later ages. Most notably, perhaps, they are profoundly ecclesial. The church, the assembly, is praying to God the Father, praising and giving thanks for the

---

12. As translated by Aaron Milavec, *The Didache: Faith, Hope, and Life of the Earliest Christian Communities, 50–70 C.E.* (New York/Mahwah, NJ: Newman Press, 2003), 30–35; also Milavec, *The Didache: Text, Translation, Analysis, and Commentary* (Collegeville, MN: Liturgical Press, 2003), 22–25.

13. As Paul Bradshaw points out, there have been four principal explanations: "1. that it is only ancillary to the Eucharist proper . . . 2. that it is a quite different kind of Eucharist . . . 3. that it is an agape and not a Eucharist . . . 4. that it is an early form of Eucharist." See Paul F. Bradshaw, *Eucharistic Origins* (Oxford: Oxford University Press, 2004), 24–32.

gifts of creation and for the at least implicitly redemptive gifts of knowledge and immortality revealed to us through Jesus. They are prayers of praise and blessing over both the cup and the loaf (note the order: cup first). There is also a eucharistic presence, although at this prechristological stage it is not the eucharistic presence of the divine Jesus but the "eucharistic" presence of the holy name of the Father tabernacled in our hearts (*Did.* 10.2). Quite prominent also are intercessions for the unity and flourishing of the church. In addition, these prayers have an eschatological thrust to them of the kind commonly found in the mainstream anaphoras of later ages. And finally, though not in the trinitarian way that eventually became normative, these relatively brief prayers, interspersed with six different doxologies, are doxological through and through. Thus, at the end of this first "chapter" in our story—taking the New Testament as the introduction to the story—of the Eucharist and the Trinity in the life of the church, the church, as praying assembly, is indeed fully present and active. But the Trinity is present only in the most inchoative of senses—for Christ is not yet portrayed as the divine Christ, and the trinitarian Holy Spirit is at most only implicitly, if at all, adumbrated in the mention of the "Spirit-sent food and drink"—*pneumatikēn trophēn kai poton* (10.3).

A whole century passes before, with Justin (ca. 165) describing in his *First Apology* how the presider "sends up prayers and thanksgivings to the best of his ability," we encounter what may be our earliest clear witness to the trinitarian *form* of eucharistic praying: "Then bread and a cup of water and (a cup) of mixed wine are brought to him who presides over the brethren, and he takes them and sends up praise and glory to the Father of all in the name of the Son and of the Holy Spirit, and gives thanks at some length that we have been deemed worthy of these things from him."[14] But this is just a very brief description of what went on, not the actual prayer or prayers used by Justin's presider. For this was still long before the time when extemporaneous eucharistic praying was replaced by carefully composed set prayers to which the presider was expected to adhere. But, although this particular form of praying in Justin is obviously trinitarian, we cannot assume that trinitarian eucharistic praying was common, let alone the rule, in the churches of the second century. As Bradshaw has pointed out, we have very few examples of liturgical texts that can be confidently dated prior to the middle of the fourth century, and it is only toward the end of that century that we find significant evidence of attempts at uniformity in eucharistic praying.[15] Indeed, what

---

14. Justin, *1 Apol.* 65.1. Quoted from R. C. D. Jasper and G. J. Cuming, *Prayers of the Eucharist: Early and Reformed*, 3rd ed. (Collegeville, MN: Liturgical Press, 1990), 28.

15. See Paul F. Bradshaw, "God, Christ, and the Holy Spirit in Early Christian Praying," in *The Place of Christ in Liturgical Prayer: Trinity, Christology, and Liturgical Theology*, ed. Bryan D. Spinks (Collegeville, MN: Liturgical Press, 2008), 53–54.

meager evidence we do have from these centuries suggests that not trinitarian but rather binitarian praying—to the Father and to or through the Son—was what was most common.

> The alleged standard formula "through Christ and in the Holy Spirit" was anything but universal. . . . The main reason why the Holy Spirit is less frequently mentioned in early sources seems to be because there was not then as completely clear a differentiation between what later orthodoxy would regard as the Second and Third persons of the Holy Trinity. The Spirit could be thought of as the Spirit of God or of Christ, and hence to speak of Christ was the same as to speak of his spirit, and vice versa. Thus, when in some third-century Syrian texts we encounter references to the invocation of the Spirit, that invocation seems to be no more than a regional variation of the invocation of the Logos found in other sources.[16]

The Epiclesis

It is not until we are well into the golden age of patristic theology in the fifth century that we encounter eucharistic prayers that have a full, consecratory epiclesis of the kind that is implied in that summary of the church's eucharistic celebrations with which I opened this chapter. The main lines of the story of how this came about can be patched together from a variety of studies.[17] Basically, it took four centuries—well into the fifth century—before, according to the evidence we have, at least some parts of the Christian church had, in their eucharistic praying, become at least implicitly aware of the reasonably full breadth, height, and depth of the mystery of the Trinity in the life of the church. But the new detail that scholars have been (and still are) uncovering since McKenna's first edition in 1975 warns us that we are still struggling to tell this story with appropriate accuracy and nuance. As to the bottom-line historical facts that constitute the basis of the story we would like to tell, our knowledge is, frankly, both meager and in flux. For the purposes of this article, I will touch down at just a few points in this early period and then, relying on the work that other scholars have done, venture some necessarily tentative summarizing remarks before going on to the full richness of trinitarian eucharistic praying in the mature anaphoras of the patristic golden age. I will

16. Ibid., 62.

17. E.g., John H. McKenna, CM, *The Eucharistic Epiclesis: A Detailed History from the Patristic to the Modern Era*, 2nd ed. (Chicago/Mundelein, IL: Hillenbrand Books, 2009); W. O. E. Oesterley, *The Jewish Background of the Christian Liturgy* (Oxford: Clarendon, 1925; repr., Gloucester, MA: Peter Smith, 1965), esp. chap. 9, "The Origin of the Epiclesis," 205–30; and Bradshaw, *Eucharistic Origins*.

present, first, some examples of early eucharistic epicletic praying and, second, some examples of developed—that is, consecratory—eucharistic epicleses.[18]

Early Eucharistic Epicletic Praying

To begin, we note the at least general validity of the remark that "from the beginning what was later known as the *Epiclesis* was in its essence a prayer for the Divine Presence among the worshippers during their most solemn act of worship."[19] In other words, the sanctification of the worshipers, whether or not in recognizably epicletic form, was always a central goal and purpose of eucharistic praying. Praying for the sanctification of the elements was, for the most part, a relatively late arrival to this development. This enables us to see the prayer of *Didache* 10.2, "We give you thanks, holy Father, for your holy name, which you tabernacle in our hearts," as a possible precursor to the epiclesis. It is remarkable that Oesterley, who convincingly argues[20] that the Jewish "*Shekhinah* conception, teaching the truth of the Divine Presence among the worshippers," is behind the earliest forms of Christian epicletic praying, did not notice[21] that this is possibly what we inchoatively have in *Didache* 10.2.

Second, we note the likely accuracy of Bradshaw's surmise that, just as there was an apparent wide diversity of eucharistic practice and praying, so too "there may not have been a single original form of epiclesis."[22]

Oesterley rightly points out that Justin, despite his witness in *1 Apology* 65 to the trinitarian *form* of eucharistic praying, seems in that description to be "unconscious of any idea of prayer being offered for the descent of the Holy Spirit upon the elements." But he does go on in *1 Apology* 66 to speak "directly of the effect of reception upon the worshippers."[23] A few years later Irenaeus (whether or not he knew the work of Justin is unknown) gives witness to a theology that is somewhat more developed: "For as the bread which is

18. For the sake of expository clarity I assume a hypothetical, theological progression from (putatively) earlier "soft" epicleses to the (putatively) later "hard," consecratory epicleses. In actual fact, however, some later (at least chronologically more mature) eucharistic prayers have a "soft," nonconsecratory epiclesis. A classic example of this situation is the Roman *Canon Missae*, which was taking its present shape in late antiquity and the early Middle Ages. It has no epiclesis of the Holy Spirit at all but rather a divine epiclesis that is at best, apparently—especially from its location *before* the explicitly consecratory words of institution—only implicitly and inchoatively consecratory.

19. Oesterley, *Jewish Background*, 217–18.

20. Ibid., 218–30, esp. at 229.

21. Ibid., 217.

22. Bradshaw, *Eucharistic Origins*, 128.

23. Oesterley, *Jewish Background*, 217.

produced from the earth, when it receives the invocation of God, is no longer bread, but the Eucharist, consisting of two realities, earthly and heavenly; so also our bodies, when they receive the Eucharist, are no longer corruptible, having the hope of the resurrection to eternity."[24] Here we are close to finding the mature *form*, though not the content or the actual wording, of a eucharistic epiclesis. Over the bread we have both an "invocation of God"—though not of the Holy Spirit—and also benefits imparted to the worshipers—though not by invocation, but by receiving the Eucharist.

In the third century, with Origen of Alexandria, Cyprian of Carthage, and the early Syriac tradition, our witnesses become slightly less sparse. Origen explicitly witnesses to a trinitarian epiclesis, speaking of the eucharistic bread "on which has been invoked the name of God, and of Christ, and of the Holy Spirit."[25] But in Cyprian (d. 258), "the last major witness to eucharistic theology and practice in the third century,"[26] we come up empty. Despite the relatively lengthy *Epistle 63*, dedicated to eucharistic questions, there is no mention of the Trinity in relation to the Eucharist, nor any mention of anything epicletic in eucharistic praying. Cyprian's overriding concern—and indeed in what now strikes us as a simplistically historicizing way—that Christians in the Eucharist are supposed to be doing precisely what the Lord did the night before he died seems to crowd out any mention of the Trinity or the Holy Spirit.

Only the early Syriac tradition saves our search for third-century evidence from coming up almost completely empty. The third-century *Didascalia Apostolorum* spoke of the Eucharist being "accepted and sanctified through the Holy Spirit."[27] Then, as Bradshaw points out,[28] the (probably) East Syrian *Acts of Thomas* contains a wide variety of petitionary prayers and acclamations, two of which are addressed to the Holy Spirit, one from a baptism, the other from a bread-only Eucharist that reads: "<Come gift of the Most High;> Come perfect compassion; Come fellowship of the male; <Come, Holy Spirit:> . . . Come and partake with us in this Eucharist which we celebrate in thy name, and in this love-feast in which we are gathered together at thy call."[29] Although such direct invocations (not characteristic either of Jewish or Greco-Roman prayers of that time) for the deity to be present may have their parallels in the

---

24. Irenaeus, *Adversus Haereses* 4.18.5.

25. Commenting on 1 Cor. 7:5 in *Homilies on 1 Corinthians*; see Claude Jenkins, "Origen on 1 Corinthians," *JTS* 9 (1908): 502.

26. Bradshaw, *Eucharistic Origins*, 114.

27. *Didascalia Apostolorum* 6.21 (ET), from *The Liturgical Portions of the Didascalia*, ed. Sebastian Brock and Michael Vasey (Nottingham: Grove Books, 1982), 32.

28. Bradshaw, *Eucharistic Origins*, 126.

29. *Acts of Thomas* 50, in *New Testament Apocrypha*, vol. 2, ed. Wilhelm Schneemelcher, trans. R. McL. Wilson, 2nd ed. (Louisville: Westminster John Knox, 1992), 359–60.

magic spells of the ancient Mediterranean world, Bradshaw points out that the most likely antecedent for an early Christian direct invocation of this kind is probably the Aramaic *marana tha* (Our Lord, come!) of 1 Corinthians 16:22 and *Didache* 10.6, and the Greek "Come, Lord Jesus!" of Revelation 22:20.[30]

At the End of the Fourth Century

In the course of the fourth century, if we insist on being rigidly critical about what is solid historical evidence, our witnesses, despite this being the century of the church's great struggle with Arianism and the century of the first two ecumenical councils (Nicaea in 325 and Constantinople I in 381), still fall far short of giving us the full picture. But by the end of the century, a more mature picture is, in some communities at least, obviously beginning to take shape. Eucharistic presiders are now, it seems, generally expected to proclaim, whether from memory or from a written text, a set eucharistic prayer rather than one of their own extemporaneous making. The "classical" structure of this prayer—ten elements in five groups, as we outlined near the beginning of this chapter—is now more easily recognizable. The words of institution, although with at least one very notable exception (in *Addai and Mari*), have become an integral, central part of the eucharistic prayers. The trinitarian structure and content of the prayers is now sufficient at least to allow us to read it back into these prayers. And finally, the epiclesis of the Holy Spirit upon the gifts to be consecrated seems now well on its way to its mature form. We will examine this in what we can see and infer from two major witnesses: first, the *Anaphora of Addai and Mari* and its close relative *Sharar*, and second, the anaphora of the *Apostolic Tradition* (*AT*) that was traditionally associated with the name of Hippolytus.

Addai and Mari *and* Sharar

Liturgical historians generally assume that *Addai and Mari* and *Sharar* contain core elements that go back to the third century, the approximate chronological midpoint between the *Didache* and the Chrysostom anaphora. However, the *Addai and Mari* and *Sharar* texts that we are using in this study represent a later stage of development that we can tentatively date to the late fourth century. The Trinity is clearly mentioned in these prayers, but sometimes in such a formulaic way that scholars suspect that these trinitarian formulas may be later insertions. In addition, when we try to relocate these prayers

---

30. Bradshaw, *Eucharistic Origins*, 126.

back into their original (late third- to late fourth-century) *Sitz im Leben*, we have to ask whether they are really trinitarian in a fully conscious way, or perhaps only binitarian, or perhaps, at times, even only unitarian in the sense of addressing God without consciousness of a distinction of trinitarian persons. We are still far from the way in which the Chrysostom anaphora was apparently formulated in order, among other things, to hammer home trinitarian orthodoxy.

In the opening dialogue of *Addai and Mari* the priest proclaims: "The grace of our Lord <Jesus Christ and the love of God the father, and the fellowship of the Holy Spirit be with us all now and ever world without end>."[31] The manuscript evidence suggests that this formulaic trinitarian prayer might not be original. However, in the very first sentence of the "preface" that follows, we read: "Worthy of glory from every mouth and thanksgiving from every tongue is the adorable and glorious name of the Father and of the Son and of the Holy Spirit. He created the world through his grace . . ."[32] and so on. This is thoroughly trinitarian, but it would be a mistake to read back into it the more mature understanding and more precise formulations of later times.[33] "Name" in the singular, not the plural, is a common primitive Christian way of speaking of/to the one God of Judaism and Christianity, and it is to this Name that the rest of the preface seems to be addressed.

Immediately after the Holy, Holy, Holy, the prayer (which the priest prays privately) shifts its address to the Lord (Jesus), who has

> put on our human nature to give us life through your divine nature; you raised us from our lowly state; you restored our Fall; you restored our immortality; you forgave our debts; you justified our sinfulness; you enlightened our intelligence. You, our Lord and our God, conquered our enemies, and made the lowliness of our weak nature to triumph through the abundant mercy of your grace.
>
> (*aloud*) And for all <your helps and graces towards us, let us raise to you praise and honor and thanksgiving and worship, now and ever and world without end>. *People:* Amen.[34]

31. Jasper and Cuming, *Prayers of the Eucharist*, 42.
32. Ibid.
33. In later times, reflecting a more mature trinitarian theology, this obviously early and relatively vague form of trinitarian praying was amplified (corrected?) by the following prayer inserted immediately after the Holy, Holy, Holy as the opening words of the post-*sanctus* anaphora: "Blessed are you, God, true Father, in whom is named all paternity in heaven and on earth. Blessed are you, eternal Son, through whom all things were made. Blessed are you, Holy Spirit, the principle from which all things are sanctified" (translation mine from *Prex Eucharistica: Textus e variis liturgiis antiquioribus selecti*, ed. Anton Hänggi and Irmgard Pahl [Fribourg: Editions Universitaires, 1968], 377).
34. Jasper and Cuming, *Prayers of the Eucharist*, 42–43.

On the assumption that this represents more or less how this anaphora was prayed at the end of the fourth century, it gives witness to that form of binitarian praying (i.e., to the Father and to the Son) that was fairly common in early Christianity[35] and that continues to this day, not just in this anaphora but also in some contemporary eucharistic prayers in use, for example, in the Maronite Church.

In the closely related anaphora of *Sharar*, the whole prayer after the *sanctus* remains addressed to Christ; but here, in *Addai and Mari*, the prayer goes back to addressing God the Father, but with continued reference to Jesus: "the body and blood of your Christ," "our Lord Jesus Christ, your beloved Son," "the precious blood of our Christ," and so on.

Toward the end of the anaphora, not precisely in the place that became its "classical" location in the later anaphoras of the Eastern churches—because here, as in *Sharar*, it (D 8) comes after rather than before the diptychs or intercessions (D 9)—we find a "soft" epiclesis of the Holy Spirit:

> May your Holy Spirit, Lord, come and rest on this offering of your servants, and bless and sanctify it, that it may be to us, Lord, for remission of debts, forgiveness of sins, and the great hope of resurrection from the dead, and new life in the kingdom of heaven, with all who have been pleasing in your sight.[36]

The designation "soft epiclesis" alerts us to the fact that, although the prayer is clearly calling upon God to send the Spirit upon the eucharistic offering, it is not explicitly requesting that the Spirit actually transform it.[37] Nor is it yet clear that the Spirit is now explicitly understood—as later became the case—to be an agent somehow "distinct" from the other trinitarian persons. But we do find clearly verified what we asserted earlier, namely that "the sanctification of the worshippers, whether or not in recognizably epicletic form, was always a central goal and purpose of epicletic praying." *Addai and Mari* closes with a full trinitarian doxology that, because of its formulaic nature, may be a later insertion. But the presence of practically the identical doxology in *Sharar*

---

35. See Spinks, *Place of Christ in Liturgical Prayer*, esp. chap. 1, "The Place of Christ in Liturgical Prayer: What Jungmann Omitted to Say," by Bryan D. Spinks, pp. 1–19; chap. 2, "The Binitarian Pattern of Earliest Christian Devotion and Early Doctrinal Development," by L. W. Hurtado, pp. 23–50; chap. 3, "God, Christ, and the Holy Spirit in Early Christian Praying," by Paul Bradshaw, pp. 51–64; and chap. 5, "Prayers Addressed to Christ in the West Syrian Tradition," by Baby Varghese, pp. 88–111.

36. Jasper and Cuming, *Prayers of the Eucharist*, 43.

37. It is noteworthy that the words "bless and sanctify it" are not found in (the likely more primitive) *Sharar*, thus suggesting that the *Addai and Mari* text we are using may represent evidence of a beginning transition from a "soft" to a "hard" (i.e., explicitly consecratory, transformatory) epiclesis.

suggests that, if indeed an insertion, it was probably early enough to have been in place by the end of the fourth century, at which time there would be nothing theologically anachronistic about it: "One holy Father, one holy Son, one holy Spirit. Glory be to the Father and to the Son and to the Holy Spirit to the ages of ages. Amen."[38]

The Anaphora of the Apostolic Tradition

I have elsewhere written of the "mystery" of this anaphora, using "mystery" in its popular secular sense rather than in its liturgical-sacramental sense.[39] This anaphora is from chapter 4 of the *Apostolic Tradition*, a church order compiled from various earlier sources probably in Syria (probably Antioch) by an apparently Arian redactor between the years 375 and 380. Recognizing this, critical historians increasingly disassociate this anaphora from the historical Hippolytus (ca. 170–ca. 236). Doctrinally, theologically, and liturgically (as a remarkably mature, complete eucharistic prayer), it would stand out as a blatant, somewhat inexplicable anachronism if it were to be located in the early third century. But in the late fourth century, just before Constantinople I in 381, it is quite at home with what we know about the theology (quite a bit) and liturgy (admittedly meager) of that time. Bradshaw, Johnson, and Phillips sum all this up by pointing out that "if this prayer does belong to the third century in its present form, it is very advanced for its age, having some features that are otherwise first encountered only in the fourth century or later."[40] Thus it would seem to be a fairly safe assumption that the prayer as a whole came together in this form in the last quarter of the fourth century.

Three points in this brief, compact prayer are significant for our theme: its first two sentences, the epiclesis, and the closing doxology. The opening two sentences read:

> We render thanks to you, O God, through your beloved child Jesus Christ, whom in the last times you sent to us as a savior and redeemer and angel of your will; who is your inseparable Word, through whom you made all things, and in whom you were well pleased. You sent him from heaven into a virgin's womb; and conceived in the womb, he was made flesh and was manifested as your Son, being born of the Holy Spirit and the Virgin.[41]

---

38. Jasper and Cuming, *Prayers of the Eucharist*, 44.
39. Daly, "Trinitarian Theology in Early Christian Anaphoras," 260–62.
40. *The Apostolic Tradition: A Commentary*, ed. Paul F. Bradshaw, Maxwell E. Johnson, and L. Edward Phillips (Minneapolis: Fortress, 2002); see esp. 37–48, here at 44.
41. Jasper and Cuming, *Prayers of the Eucharist*, 35.

This is trinitarian, at least in the sense that the three persons of the Trinity are mentioned, but not in the sense that reflects anything beyond what was already there in the New Testament, except for the final phrase: "born of the Holy Spirit and the Virgin." This is a wording that "is in line with several later creedal formulae, including the Niceno-Constantinopolitan Creed of 381," but not with earlier versions (for the wording in this first part of the anaphora is quite primitive).[42] If so, this wording would seem to be an insertion into earlier, traditional forms of praying, an example of *lex credendi* influencing *lex orandi*.

The epiclesis, located precisely—except for the absence of diptychs or intercessions (D 9)—where it is found in the later, more mature anaphoras, is immediately followed by the concluding doxology:

> And we ask that you would send your Holy Spirit upon the offering of your holy Church, that, gathering her into one, you would grant to all who receive the holy things (to receive) the fullness of the Holy Spirit for the strengthening of faith in truth; that we may praise and glorify you through your child Jesus Christ; through whom be glory and honor to you, to the Father and the Son, with the Holy Spirit, in your holy Church, both now and to the ages of ages.[43]

This is a "soft," nonconsecratory epiclesis, more or less of the kind that we found in the (roughly contemporaneous?) anaphora of *Addai and Mari* that we treated a few pages above.

The concluding doxology is similarly remarkable, both in what it says (reflecting the conservative, traditional mode of eucharistic praying that seems to be characteristic of the little that we know of fourth-century eucharistic praying) and in what it does not say (it does not seem to take sides with this or that side of the then-raging christological and trinitarian controversies). Chronologically, the relatively final form of this anaphora that we are studying was probably taking shape at the height of the Arian crisis. But there is no indication that it was affected by that crisis. Although it may indeed have been more congenial to Arian than to Nicaean sensitivities, there is no evidence to suggest that this apparent congeniality to Arian sensitivities, rather than traditional liturgical conservatism, was the reason behind the way it expressed itself. In the development of eucharistic praying, we are apparently still not yet at that stage in which the anaphora itself could become a means of expressing or insisting on creedal orthodoxy. Quite different will be the situation in the anaphora found in book 8 of the *Apostolic Constitutions* (*AC*) and in the anaphora of Chrysostom.

42. Ibid., 46.
43. Ibid., 35.

The Anaphora of Book 8 of the Apostolic Constitutions

Although the Arian redactor of the *Apostolic Constitutions* apparently did not insert (or include) Arian formulations in his redaction of the so-called anaphora of Hippolytus in *AT* 4, he did so quite obviously in his redaction/ adaptation of this anaphora in *AC* 8. Some characteristics of neo-Arian religion obviously present in this anaphora are as follows:

(1) a close affinity to a theologically conservative Jewish Christianity; (2) an unusually jealous and intense worship of the one true God, or, as Kopecek put it, an "intensely consistent monotheism"; (3) the liturgical role of the Son as the primary worshipper of the Father; (4) placing restrictions on the worship of the Son; (5) a tendency to downplay affective worship in favor of consciously intellectual worship.[44]

The second, third, and fifth of these characteristics are obvious in the opening paragraphs of the preface:

It is truly fitting and right to praise you before all things, essentially existing God, existing before created things, from whom all fatherhood in heaven and on earth is named, alone unbegotten, without beginning, without lord or master, lacking nothing, provider of all good things, greater than every cause and origin, always being in one and the same mode, from whom all good things came into being as from a starting point.

For you are knowledge, without beginning, eternal vision, unbegotten hearing, untaught wisdom, first in nature, alone in existence, too great to be numbered. You brought all things from non-existence into existence through your only-begotten Son; and him you begat without an intermediary before all ages by your will and power and goodness, your only-begotten Son, the Word of God, living wisdom, the firstborn of all creation, the angel of your great purpose, your high-priest <and notable worshipper>, king and Lord of all rational and sentient nature, who was before all, through whom are all.[45]

The words in angle brackets, "<and notable worshipper>," are not found in later, non-Arian editions of the *Apostolic Constitutions*. This theme of the Son as worshiper of the Father—congenial to Arians but probably not to Nicaeans—is also found at the end of the lengthy preface: "For all things glory

---

44. Cited from Daly, "Trinitarian Theology in Early Christian Anaphoras," 264–65, where I am summarizing from Thomas A. Kopecek, "Neo-Arian Religion: The Evidence of the Apostolic Constitutions," in *Arianism: Historical and Theological Reassessments; Papers from the Ninth International Conference on Patristic Studies, September 5–10, 1983, Oxford, England*, Patristic Monograph Series 11 (Philadelphia: Philadelphia Patristic Foundation, 1985), 155–60.

45. Jasper and Cuming, *Prayers of the Eucharist*, 104–5.

be to you, almighty Lord. You are worshipped <by every bodiless and holy order, by the Paraclete, and above all by your holy child Jesus the Christ, our Lord and God, your angel and the chief general of your power, and eternal and unending high priest.>"[46]

To confirm that we are now at a time—the late fourth and into the fifth century—when, in the eucharistic prayers, doctrine, specifically trinitarian doctrine, is beginning to influence the formulation of these prayers—*lex credendi* influencing *lex orandi*—we have only to compare their doxologies. In *AC* 8, at least as it came from the hand of its Arian redactor, there are two obviously Arian-influenced doxologies:

> We beseech you [God] . . . that you keep us all in piety, and gather us together in the kingdom of your Christ, who is the God of all sensible and intellectual nature, our king . . . for through him to you is all glory, reverence, and thanksgiving, *and because of you and after you* [*dia se kai meta se*] honor and worship is to him in the Holy Spirit.[47]

> For to you is glory, praise, magnificence, reverence, and worship, and after you and because of you [*dia se kai meta se*] to your child Jesus, our lord and king, through whom worthy thanksgiving is owed to you from every rational and holy nature in the Holy Spirit.[48]

In striking contrast, the doxologies at the end of the anaphoras of Chrysostom and Basil clearly insist (though not quite as aggressively as the Arian redactor of *AC* 8 insisted on his view) on a Nicaean understanding of the equality of the Son with the Father: ". . . and grant us with one mouth and one heart to glorify and hymn your all-honorable and magnificent name, the Father, [and] the Son, and the Holy Spirit, <now and always to the ages of ages>."[49] As they are again in our own day—witness our struggles to find nonsexist, inclusive trinitarian formulations—the doxologies in our late fourth/early fifth-century anaphoras, as evidenced also by the large number of manuscript variants in these particular texts, had become a polemical battleground. When the dust had settled, one tended to find various forms of what became the classical formula: *to* the Father, *in/through/with* the Son, *and* (plus at times various other of these prepositions) the Holy Spirit. Remarkably, the possibly quite

---

46. Ibid., 108.

47. *AC* 8.12.50 (from the Greek Vatican Codex 1506; SC 336:204), as cited in Kopecek, "Neo-Arian Religion," 170.

48. *AC* 8.15.9 (from the Greek Vatican Codex 1506; SC 336:214), as cited in Kopecek, "Neo-Arian Religion," 171.

49. Jasper and Cuming, *Prayers of the Eucharist*, 123, 134.

early doxology at the end of the *Apostolic Tradition*, even though it comes to us through the hand of an Arian redactor, seems to reflect these major Arian and Nicaean concerns in a remarkably constructive tension: ". . . that we may praise and glorify you through your child Jesus Christ; through whom be glory and honor to you, to the Father and the Son, with the Holy Spirit, in your holy Church, both now and to the ages of ages."[50]

But to come back to the development of the epiclesis, it seems not to have been affected by the Arian-Nicaean controversy, and instead seems to reflect simply the growing theological awareness of the Spirit as, within the unquestioned unity of the Trinity, a reality, indeed an "agency" that is somehow distinct from the Son/Logos. We have already pointed out how the epiclesis of the *Apostolic Tradition* is indeed an epiclesis of the Holy Spirit, but also how, in line with the earlier tradition, it has remained a "soft"—that is, nonconsecratory—epiclesis. In *AC 8*, however, the epiclesis is explicitly consecratory:

> And we beseech you to look graciously upon these gifts set before you, O God who need nothing, and accept them in honor of your Christ; and to send down your Holy Spirit upon this sacrifice, the witness of the sufferings of the Lord Jesus, that he may make this bread body of your Christ, and this cup blood of your Christ; that those who partake of it may be strengthened to piety, obtain forgiveness of sins, be delivered from the devil and his deceit, be filled with Holy Spirit, become worthy of your Christ, and obtain eternal life, after reconciliation with you, almighty Master.[51]

Compare this with the epiclesis in Chrysostom:

> We offer you also this reasonable and bloodless service, and we pray and beseech and entreat you, send down your Holy Spirit on us and on these gifts set forth; and make this bread the precious body of your Christ, [changing it by your Holy Spirit,] Amen; and that which is in this cup the precious blood of your Christ, changing it by your Holy Spirit, Amen; so that they may become to those who partake for vigilance of soul, for fellowship with the Holy Spirit, for the fullness of the kingdom <of heaven>, for boldness toward you, not for judgment or condemnation.[52]

---

50. Ibid., 35. The exposition here follows very closely what I presented in "Trinitarian Theology in Early Christian Anaphoras," 264–67, where I summed up the situation by writing: "Continuing the primitive reference to Jesus as 'child/*pais*' was obviously congenial to Arian sensitivity, as was also the idea/concept of *through* Christ. However, the Arians took pains to avoid giving glory *to* the Son, which the orthodox Niceans made a point of doing, without the Arian qualifications *because of* and *after* the Father."

51. Jasper and Cuming, *Prayers of the Eucharist*, 111.

52. Ibid., 133.

The Anaphora of Chrysostom

Whether or not this anaphora was actually authored by Chrysostom, or to whatever extent it may have been—for perhaps he simply brought it with him from Antioch when he became patriarch of Constantinople in 398—it is not only the prayer with which the contemporary Orthodox Churches celebrate their Divine Liturgy; it has also become, in the recent liturgical renewal experienced by the mainline Christian churches, the most frequently used classical model of a full, mature eucharistic prayer.[53] One easily identifies in it the five-group/ten-element structure I outlined above (see "The Eucharistic Prayer") and also, within and through that structure, its obvious trinitarian content.[54]

A 1 The grace of our Lord Jesus Christ, and the love of God the Father, and the fellowship of the Holy Spirit be with you all.

> *People:* And with your spirit.
>
> *Priest:* Let us lift up our hearts.
>
> *People:* We have them with the Lord.
>
> *Priest:* Let us give thanks to the Lord.
>
> *People:* It is fitting and right <to worship the Father, the Son, and the Holy Spirit, the consubstantial and undivided Trinity>.

2 *The priest begins the holy anaphora:* It is fitting and right to hymn you, <to bless you, to praise you,> to give you thanks, to worship you in all places of your dominion. For you are God, ineffable, inconceivable, invisible, incomprehensible, existing always and in the same way, you and your only-begotten Son and Your Holy Spirit. You brought us out of non-existence into existence; and when we had fallen, you raised us up again, and did not cease to do everything until you had brought us up to heaven, and granted us the kingdom that is to come. For all these things we give thanks to you and to your only-begotten Son and to your Holy Spirit, for all that we know and do not know, your seen and unseen benefits that have come upon us.

We give you thanks also for this ministry; vouchsafe to receive it from our hands, even though thousands of archangels and ten thousands of angels stand before you, cherubim and seraphim, with six

---

53. This is true even of the new eucharistic prayers 2–4 of the contemporary Roman rite. For although these prayers insert an epiclesis of the Holy Spirit *before*, rather than after, the words of institution, they conform in other respects not to the more "Egyptian" structure of the *Canon Missae*/Roman Eucharistic Prayer 1 but to the more Antiochian, anamnesis-epiclesis/protasis-apodasis structure that is modeled in the Chrysostom prayer.

54. The absence of B 5 (preliminary epiclesis) is not a lack but a virtue, since the epiclesis has its proper place after the words of institution and ensuing anamnesis offering prayer, and not at this point as in the somewhat less elegant (my opinion!) Egyptian structure that eventually developed into the Roman Canon and its analogues.

wings and many eyes, flying on high, (*aloud*) singing the triumphal hymn <proclaiming, crying, and saying>:

3 *People:* Holy, <holy, holy, Lord of Sabaoth; heaven and earth are full of your glory. Hosanna in the highest. Blessed is he who comes in the name of the Lord. Hosanna in the highest>.

B 4 *The priest privately:* With these powers, Master, lover of man, we also cry and say: holy are you and all-holy, and your only-begotten Son, and your Holy Spirit; holy are you and all-holy and magnificent is your glory; for you so loved the world that you gave your only-begotten Son that all who believe in him may not perish, but have eternal life.

C 6 When he had come and fulfilled all the dispensation for us, on the night in which he handed himself over, he took bread in his holy and undefiled and blameless hands, gave thanks, blessed, broke, and gave it to his holy disciples and apostles, saying, (*aloud*) "Take, eat; this is my body, which is <broken> for you <for forgiveness of sins." *People:* Amen>. <*privately*> Likewise the cup also after supper, saying, (*aloud*) "Drink from this, all of you; this is my blood of the new covenant, which is shed for you and for many for the forgiveness of sins."

People: Amen.

D 7 *The priest, privately:* We therefore, remembering this saving commandment and all the things that were done for us: the cross, the tomb, the resurrection on the third day, the ascension into heaven, the session at the right hand, the second and glorious coming again; (*aloud*) offering you your own from your own, in all and for all,

People: we hymn you, <we bless you, we give you thanks, Lord, and pray to you, our God>.

8 *The priest says privately:* We offer you also this reasonable and bloodless service, and we pray and beseech and entreat you, send down your Holy Spirit on us and on these gifts set forth; and make this bread the precious body of your Christ, [changing it by your Holy Spirit,] Amen; and that which is in this cup the precious blood of your Christ, changing it by your Holy Spirit, Amen; so that they may become to those who partake for vigilance of soul, for fellowship with the Holy Spirit, for the fullness of the kingdom <of heaven>, for boldness toward you, not for judgement or condemnation.

9 We offer you this reasonable service also for those who rest in faith, <forefathers,> Fathers, patriarchs, prophets, apostles, preachers, evangelists, martyrs, confessors, ascetics, and all the righteous <spirits> perfected in faith;

(*aloud*) especially our all-holy, immaculate, highly glorious, Blessed Lady, Mother of God and ever-Virgin Mary; <diptychs of the dead;>

Saint John the <prophet,> forerunner, and Baptist, and the holy, <glorious,> and honored Apostles. . . .

[The prayer continues with extensive intercessions (diptychs) for all the members of the Communion of Saints, for the living and the dead, for church and government leaders, for all in particular need of prayers and help, etc., until it ends:]

E 10 . . . and send out your mercies upon us all, *(aloud)* and grant us with one mouth and one heart to glorify and hymn your all-honorable and magnificent name, the Father, the Son, and the Holy Spirit, <now and always and to the ages of ages>.

People: Amen.[55]

Conclusion

As we, from the vantage point of contemporary eucharistic theology, look back to what was happening from Jesus's apparent practice of open table fellowship up to the theologically nuanced eucharistic prayers that were taking shape by the beginning of the fifth century, we become aware of an extraordinary theological development. The earliest eucharistic prayers in *Didache* 9 and 10 were, by later standards, not only prechristological but also, to a large extent, binitarian rather than trinitarian. To the extent that we can conclude anything from meager historical evidence, this situation apparently lasted until well into the third century, when Origen became the first to point out the specific role of the Holy Spirit in the unfolding of the eucharistic event. In sum, the historical evidence suggests not only an apparent wide diversity of eucharistic practice and praying but also the absence of any original form of the epiclesis.

However, by the end of the fourth century—when the earlier practice of relatively extemporaneous eucharistic praying had been replaced by the recitation of carefully crafted "set" eucharistic prayers, in which, in contrast to apparent pre-Nicene practice, Jesus's words of institution also now held a central place—all the "new" eucharistic prayers, despite variations that persist to our own day, manifested the basic euchological (relating to formal ritual prayer) structure of ten elements in five groups that we outlined in the early pages of this chapter.

55. Except for the group and element designations in the left margin, the text is taken as printed in Jasper and Cuming, *Prayers of the Eucharist*, 131–34, who note (p. 130) that, following the eighth-century Barberini manuscript, and with the people's part supplied from modern editions, this text "differs from the Barberini text only in a few additions and completions, here in angle brackets, and the omission of two phrases, here in square brackets."

I have begun to point out how christological and trinitarian euchology, with its trinitarian doxologies, began to be a place where the struggle between Arianism and Nicene orthodoxy could become visible. In this development, however, different theological understandings of the Eucharist were apparently not at issue. The Eucharist was an ecclesial event. Its purpose was, as became increasingly clear (and as Augustine later put it), the transformation of the participants into the ecclesial body of Christ. The transformation of the elements of bread and wine into the body and blood of Christ, seen as the means and ground of this transformation of the participants, while expressed with varying degrees of explicitness in various of these prayers, was not an issue that had to be argued about. The Eucharist itself was not a battleground. This held true at least until the end of the fifth century, when Pope St. Gelasius felt free to assume what was basically a theory of eucharistic consubstantiation in his fight against the (for him much more threatening) Monophysite denial of the two natures of Christ.[56]

56. See Kilmartin, *Eucharist in the West*, 31–58, or, more briefly, Edward J. Kilmartin, "The Eucharistic Theology of Pope Gelasius I: A Nontridentine View," *Studia Patristica* 29 (Leuven: Peeters, 1997), 283–89.

3

The Nascent "Trinitarian" Worship of *Martyrdom of Polycarp* 14 and Ephesians 1

Paul A. Hartog

In 1899, J. Armitage Robinson, who would later become the dean of Westminster Abbey and then of Wells Cathedral, investigated the "dignified Prayer" that Polycarp allegedly uttered from his execution stake (*Martyrdom of Polycarp* 14).[1] Robinson compared Polycarp's prayer with early liturgical sources, believing that this was a path "worth pursuing," and one that might cast light upon "the history of the beginnings of liturgical worship."[2]

A fresh examination of Polycarp's prayer still remains a path "worth pursuing." This essay makes two preliminary assumptions. First, the wording of the prayer as found in the *Martyrdom of Polycarp* does not represent the *ipsissima verba* of Polycarp's final minutes of life.[3] Martyrologies commonly included final prayers (cf. *4 Macc.* 6:27–29; *Martyrdom of Carpus, Papylus, and Agathonice* 41; *Martyrdom of Pionius* 21.7–9; etc.), but these

---

1. J. Armitage Robinson, "Liturgical Echoes in Polycarp's Prayer," *Expositor* 64 (1899): 63–72. See also James Kleist, "An Early Christian Prayer," *Orate Fratres* 22 (1948): 201–6.
2. Robinson, "Liturgical Echoes," 64–65.
3. Ibid., 72.

prayers did not necessarily reproduce the exact words of the dying martyrs.[4] Second, the wording of the prayer resembles various early liturgical materials.[5] I will not spend time arguing the case for either one of these two basic assumptions, since the former seems self-evident and the latter seems well established.[6] Instead, I will concentrate upon the triadic characteristics and formulations and attempt to place this nascent "trinitarian" worship within broad historical context.[7] By doing so I will rectify one of Robinson's own historical claims.

Overview of Polycarp's Triadic Prayer

Three portions of "Polycarp's" prayer provide the materials for our examination of nascent "trinitarian" worship. First, the address is directed toward the "Lord God Almighty," who is further described as "Father of your beloved and blessed child [*pais*] Jesus Christ."[8]

Second, the heart of the prayer declares, "I bless you for making me worthy of this day and hour, that I may receive a share among the number of the martyrs in the cup of your Christ, unto the resurrection of eternal life in both soul and body and in the immortality of the Holy Spirit."[9] This

4. See David Tripp, "The Prayer of St Polycarp and the Development of Anaphoral Prayer," *Ephemerides Liturgicae* 104 (1990): 97.

5. Michael Holmes, "The *Martyrdom of Polycarp* and New Testament Passion Narratives," in *Trajectories through the New Testament and the Apostolic Fathers*, ed. Andrew Gregory and Christopher Tuckett (Oxford: Oxford University Press, 2005), 414.

6. See Hans Lietzmann, "Ein liturgisches Bruchstück des zweiten Jahrhunderts," *ZWT* 54 (1912): 56–61; W. Reuning, *Zur Erklärung des Polykarpmartyriums* (Darmstadt: Winter, 1917), 31–43; Robinson, "Liturgical Echoes," 63–73; Robinson, "The 'Apostolic Anaphora' and the Prayer of St Polycarp," *JTS* 21 (1920): 97–108; Robinson, "The Doxology in the Prayer of St Polycarp," *JTS* 24 (1923): 141–44; Tripp, "Prayer of St Polycarp," 97–132; J. W. Tyrer, "The Prayer of St Polycarp and Its Concluding Doxology," *JTS* 23 (1922): 390–92; Leslie Barnard, "In Defence of Pseudo-Pionius' Account of Polycarp's Martyrdom," in *Studies in Church History and Patristics* (Thessaloniki: Patriarchikon Hydryma Paterikon Meleton, 1978), 224–41; Gerd Buschmann, "Traditionsgeschichtliche Analyse des Gebets in MartPol 14," *JECS* 5 (1997): 181–221; Buschmann, *Das Martyrium des Polykarp*, KAV 6 (Göttingen: Vandenhoeck & Ruprecht, 1998), 226–57.

7. "Trinitarian" is anachronistic, of course. On "nascent 'trinitarianism'" (which would not carry the connotations of the developed doctrine), see Mark Carpenter, "A Synopsis of the Development of Trinitarian Thought from the First Century Church Fathers to the Second Century Apologists," *TJ* 26 (2005): 293–319.

8. Parallel uses of "Lord God Almighty" (including three vocative uses) are found in Rev. 4:8; 11:17; 15:3; 16:7; 21:22.

9. English translations of the apostolic fathers come from Bart Ehrman, *The Apostolic Fathers*, vols. 1–2, LCL 24–25 (Cambridge, MA: Harvard University Press, 2003); quotation here is from 1:387.

section, which is addressed to the Father, also mentions both Christ and the Holy Spirit. Robinson noted parallels between this material and early liturgical uses of "counted worthy" (*katēxiōsas*), "this hour," and "eternal life."[10] The martyrological language of "the cup of your Christ" echoes the Gospel accounts of Jesus's death (cf. Matt. 26:39, 42; Mark 14:36; Luke 22:42; John 18:11).[11]

Third, the prayer's closing exclaims, "I praise you, I bless you, I glorify you, through the eternal and heavenly high priest Jesus Christ, your beloved child (*pais*), through whom be glory to you, with him and the Holy Spirit, both now and for the ages to come. Amen." J. B. Lightfoot highlighted similar material in the *Apostolic Constitutions*, including the phrase "through the great High Priest."[12] But the position of Jesus Christ as high priest already appears in the doxological material of *1 Clement* 61. Interpreters of *Martyrdom of Polycarp* 14 have also noted the threefold "I praise you, I bless you, I glorify you."[13] Moreover, *Martyrdom of Polycarp* 14 concludes with triadic doxological praise: "through whom be glory to you, with him and the Holy Spirit (*di' hou soi syn autō kai pneumati hagiō*), both now and for the ages to come."

On the one hand, the labeling of Jesus Christ as God's beloved *pais* seems to reflect an early quality. Robinson himself insisted that it had not been "sufficiently recognized" that "the title [*pais*] perpetually recurs in primitive eucharistic formulae."[14] On the other hand, the threefold nature of the doxology—and especially the inclusion of the Holy Spirit in the doxology—seems to reflect a later liturgical character.[15] Robinson argued that this clause, at least, "was not written within the limits of the second century."[16] "The beauty of this famous Martyrdom," he cautioned, "must not deter us from a fresh investigation of its genuineness."[17]

---

10. Robinson, "Liturgical Echoes," 70–71. Cf. Jesus's understanding of the coming "hour" in the Gospel of John. On being "counted worthy" (along with references to "cup" and Jesus as a *puer*) in the *Apostolic Tradition*, see Tripp, "Prayer of St Polycarp," 121–22. For a description of the doxological variations within the recensions of the *Apostolic Tradition*, see R. H. Connolly's untitled addendum to "The Doxology in the Prayer of St Polycarp," *JTS* 24 (1923): 144–46; M. A. Smith, "The Anaphora of 'Apostolic Tradition' Reconsidered," StPatr 10 (Berlin: Akademie-Verlag, 1970): 426–30.

11. See also Matt. 20:22–23; Mark 10:38–39.

12. As noted by Robinson, "Liturgical Echoes," 65. Pol. *Phil.* 12.2 calls Jesus the "eternal high priest."

13. See Robinson, "Liturgical Echoes," 64, 71.

14. Ibid., 67.

15. On the textual variants, see below.

16. Robinson, "Apostolic Anaphora," 102.

17. Ibid., 104.

Parallels with *Pais*

Martyrdom of Polycarp 14 twice refers to Jesus Christ as God's *pais* ("child" or "servant").[18] David Tripp argued that the use of this label is one element that is demonstrably "pre-Polycarpian" because of its "antiquity."[19] For example, Acts 4:27 and 30 refer to Jesus as God's "holy servant [*pais*]." Later texts regularly avoided the christological use of *pais* and instead favored *ho [monogenēs] huios*.[20] "Despite the possibility of deliberate 'archaism,'" maintained Tripp, "the presence of the term in the prayer is best seen as a symptom of the prayer being rooted in public tradition."[21]

First Clement calls Jesus Christ the *pais* of God three times within one chapter alone (chap. 59). Verse 2 declares, "We will ask with a fervent prayer and petition that the Creator of all safeguard the number of those counted among his elect throughout the entire world, through his beloved child [*dia tou ēgapēmenou paidos autou*] Jesus Christ, through whom he called us out of darkness into light, from ignorance into the knowledge of his glorious name." Verse 3 addresses God as follows: "the one who multiplies the nations upon the earth and who from all has chosen those who love you through Jesus Christ, your beloved child [*tou ēgapēmenou paidos sou*]." The final verse beseeches, "Let all the nations know you, that you alone are God, that Jesus Christ is your child [*ho pais sou*]" (59.4). This prayer of *1 Clement* (which continues through chap. 61) closes with this doxological statement: "You who alone can do these things for us, and do what is more abundantly good, we praise you through the high priest and benefactor of our souls, Jesus Christ, through whom the glory and majesty be yours both now and for all generations and forever. Amen."[22]

The *Didache* describes Jesus as God's *pais* three times, also within a context of prayer. *Didache* 9.2 declares, "We give you thanks, our Father, for the holy vine of David, your child [*tou paidos sou*], which you made known to us through Jesus your child [*tou paidos sou*]. To you be the glory forever." Since this passage uses *tou paidos sou* not only of Jesus but also of King David, Robinson argued that the phrase should probably not be translated within context as "your son" but rather as "your servant."[23] On the other hand, 2 Samuel 7:14 and Psalm 2:7 use "son" of God as a Davidic title (cf. Ps. 89:26–27).

---

18. See Joachim Jeremias, "Ἀμνὸς τοῦ θεοῦ—παῖς θεοῦ," *ZNW* 34 (1935): 115–23. Cf. *Mart. Pol.* 20.2.

19. Tripp, "Prayer of St Polycarp," 103.

20. As noted by Robinson himself in "Liturgical Echoes," 69; cf. 72.

21. Tripp, "Prayer of St Polycarp," 103.

22. Ehrman has "You who alone can to [*sic*] do these things for us. . ." (*Apostolic Fathers*, 1:147). Cf. the glory ascribed to Jesus Christ in *1 Clem.* 20.11–12 and Ign. *Smyrn.* 1.1.

23. Robinson, "Liturgical Echoes," 67.

The *Didache* continues, "We give you thanks, our Father, for the life and knowledge that you made known to us through Jesus your child [*tou paidos sou*]. To you be the glory forever" (9.3).[24] The next chapter of the *Didache* adds, "We give thanks, holy Father, for your holy name which you have made reside in our hearts, and for the knowledge, faith, and immortality that you made known to us through Jesus your child [*tou paidos sou*]. To you be the glory forever" (10.2).[25]

Robinson observed that all of these christological uses of *pais* within *1 Clement*, the *Didache*, and *Martyrdom of Polycarp* are found in prayers.[26] He also remarked that all three texts closely connect the christological use of *pais* with God's granting of "knowledge" (*gnōsis* or *epignōsis*).[27] Robinson noted a further parallel between *1 Clement* and the *Didache*, but one not found in Polycarp's final prayer: a concern for the universal church (cf. *1 Clem.* 59.2; *Did.* 9.4).[28] What Robinson failed to note, however, is that concern for the universal church does appear in Polycarp's previous prayer as depicted in *Martyrdom of Polycarp* 8.1: "Then he finished his prayer, having remembered everyone he had ever met, both small and great, reputable and disreputable, as well as the entire universal church [*tēn oikoumenēn katholikēs ekklēsias*] throughout the world."[29]

Furthermore, Robinson failed to underscore the doxological contexts of the christological uses of *pais* in both *1 Clement* and the *Didache*. The setting within *1 Clement* (chaps. 58–65) contains four doxologies, all of which ascribe glory to God (the Father) through Jesus Christ (58.2; 61.3; 64; 65.2). The Holy Spirit is not mentioned in the final three. Nevertheless, *1 Clement* 58.2—the passage immediately before the prayer of 59.1–61.3—states, "For as God, the Lord Jesus Christ, and the Holy Spirit all live—as do the faith and hope of those who are chosen . . . the number of those who will be saved through Jesus Christ. Through whom be glory to him forever and ever. Amen."[30] This doxological material ascribes glory through Jesus Christ to God (the Father) alone, yet it does mention God (the Father), the Lord Jesus Christ, and the Holy Spirit in the introductory remarks.

It is also noteworthy that *1 Clement* 61.3 adds, "We praise through the high priest [*dia tou archiereōs*] and benefactor of our souls, Jesus Christ." This

---

24. See Klaus Gamber, "Die 'Eucharistia' in der Didache," *Ephemerides Liturgicae* 101 (1987): 3–32.

25. Note that the glory is directed to the Father.

26. Robinson, "Liturgical Echoes," 67–68.

27. Ibid., 68. See also Barnard, "In Defence," 237–40.

28. See Robinson, "Liturgical Echoes," 68.

29. Cf. John 17:20–24. On the "catholic" church, see Ign. *Smyrn.* 8.2; *Mart. Pol.* 8.1; 16.2; 19.2.

30. Cf. Tyrer, "Prayer of St Polycarp," 391.

wording resembles *Martyrdom of Polycarp* 14.3: "I glorify you through the eternal and heavenly high priest [*dia tou aiōniou kai epouraniou archiereōs*] Jesus Christ, your beloved child [*paidos*], through whom be glory to you."

Besides the relevant uses within *1 Clement* and the *Didache*, Robinson examined the second-century christological use of *pais* within the *Epistle to Diognetus* 8.9–11 and in the *Acts of Thecla* 24, and his investigation broadened forward to include the *Apostolic Tradition* (the so-called *Egyptian Church Order*) and the *Apostolic Constitutions*.[31] Robinson concluded that "the title [*pais*] perpetually recurs in primitive eucharistic formulae" and "is repeatedly found in the very earliest liturgical forms that have come down to us."[32] One might add *Epistle of Barnabas* 6.1, 92; Justin's *1 Apology* 50 (cf. 35); and multiple instances throughout Justin's *Dialogue with Trypho* as early nonliturgical parallels to the christological use of *pais*.[33]

The Doxology's Inclusion of the Spirit

Robinson argued that the doxology's inclusion of the Holy Spirit with the Father and the Son seems to betray a later character. He found the doxology "unfamiliar and even startling to our ears," and later expressed "increasing astonishment" at the "remarkable form and substance."[34] He pronounced that an appearance in the year 156 (a commonly accepted date for Polycarp's martyrdom) would be "no less than amazing."[35] Therefore, Robinson (like others) advocated an interpolation theory in order to solve the tension.[36]

Robinson highlighted later parallels, including numerous examples within the *Canons of Hippolytus* and the *Apostolic Tradition*, and he drew attention to the "stereotyped formula" in the Ethiopic Liturgy.[37] Robinson found only one other instance of *di' hou soi syn autō kai pneumati hagiō* (as found in Polycarp's final prayer), a single occurrence within the anaphora (rather than concluding doxology) of the *Liturgy of St. Mark*.[38] Greek fragments of this liturgy are

31. Robinson, "Liturgical Echoes," 65–69.

32. Ibid., 66–67.

33. See Tripp, "Prayer of St Polycarp," 108.

34. Robinson, "Liturgical Echoes," 71; Robinson, "Doxology," 141–42.

35. Ibid., 144. On the date of *Martyrdom of Polycarp*, see Boudewijn Dehandschutter, *Polycarpiana* (Leuven: Leuven University Press, 2007), 56–60.

36. Robinson, "Doxology," 144. See also James Donaldson, *The Apostolical Fathers* (London: Macmillan, 1874), 211–19.

37. Robinson, "Liturgical Echoes," 71–72.

38. Robinson's translation of the pertinent passage from the *Liturgy of St. Mark* (a composite liturgy from Egypt) was as follows: "through whom to thee, with him and the Holy Spirit, we give thanks and offer" ("Apostolic Anaphora," 103).

extant from the fourth or fifth centuries.[39] Robinson concluded, "If then this Martyrdom [of Polycarp] was indeed written shortly after A.D. 156, we have the surprising phenomenon that the earliest doxology in which the Holy Spirit is mentioned *at all* presents us with the stereotyped formula of the Ethiopic Church, a formula which also occurs once in the so-called Liturgy of St. Mark."[40]

In most scholarly reconstructions, our manuscripts of *Martyrdom of Polycarp* include appended materials, and the doxologies in these addenda include textual variants. Many scholars believe that chapter 21 was an early addition, and most conclude that chapter 22 was appended later.[41] *Martyrdom of Polycarp* 21.1 includes a doxology that is directed toward Christ alone: "To him be the glory, honor, greatness, and the eternal throne, from one generation to the next. Amen."[42] *Martyrdom of Polycarp* 22 includes two more doxologies (22.1 and 22.3). In most Greek manuscripts, the first doxology declares, "We bid you farewell, brothers, you who conduct yourselves in the word of Jesus Christ according to the gospel; with him be glory to God, both Father and Holy Spirit, for the salvation of his holy chosen ones" (22.1).[43] Codex Parisinus (tenth century), however, omits *kai patri kai hagiō pneumati* ("both Father and Holy Spirit"). Michael Holmes sides with this reading, thus rendering the final phrase simply as "with whom be glory to God for the salvation of the holy elect."[44] In most manuscripts, the second doxology states, "To him [the Lord Jesus Christ] be the glory with the Father and the Holy Spirit forever and ever. Amen" (22.3).[45] Codex Mosquensis, however, ends with "To him be the glory, with the Father and the Son and the Holy Spirit, forever and ever. Amen."[46]

The Greek manuscript tradition of *Martyrdom of Polycarp* 14.3 itself may include a textual emendation. Eusebius's duplication of Polycarp's martyrdom

---

39. See George Cuming, *The Liturgy of St. Mark* (Rome: Pontificium Institutum Studiorum Orientalum, 1990), xxiv.

40. Robinson, "Apostolic Anaphora," 104 (emphasis added). In response to Robinson's description of "the surprising phenomenon" of this "stereotyped doxology," which sounds "somewhat strange to our modern ears," F. E. Brightman cited similar ("some of them even more 'strange'") doxologies in later authors (in his addendum to "The Prayer of St. Polycarp and Its Concluding Doxology," *JTS* 23 [1922]: 392).

41. See the editions by Schoedel, Musurillo, Buschmann, and Dehandschutter.

42. Tripp reasons, "The original ending of the *Martyrdom* (xxi.1) has a doxology to the Christ only; the author was not anxious about Trinitarian formulae!" ("Prayer of St Polycarp," 103). One could use the same evidence to demonstrate that the author was not set upon ascribing glory to the Father alone (*through* the Son and Spirit), because chap. 21 clearly attributes glory *to* the Son.

43. Cf. Ehrman, *Apostolic Fathers*, 1:397.

44. Lightfoot agreed with this omission (J. B. Lightfoot, *Apostolic Fathers: Clement, Ignatius and Antioch* [London: Macmillan, 1889], 2:3, 400).

45. Codex Hierosolymitanus adds *tō* before both *patri* and *hagiō pneumati*.

46. The epilogue of Codex Mosquensis (thirteenth century) is quite distinct from the other manuscripts.

reads "*through* [*en*] the Holy Spirit" instead of "*and* [*kai*] the Holy Spirit."[47] Such textual variants are relatively common in doxological passages (as seen in the alternative renditions of *Mart. Pol.* 22 above). Even within *Martyrdom of Polycarp* 14.3, just several words earlier, some Greek manuscripts (along with Eusebius and the Latin translation) have *di' hou* while other Greek manuscripts have *meth' hou*.

Robinson maintained that Eusebius's rendition of *Martyrdom of Polycarp* 14 ("*through* the Holy Spirit") altered an original "and" to "through," involving "a change which would be in harmony with his dogmatic position."[48] Tripp, however, reasons that "it is fairly safe to take 'in' ['through'] as closer to the original," because "the 'and' of the MSS reflects the anxious assertion of homoousian orthodoxy typical of the fourth and later centuries."[49] It may be impossible now to determine the exact wording of the original with full certainty because of the frequency of revisions in such doxological passages as well as the reasonable arguments that can be mustered on both sides.

Nevertheless, Robinson argued, "The Latin version supports the 'and' reading of the text, which doubtless must be accepted."[50] The use of "doubtless" overstates Robinson's case, but the Latin translation does serve as a counterwitness to Eusebius.[51] If the Greek manuscript tradition reflects an alteration, the text must have been changed before the archetype of the Greek manuscripts and before the translation into Latin. Alternatively, one may (like Robinson) accept that *kai* represents the original, under the supposition that Eusebius modified "and" to "through," perhaps for his own theological purposes. Buschmann, Dehandschutter, Ehrman, Holmes, Lake, and Musurillo all side with the "and" reading of the Greek manuscript tradition (and Latin translation) against the Eusebian "through."

Examples Including the Holy Spirit

Robinson described *Martyrdom of Polycarp* 14 as a "stereotyped doxology," and he declared that an examination of early Christian doxologies would be

---

47. Lake's translation misses this nuance (Kirsopp Lake, *Eusebius: The Ecclesiastical History*, LCL 153 [Cambridge, MA: Harvard University Press, 1965], 1:355).

48. Robinson, "Apostolic Anaphora," 103.

49. Tripp, "Prayer of St Polycarp," 103; cf. Tyrer, "Prayer of St Polycarp," 391. Tyrer compares Basil, *On the Holy Spirit* 29.72.

50. Robinson, "Apostolic Anaphora," 103. In a later article, Robinson also accepted the textual judgment of "and" as found in Zahn, Lightfoot, and Harnack ("Doxology," 144).

51. Codex Mosquensis agrees with Eusebius, while the other seven extant manuscripts have "and."

"an admirable introduction to the study of Christian doctrine."[52] "Moreover," continued Robinson, "the answer to some interesting questions would then appear at a glance. What, for example, is the earliest reference *of any kind* in a doxology to the Holy Spirit?" He claimed that no reference to the Spirit existed "in the doxologies of the New Testament, nor in the numerous doxologies of the Epistle of Clement of Rome."[53] And he doubted whether any doxology mentioning the Spirit could be securely dated before Clement of Alexandria or Hippolytus (cf. Clement of Alexandria, *Paedagogus* 3.101.2; *Quis dives salvetur* 42; Hippolytus, *Against Noetus* 18).[54]

David Tripp cited a passage in the *Acts of Apollonius*: "I thank my God . . . and his only-begotten Son Jesus Christ and the Holy Spirit, even for this sentence of yours, which will be for my salvation." But overall, the extant *Acta* is likely a late, redacted version.[55] Moreover, this prayer, as found in the *Acts of Apollonius*, is not strictly "doxological" (it lacks the *doxa* word group). Certainly remaining of interest are the early "trinitarian" baptismal formulae found in Matthew 28:19, *Didache* 7.1–3, and Justin, *1 Apology* 61.

Fernand Cabrol examined doxological materials in the *Odes of Solomon* that include the Holy Spirit.[56] And J. W. Tyrer summoned even more significant materials in Justin Martyr. Justin describes Christians as worshipers of the Father, Son, and Spirit (*1 Apology* 6; 13). According to *1 Apology* 65, the eucharistic celebrant, after receiving the bread and the cup, "sends up praise and glory to the Father of all through the name of the Son and the Holy Spirit, and makes thanksgiving [*eucharistian*] for being accounted worthy [*katēxiōsthai*] of these gifts from Him."[57] Two chapters later, Justin says,

---

52. Robinson, "Apostolic Anaphora," 102.

53. Ibid. But cf. *1 Clem.* 58 (as discussed above), which refers to the Spirit within its doxology, although ascribing glory directly to the Father alone.

54. Robinson, "Apostolic Anaphora," 102. Cf. R. H. Connolly, "The Eucharistic Prayer of Hippolytus," *JTS* 39 (1938): 358–69; Tripp, "Prayer of St Polycarp," 119–23. See also the similar doxological material in Origen, as discussed in Fernand Cabrol, "La doxologie dans la prière chrétienne des premiers siècles," *RSR* 18 (1928): 18. Cf. Tripp's discussion of the eucharistic prayer of Serapion ("Prayer of St Polycarp," 124–28). Tripp believed that the *Apostolic Tradition* and the material in Serapion reveal "two distinct ways in which the three-fold pattern" found in *Martyrdom of Polycarp*, Justin, and Irenaeus "was developed (or enriched, or expanded, or overloaded, as you prefer)."

55. Tripp, "Prayer of St Polycarp," 104n18. Apollonius is believed to have been executed around AD 185. Tripp (along with others) treated the *Acta* material as second-century material. But the extant text is probably based upon an earlier nonextant rendition. See Victor Saxer, "L'apologie au Sénat du martyr romain Apollonius," *Mélanges de l'École française de Rome—Antiquité* 96 (1984): 107–38. Tripp also notes that the *Vercelli Acts of Peter* includes a triadic baptismal formula ("Prayer of St Polycarp," 117).

56. Cabrol, "La doxologie," 15–16.

57. One notes the liturgical language of being "counted worthy," a notion already found in Justin, *1 Apol.* 65 (cf. 1 Cor. 11:27; *Mart. Pol.* 14). Tripp notes that Tyrer "reasonably infers

"And over all our food we bless the Maker of all things through His Son Jesus Christ and through the Holy Spirit" (*1 Apology* 67).[58]

Based upon this material, Tyrer inferred that the Son and Holy Spirit were already established within threefold doxologies in ecclesial public prayers by the mid-second century.

> Further, Justin is professedly giving a description of Christian worship, not in some one church only but everywhere, which his wide experience as a traveller entitled him to do. Hence none of the usages he mentions can have been of very recent origin; all must have been at least fifteen to twenty years old. And this brings us to 130–140 as the latest possible date for the rise of the threefold doxology.[59]

Robinson graciously acknowledged, "I had rather forgotten Justin, and I am grateful to my critic for jogging my memory."[60] Yet Robinson rightly noted that these examples from Justin Martyr are not *exact* parallels to the Greek manuscript tradition of *Martyrdom of Polycarp*, since Justin directs glory *to* the Father *through* the Son and *through* the Holy Spirit.[61]

Ephesians 1:3–14

Ephesians 1:3–14 may cast further light upon the discussion (even though there is no direct dependence).[62] Buschmann has noted that both Ephesians 1 and *Martyrdom of Polycarp* 14 are "thanksgiving prayers" or "hymns," both

---

from Justin's words a final Trinitarian doxology, but mistakenly limits the sense to that; Justin is characterising the entire prayer" ("Prayer of St Polycarp," 107n23). See E. C. Ratcliff, "The Eucharistic Institution Narrative of Justin Martyr's *First Apology*," *JEH* 22 (1971): 97–102.

58. Tyrer did not remark upon *1 Apol.* 67, but the parallel was discussed by Robinson ("Doxology," 143) and by Tripp ("Prayer of St Polycarp," 104). Cf. Justin, *Dial.* 29.1. Tripp believes a "schema" or "a pattern of anaphoral prayer" underlies *Martyrdom of Polycarp*, Justin, and Irenaeus, although it is not the same pattern as is found in the second-century apocryphal literature ("Prayer of St Polycarp," 115–18). Cf. David Gill, "A Liturgical Fragment in Justin, Dial. 29.1," *HTR* 39 (1966): 98–100. See also Justin, *Dial.* 41.

59. Tyrer, "Prayer of St Polycarp," 390. On the other hand, Tripp refers to the "Asian character" of Justin's "liturgical data" ("Prayer of St Polycarp," 104n17).

60. Robinson, "Doxology," 143.

61. Ibid. As discussed above, Robinson adopted the *kai* reading in *Mart. Pol.* 14.3 (rather than the Eusebian *en*).

62. Ephesians was available in Smyrna, as demonstrated by Polycarp's use in Pol. *Phil.* 1.3. See Kenneth Berding, *Polycarp and Paul*, VCSup (Leiden: Brill, 2002), 42–44; Paul Hartog, *Polycarp and the New Testament*, WUNT 134 (Tübingen: Mohr Siebeck, 2002), 177; Michael Holmes, "Polycarp's *Letter to the Philippians* and the Writings That Later Formed the New Testament," in *The Reception of the New Testament in the Apostolic Fathers*, ed. Andrew Gregory and Christopher Tuckett (Oxford: Oxford University Press, 2005), 210–11.

locate knowledge in Christ, both include eulogies, and both mention the prior purpose and plan of God.[63]

Ephesians 1:3–14 is one long sentence in Greek, made up of 202 words.[64] The text has been variously described as a hymn, a eulogy, or a benediction.[65] Honoré Coppieters and Joseph Bover have labeled the passage as a "doxology."[66] Most interpreters acknowledge that the style seems to reflect early Christian worship.[67] Some have further commented upon similarities between Ephesians 1:3–14 and Jewish *berakoth*, blessings or eulogies praising God for his goodness.[68] Many scholars have also recognized a basic triadic structure within the Ephesians passage.[69] According to Ralph Martin, "A threefold division is both

63. Buschmann, *Das Martyrium des Polykarp*, 240, 266, 276, 277, 279, 287. See also Buschmann, "Traditionsgeschichtliche Analyse," 199.

64. Eduard Norden, *Agnostos Theos* (Leipzig: Teubner, 1913), 253n1.

65. See Friedrich Lang, "Die Eulogie in Epheser 1,3–14," in *Studien zur Geschichte und Theologie der Reformation*, ed. Luise Abramowski and Johann Friedrich Gerhard Goeters (Neukirchen-Vluyn: Neukirchener Verlag, 1969), 7–20; Stanislas Lyonnet, "La bénédiction de Eph. i,3–14 et son arrière-plan judaïque," in *À la rencontre de Dieu*, ed. André Barucq et al. (Le Puy: Xavier Mappus, 1961), 341–52; Christian Maurer, "Der Hymnus von Epheser I als Schlüssel zum ganzen Briefe," *EvT* 11 (1951–52): 151–72; J. T. Sanders, "Hymnic Elements in Ephesians 1–3," *ZNW* 56 (1965): 214–32; Rudolf Schnackenburg, "Die grosse Eulogie Eph. 1,3–14: Analyse unter textlinguistischen Aspekten," *BZ* 21 (1977): 67–87; Léonard Ramaroson, "'La grande bénédiction' (Ep 1,3–14)," *ScEs* 33 (1981): 93–103; Jan Harm Barkhuizen, "The Strophic Structure of the Eulogy of Ephesians 1:3–14," *HvTSt* 46 (1990): 390–403; Chantal Reynier, "La bénédiction en Éphésiens 1,3–14: Election, filiation, rédemption," *NRTh* 118 (1996): 182–99.

66. Honoré Coppieters, "La doxologie de la lettre aux Éphésiens," *RB* (1909): 85–88; Joseph Bover, "Doxologiae Epistolae ad Ephesios logica partitio," *Bib* 2 (1921): 458–60. For a distinction between "doxology," "benediction," and "eulogy," see Reinhard Deichgräber, *Gotteshymnus und Christushymnus in der frühen Christenheit* (Göttingen: Vandenhoeck & Ruprecht, 1967), 64–76. Texts such as Matt. 28:19–20, 2 Cor. 13:13–14, 2 Thess. 2:13–14, and 1 Pet. 1:1–2 closely connect the Father, Son, and Spirit but are not "doxologies."

67. See Kathryn Sullivan, "'Blessed Be the God and Father of Our Lord Jesus Christ' Εὐλογητὸς ὁ θεός (Eph 1:3–14)," in *Liturgy for the People*, ed. William Leonard (Milwaukee: Bruce, 1963): 29–37; Andrew Lincoln, *Ephesians*, WBC 42 (Dallas: Word, 1990), 44; Peter O'Brien, *The Letter to the Ephesians*, PNTC (Grand Rapids: Eerdmans, 1999), 91; Ernest Best, "The Use of Credal and Liturgical Materials in Ephesians," in *Worship, Theology and Ministry in the Early Church*, ed. Michael Wilkins and Terence Paige (Sheffield: JSOT Press, 1992), 56–58; Harold Hoehner, *Ephesians* (Grand Rapids: Baker Academic, 2002), 159.

68. See Lyonnet, "La bénédiction," 341–52. Cf. the shorter eulogies in the letter openings of 2 Corinthians (1:3–4) and 1 Peter (1:3), including the triadic nature of 1 Peter 1:3. See also J. Coutts, "Ephesians i.3–14 and I Peter i.3–12," *NTS* 3 (1957): 115–27. Best comments, "If, as is probable, 1 Pet 1.3ff is dependent on neither 2 Cor 1.3ff nor Eph 1.3ff, this increases the probability that the form was in use among Christians" (Ernest Best, *Ephesians*, ICC [Edinburgh: T&T Clark, 1998], 106; cf. Leonhard Goppelt, *Der erste Petrusbrief* [Göttingen: Vandenhoeck & Ruprecht, 1978], 48–51).

69. Hoehner, *Ephesians*, 157. Hoehner charts forty-three attempts to analyze the form and structure of the paragraph (160–61).

logical and chronological."[70] In a chronological manner, the text progresses from the pretemporal past, to the historical work of Jesus, to the contemporary application of salvation.[71] In a logical manner, the passage moves from the role of the Father to the role of the Son to the role of the Holy Spirit. This placement of the Father, Son, and Spirit is a "noticeable feature of the hymn."[72]

In "a broad sense," the Father's work is laid out in verses 3–6, the Son's provision in verses 7–12, and the Spirit's ministry in verses 13–14.[73] Martin, therefore, refers to the paragraph's "trinitarian layout, reflecting the praise of God in the threefold revelation and drawn from the worship practices of the Asian churches."[74] Martin contends that the text may be viewed as "laying the foundation on which later creeds and liturgies will be formed; out of these raw materials will be fashioned the Christian belief in and confession of 'one God in three persons.'"[75] He wisely cautions, "Yet the present passage is still a long way from a set creedal statement."[76]

C. Leslie Mitton finds "confirmation" for this triadic interpretation of Ephesians 1:3–14 "by the fact that each of the three suggested sections concludes with the phrase: *to the praise of his glory*."[77] Theodor Innitzer and Jules Cambier similarly noted a threefold structure focusing upon Father, Son, and Spirit, with each section ending with "to the praise of his glory."[78] Harold Hoehner concludes, "Certainly, this eulogy shows development, for one sees that the refrain 'to the praise of his glory' (vv. 6, 12, 14) is given after discussing each person of the Trinity in the order of the Father, Son, and Holy Spirit."[79] The glory ultimately seems directed to the Father in all three cases, although

70. Ralph Martin, *Ephesians, Colossians, and Philemon*, IBC (Atlanta: John Knox, 1991), 16.

71. Ibid., 13–14.

72. Arthur Patzia, *Ephesians, Colossians, Philemon*, Understanding the Bible Commentary Series (Grand Rapids: Baker Books, 2011), 149.

73. Ibid., 149.

74. Martin, *Ephesians*, 14. See also Eph. 2:18–22; 4:4–6; 5:18–20. "Paul does much the same in Ephesians 1, turning older Jewish prayer formulae to new use with a focus on Jesus, meditating on and exulting in God's work in Christ until, with the mention of the Spirit, the trinitarian picture is complete" (N. T. Wright, *Bringing the Church to the World* [Minneapolis: Bethany House, 1992], 211). Cf. Rom. 15:30; 1 Cor. 12:4–6; 2 Cor. 13:14; Gal. 4:6; 2 Thess. 2:13–14.

75. Martin, *Ephesians*, 14.

76. Ibid.

77. C. Leslie Mitton, *Ephesians*, NCBC (Grand Rapids: Eerdmans, 1982), 44. Cf. M. Coune, "À la louange de sa gloire. Eph 1, 3–14," *AsSeign* 46 (1974): 37–42; François Dreyfus, "Pour la louange de sa gloire (*Ep 1,12.14*): L'origine vétéro-testamentaire de la formule," in *Paul de Tarse, apôtre du nôtre temps*, ed. Lorenzo de Lorenzi (Rome: Abbaye de S. Paul, 1979), 233–48.

78. Jules Cambier, "La bénédiction d'Eph 1:3–14," *ZNW* 54 (1963): 58–104; Theodor Innitzer, "Der 'Hymnus' im Epheserbriefe (1, 3–14)," *ZKT* 28 (1904): 612–21.

79. Hoehner, *Ephesians*, 159; cf. 245. The exact language of "each person of the Trinity" obviously imports later terminology.

focused through the redemptive ministry of the Son and the efficacious role of the Spirit.[80]

Conclusion

In 1920, J. Armitage Robinson asked, "What, for example, is the earliest reference *of any kind* in a doxology to the Holy Spirit? There is none in the doxologies of the New Testament, nor in the numerous doxologies of the Epistle of Clement of Rome."[81] In the same article, Robinson also maintained that *Martyrdom of Polycarp* contains "the earliest doxology in which the Holy Spirit is mentioned *at all.*"[82] Curiously, some seventeen years prior, Robinson *himself* composed a commentary that *repeatedly* described Ephesians 1:3–14 as a "doxology" *and* noted the passage's references to the Holy Spirit.

Robinson published his commentary on Ephesians in 1903, with a revised edition appearing in 1904. On multiple occasions, this commentary described Ephesians 1:3–14 as a "doxology" (or "great doxology").[83] Robinson did not comment upon how the phrase "to the praise of his glory" closes three sections of the "doxology," focusing upon the three "trinitarian" members.[84] Nevertheless, his commentary on Ephesians 1:14 noted: "At last the great doxology comes to its close with the repetition for the third time of the refrain, '*to the praise of His glory.*'"[85]

Perhaps Robinson's own work should have qualified his description of the "startling," "amazing," and "astonishing" novelty of the "trinitarian" nature of *Martyrdom of Polycarp* 14.[86] The Greek manuscript tradition of *Martyrdom of Polycarp* 14 ("and the Spirit") does differ from the work of Justin Martyr ("through" the Spirit). And this conglorification of the Spirit as found in the Greek manuscript tradition of *Martyrdom of Polycarp* definitely goes beyond the relevant, though seminal, materials in both Ephesians and *1 Clement*. Nevertheless, the nascent "trinitarianism" of *Martyrdom of Polycarp* 14 does

---

80. Cf. Eph. 3:20–21.

81. Robinson, "Apostolic Anaphora," 102 (emphasis added).

82. Ibid., 104 (emphasis added).

83. J. Armitage Robinson, *Commentary on Ephesians*, 2nd ed. (London: Macmillan, 1904), 13 ("a doxology"), 18 ("the great doxology"), 19 ("this great doxology"), 34 ("his doxology"), 36 ("the great doxology"), 37 ("doxology").

84. Again, using "trinitarian" anachronistically.

85. Ibid., 36 (emphasis in the original).

86. William Schoedel insisted, "There seems to be no clear evidence that elements in the prayer are beyond the range of possibilities in the middle of the second century" (*Polycarp, Martyrdom of Polycarp, Fragments of Papias*, The Apostolic Fathers: A New Translation and Commentary 5 [New York: Nelson, 1967], 70–71). See also Barnard, "In Defence," 15.

not spring forth suddenly, like Athena full-grown from the head of Zeus.[87] Robinson may very well have been correct that *Martyrdom of Polycarp* 14 was not written in AD 156 or so (within a year of Polycarp's death). I would lean toward including the prayer, or at least its bulk, as original rather than an interpolation, without entirely dismissing the possibility of later redacting. Yet I am inclined to date the general composition of *Martyrdom of Polycarp* tentatively in the coming decades, or at least years, following Polycarp's death.[88]

The doxological language of Ephesians 1 does not ascribe glory to the Father, Son, and Holy Spirit through conglorification. It merely mentions the salvific work of the Father, Son, and Spirit in the plan of grace, concluding three sections with the thrice-repeated "to the praise of his glory." The phrase seems directed to the Father in all three cases, although focused through the redemptive and effective works of the Son and Spirit.[89] Nevertheless, Ephesians (along with *1 Clement*) may be placed along a multifaceted trajectory that leads through *Martyrdom of Polycarp* (and Justin's *First Apology*) and on to the fourth century's abbreviated and polished *kai*-connected formula: "Glory [be] to the Father, and to the Son, and to the Holy Spirit."[90]

Rather than pinpointing the exact dating of developments, one could focus upon the nature and impetuses of development. The "doxological" nature of these important texts positively demonstrates the role of worship within the progressive development of nascent "trinitarian" language and doctrine. The possibility that the wording of *Martyrdom of Polycarp* 14 was emended (from

87. Cecil John Cadoux claimed, "Whether we read with Eusebios 'in the Holy Spirit' or with the MSS. 'and to the Holy Spirit,' the rarity of the formula does not discredit either the early date of *Mart. Polyc.* or the *substantial* accuracy of the report" (*Ancient Smyrna* [Oxford: Basil Blackwell, 1938], 362n1). Cf. Hippolyte Delehaye, *Les passions des martyres et les genres littéraires*, SA 13B (Brussels: Société des Bollandistes, 1920), 15–16.

88. *Mart. Pol.* 18.3 is commonly cited as proof that the work was written within one year of Polycarp's execution, but this argument does not necessarily hold (although space does not permit a response here).

89. One is reminded of Basil, *On the Holy Spirit*, chaps. 7, 23–26.

90. When this chapter was presented as a paper at the 2008 Pappas Patristic Conference, relevant materials such as the following had not yet been published: Candida R. Moss, "On the Dating of Polycarp: Rethinking the Place of the *Martyrdom of Polycarp* in the History of Christianity," *Early Christianity* 1 (2010): 539–74; Albertus G. A. Horsting, "Transfiguration of Flesh: Literary and Theological Connections between Martyrdom Accounts and Eucharistic Prayers," in *Issues in Eucharistic Praying in East and West*, ed. Maxwell E. Johnson (Collegeville, MN: Liturgical Press, 2011), 307–26; Paul F. Bradshaw and Maxwell E. Johnson, *The Eucharistic Liturgies: Their Evolution and Interpretation* (Collegeville, MN: Liturgical Press, 2012), 54–56; Maxwell E. Johnson, "Sharing 'The Cup of Christ': The Cessation of Martyrdom and Anaphoral Development," in *Studies on the Liturgies of the Christian East*, ed. Steven Hawkes-Teeples, Bert Groen, and Stefanos Alexopoulos, Early Christian Studies 18 (Leuven: Peeters, 2013), 109–26; Jesse Hoover, "False Lives, False Martyrs: 'Pseudo-Pionius' and the Reading of the *Martyrdom of Polycarp*," VC 67 (2013): 1–28.

"through" to "and") does not undermine this general point. Rather, if such an emendation took place, it also would have been influenced by the worship life of the church. This present study thus buttresses those investigations that have emphasized the role of worship in the development of early Christian "trinitarianism."

4

GREGORY OF NYSSA ON KNOWING THE TRINITY

NONNA VERNA HARRISON

As created beings, can we come to know God as Trinity? It seems we can, because the church glorifies God as Father, Son, and Holy Spirit. Moreover, Christians are taught to address each of these three in prayer. Our Lord taught his disciples to pray, "Our Father who art in heaven, hallowed be thy name. Thy kingdom come, Thy will be done, on earth as it is in heaven" (Matt. 6:9–10 RSV). In the Orthodox Church and elsewhere, many people pray the Jesus Prayer: "Lord Jesus Christ, Son of God, have mercy on me, a sinner." And Orthodox services begin with a prayer to the Holy Spirit: "Heavenly King, Comforter, Spirit of truth, who art everywhere present and fillest all things, treasury of blessings and giver of life, come and abide in us." Each of these prayers addresses a particular divine person in a specific way, as one who is known to the faithful. In our devotional life, we take it for granted that as Christians we can pray in this manner.

So, how can we understand the doctrine of the Trinity in a way that supports this practice? This question may seem simple, yet it can prove to be surprisingly difficult to answer. Let us consider the kind of answer Gregory of Nyssa would provide.

The Unknowable God and God's Knowable Attributes

If God's nature or essence is unknowable, as the Cappadocians believed, what we can know are God's activities in the created world. Thus, we can also come to know the divine attributes whose names describe how God acts in creation, such as wisdom, power, life-giver, light, compassion, and love. Gregory of Nyssa thinks of these activities and attributes that reveal God as surrounding the unknowable essence; they are *ta tou peri theou*, "the things that surround God," and are themselves divine, as we shall see.

To understand how they can reveal the Trinity, we must consider how Gregory understands them. In the letter *To Ablabius*, which explains that belief in the Trinity does not mean there are "three gods," he states that the divine nature or essence is "unnameable and ineffable."[1] He adds that all the terms for God learned through human custom or known in Scripture express "our conceptions of the divine nature" but do not "signify the divine nature itself [*autēn tēn theian physin*]." Rather, each term makes known "some one of the things that surround it [*ti tōn peri autēn*]."[2] Note that the word "things" is not in the Greek, though it is hard to avoid using it in English as a place holder for "those (= what?) that surround it." These "things" include God's attributes and activities and self-manifestations, as far as they can be perceived by humans.

Gregory gives as examples of God's attributes incorruptibility and power, and he notes that neither one names God's nature directly. "Incorruptibility" names something God is not—that is, corruptible; God does not decay. "Power" points to many diverse things that God creates.[3] Neither term tells us what the divine nature itself actually is. Yet each tells us something distinct about God. In the letter *To Eustathius on the Holy Trinity*, Gregory explains that the names of divine characteristics—for instance, terms that name him as "good, holy and eternal, as wise, righteous, guiding and powerful"—are not all synonymous. Rather, "different ones guide our thoughts by different meanings to the same reality,"[4] that is, God. Yet Gregory notes in the letters to Eustathius and Ablabius that divine attributes are one, just as the divine nature itself is one. Because they are fully divine, the three persons each possess every attribute in its fullness, not some more, others less.[5]

---

1. GNO 3.1.42. Translations not otherwise attributed are my own.
2. GNO 3.1.42–43. Gregory frequently uses this language to identify God's attributes, activities, and presence to created beings. See Verna E. F. Harrison, *Grace and Human Freedom according to St. Gregory of Nyssa* (Lewiston, NY: Edwin Mellen Press, 2000), 41–48.
3. GNO 3.1.43–44.
4. GNO 3.1.7–8.
5. GNO 3.1.8.

Moreover, these divine characteristics have a central place in Gregory's spirituality, especially virtues such as goodness, wisdom, compassion, and so forth. In *On What It Means to Call Oneself a Christian* and *On Perfection*,[6] he lists many such characteristics and emphasizes that Christians are called to acquire and practice them. He points out that humans are made in God's image and given the task of acquiring God's likeness. The virtues are originally divine and compose the primary kind of divine likeness that Christians are called to practice and perfect.

In his fourth homily *On the Beatitudes*, Gregory comments on the text, "Blessed are those who hunger and thirst for justice, for they shall be filled" (Matt. 5:6). He observes that since the virtues are all interconnected, to hunger for justice is to hunger for all the virtues. Ultimately, he says, this means yearning to receive into oneself God himself, who *is* all the virtues. And as the beatitude promises, God will fulfill this desire: "He who has received God into himself becomes full of that for which he has thirsted and hungered, in accordance with the promise of the one who said, 'I and my Father shall come and we shall make our abode with him' (John 14:23), the Holy Spirit having of course made his home there first."[7]

The Holy Spirit must be dwelling in the faithful Christian to inspire his hunger and enable his receptivity. The Son and the Father follow. So the whole Trinity indwells the blessed one, and the three divine persons are present in the virtues he practices. This text shows that the "things around" the divine essence are not merely human words or concepts but are in fact divine.[8] In the persons' act of giving themselves, the Trinity follows a specific pattern: the gift is received in the Holy Spirit, who reveals the Son, and the Son leads to the Father. Though the virtues themselves may not be endowed with the distinguishing marks of each of the persons, for Gregory the divine activity of giving certainly discloses the persons. So let us now turn to his understanding of how the Trinity is present in divine activities.

The Trinity in Action

For Gregory, the persons of the Trinity are distinguished from each other by their manner of origination. For him, as a supporter of Nicaea, the Son is

6. GNO 8.1.129–42, 173–214; V. W. Callahan, trans., *Saint Gregory of Nyssa: Ascetical Works*, FC 38 (Washington, DC: Catholic University of America Press, 1967), 81–89, 95–122.

7. GNO 7.2.122; S. G. Hall, trans., "Gregory of Nyssa, *On the Beatitudes*," in *Gregory of Nyssa: Homilies on the Beatitudes*, ed. H. R. Drobner and A. Viciano (Leiden: Brill, 2000), 56.

8. See Harrison, *Grace and Human Freedom*, 41–59.

eternally begotten from the Father, and the Spirit proceeds eternally from the Father through the Son. So their relationships of origin constitute their ongoing manner of existence, not merely a moment in their lives. In the letter *To Ablabius* Gregory describes their ways of origination and thus also how they remain related to each other in terms of causality.

> While we confess that the [divine] nature is invariable, we do not deny the difference in regard to cause and what is caused. By this alone we grasp that one [person] is distinguished from another, that is, by our belief that one is the cause and another is from the cause. Again, in that which is from the cause we recognize another distinction, for one is directly from the first cause, and another is through that which is directly from the first cause. So also the Son remains unambiguously only-begotten, and the Spirit is not excluded from being from the Father. The Son's mediation, while guarding him as only-begotten, does not shut out the Spirit from his relation by nature to the Father.[9]

Here Gregory describes how, although their divine nature is unchangeable and is identical throughout, causality distinguishes the three persons and also joins them with each other. The one who "is the cause," of course, is the Father, the ultimate source of the Godhead. The Son and the Holy Spirit are distinct from the Father in that both derive from him, but they must also be understood as distinct from each other. Gregory's explanation of this second distinction is that as only-begotten the Son alone is said to come directly from the Father, though he is also an intermediary in the origination of the Holy Spirit. Likewise, the Son ensures that the Spirit remains connected to the Father.

Gregory here describes a trinitarian theology in which the Holy Spirit proceeds from the Father through the Son. Thus the three persons are linked with each other, as it were, in a linear sequence, though the Spirit, as he says, also remains directly linked to the Father. In the letter *To Peter on the Difference between Essence and Hypostasis*, Gregory notes that, from a created perspective, a man who starts to draw the Spirit to himself also draws to himself the Son and the Father, like one who grasps the end of a chain and drags the other end along too.[10] When considered from the Father's end, this linear sequence also describes the pattern by which divine activity unfolds and is

---

9. *GNO* 3.1.55–56.

10. PG 32:332c. This letter is now attributed to Gregory of Nyssa. Its style and theological detail are the same as in his other trinitarian works. However, many manuscripts attribute it to his older brother Basil as Letter 38. The text is accordingly found among Basil's letters in the *Patrologia Graeca*. A similar but updated edition with an old but excellent English translation can be found in Roy J. Deferrari, ed. and trans., *Saint Basil: The Letters*, LCL, 4 vols. (Cambridge, MA: Harvard University Press, 1926), 1:196–227.

accomplished in the created world. As Gregory says in *To Ablabius*, "Every activity that reaches from God to the creation, and is named after our various conceptions of it, originates from the Father, and proceeds through the Son, and is perfected in the Holy Spirit."[11] Yet he also emphasizes that each divine activity "is one and not three"[12]—that is, it is not divided into three separate parts. Rather, in each activity "there occurs one movement and distribution of the good will, which passes from the Father through the Son to the Spirit."[13]

From our point of view in the created world, like the man with the chain we perceive the same sequence from the Spirit's end. Thus, as the letter *To Ablabius* says, "every good thing . . . is brought to perfection in the power of the Spirit through the only-begotten God, . . . in the movement of the divine will from the Father through the Son upon the Spirit."[14] In *To Peter*, Gregory explains the same example at some length. This text is worth examining closely. It shows how one who receives a good gift in the created world can find divine activity causing it and trace that activity from the Holy Spirit through the Son back to the Father. Moreover, through the manner of their creative activity, the recipient can discern the identifying marks of each person. The passage begins as follows. "Every good that comes to us from divine power we say is an activity of the grace that works all things in all things, as the apostle says that 'One and the same Spirit works all these things, distributing them to each one individually, as he wills' [1 Cor. 12:11]."[15] The Holy Spirit is the one who dwells in things, completing and perfecting God's creative activity. As Gregory says in the chain illustration, the Holy Spirit is also the one who brings Father and Son together to creation and who brings creatures to them. So we pray that the Spirit will "come and abide in us." This work of indwelling and connecting with others manifests his identifying mark, his origination that links him to both Father and Son.

In this passage, Gregory uses Scripture to name the presence of each divine person. As the text continues, the observer is led by Scripture to look for another person as bestower of the gift he receives.

> But if we ask whether it is from the Holy Spirit alone that the supply of goods originates and thus comes to benefit those who are worthy, we are again led by Scripture to believe that the only-begotten God is the source and cause of the supply of goods that are working in us through the Spirit. For the Holy Scripture

11. *GNO* 3.1.47–48.
12. *GNO* 3.1.51.
13. *GNO* 3.1.48–49.
14. *GNO* 3.1.51.
15. PG 32:329a–b.

has taught us that all things came into being through him [John 1:3] and in him all things hold together [Col. 1:17]. So also, when we have been lifted up to that concept, again, led by guidance inspired by God [2 Tim. 3:16], we are taught that through this power [namely, the Son] all things are brought from non-being into being.[16]

Here Gregory cites passages from John and Colossians that name Christ as the Creator. John's prologue, which names him as the Father's Logos, provides the key to this passage. For early Christians, "Son" and "Logos" had become alternative names for the same person, and both identified the same mode of origin from the Father. The Logos came forth from the Father's mind, which is ultimately another way of articulating the concept that the Son was begotten from him. As Logos, the Son also implemented the creative planning and actualization that the Father willed.

Our text continues by making this point:

We are taught that through this power [namely, the Son] all things are brought from non-being into being, though surely not from this power without origin. Rather, there is a certain power that subsists without begetting and without origin, that is cause of the cause of all things that exist. For from the Father is the Son, through whom all things exist. With him the Holy Spirit is understood too, to be present always and inseparably.[17]

In this way, one comes to recognize the presence and activity of the Father, the ultimate uncaused Cause of all things, including the Son's creative work and the Holy Spirit's gift. The Father's will sustains all the goodness of creation. So Christians pray for this will to be accomplished on earth as it is in heaven.

"Just as one who grasps one end of a chain drags the other end along as well," Gregory concludes, "thus he who draws the Spirit, . . . draws both the Son and the Father through him."[18] In this way, the Trinity is made known. In the letter *To Eustathius*, Gregory declares that the angels as well, who are themselves created beings, ascend to their vision of the Father's face through the same trinitarian path that we humans follow.

For it has been said that, "through everything the angels see the face of my Father who is in the heavens" [Matt. 18:10]. Yet it is not otherwise possible to see the hypostasis of the Father except by gazing intently through the image into it. The image of the hypostasis of the Father is the only-begotten [cf. 1 Cor.

16. PG 32:329b.
17. PG 32:329b–c.
18. PG 32:332c.

12:3], whom, in turn, one may not even approach unless his mind is illumined by the Holy Spirit. What is proven by these statements? . . . The identity of the activity in Father and Son and Holy Spirit clearly indicates the invariability of the [divine] nature.[19]

Gregory envisages the angels as seeing the face of the Father not directly but by looking at its undistorted icon, the face of the Son. Moreover, their vision is enabled by the Holy Spirit's work of illumination. The angels thus perceive and engage with all three divine persons when they look upon the Father's face. Gregory understands the angelic vision as resulting from the common activity of the three, an activity of self-revelation, of making themselves present to those who perceive them. If this is how God makes his presence known in the heights of heaven, surely he reveals himself in the same way throughout all creation.

In the letter *To Peter*, Gregory concludes that in the activities of the Trinity there is an incomprehensible communion among the persons, and simultaneously each one is distinct. So the distinction among the persons does not disrupt the continuity of the one nature, nor does the community in the common essence confuse the individuality in their distinctive properties[20]—that is, in the identifying marks of Father, Son, and Holy Spirit. Both in nature and in "the things surrounding the nature," the divine activities and self-manifestations, God is one in three, and these three are one. The Trinity remains in essence an absolute mystery, yet through divine activities the triune God is made known as far as is possible to created beings.

19. *GNO* 3.1.13.
20. PG 32:332d–333a.

PART 2

JESUS CHRIST, THE TRINITY, AND CHRISTIAN SALVATION

5

The Holy Trinity as the Dynamic of the World's Salvation in the Greek Fathers

John Anthony McGuckin

A Theology in Crisis?

The doctrine of the Trinity has been said by many scholars throughout the latter part of the twentieth century to be one that is in crisis. This, if true, is a serious state of affairs, since the Holy Trinity is the substrate of our faith, the bedrock of our salvation, the foundation and pillar of the church, the very meaning of the Christian experience. Can it possibly be true, as we are told, that the doctrine of the Trinity is in crisis? The Roman Catholic theologian Karl Rahner, assessing this issue in the years immediately following the Second Vatican Council, concluded that, in his opinion, most Catholics in his day professed a simple and unreflective tritheism. By this he did not actually mean that they were all irredeemably heretical; rather, he thought they confessed their belief in God as sublime Triunity with their voices and gave assent to it with one part of their mind, but in their actual practices of prayer and the rituals of piety they most engaged in, the reality was a monophonic focus on one of the persons of the Trinity at a time: trinitarianism, therefore, flattened down as radically successive hypostatization. Rahner's diagnosis was that when the Father was addressed, one type of theological vision was adopted (with a corresponding form of subordinationism in relation to the conceived roles of the Son and the Spirit); when the Son or Spirit was addressed directly in prayer, each was hailed as a divine agent, on his own terms, with specific "characteristics" (the Son being more "approachable" in the imagination of piety than the Father, as enhominated divinity as distinct from immaterial transcendent; "the Spirit" being a preferred form of invocation for those wishing to imagine God as endorsing their own inspirational feelings or practices, considered somehow as God's energy or activity in the world at present). This Rahner characterized as a sad state of affairs, a kind of trinitarian somnolence muffling the vision of the church at large. It is an environment where the doctrine of coequality of hypostases is given overwhelming precedence over the concept of Trinity as divine outreach of creation and salvation.

Now this is hardly sufficient as a synopsis of Rahner's own contribution to trinitarian thought (which would be a worthy study for another occasion as being the most significant contribution to the essence-energies distinction since the time of St. Gregory Palamas);[1] but I am raising the example here simply as one of his more famous "diagnoses" in the *Theological Investigations*.

In the Protestant world it is more difficult to find a commentator who could make such a telling generic diagnosis. I remember my own interest a few years back as I motored for the first time through New England and found, in a succession of towns, several notice boards outside beautiful clapboard churches announcing: "First Unitarian Church: Now Worshipping as Trinitarian." I am sure that this might have had something to do with holding on to endowment. But the concept of trinitarian Unitarianism did strike me at the

---

1. In most of his philosophical thinking Rahner argued that God could not possibly be a direct object of human thought in the way that a thing or person within the world order could be. Even so, when a human mind thought about or related to any given object, or willed any particular value, it could grasp that object, or will that end, only as the object or end related (each and every moment) to a whole complex of being in which the particular object or end made sense and was situated—only, in other words, as a particular in the "whole of being." So it was, for Rahner, that all living sentient beings had an awareness of God, in so far as by their existential interactions they not only grasped individual entities in the world, but in that very act reached out invariably also to the "whole of being" that was beyond the individualities: reached out to God, therefore, whether they knew this in such terms or not. Rahner also posited throughout his theology an important new iteration of the relationship between "transcendental" and "categorical" experience: that God, in dealing with his creation, did not give revelations about himself; rather, he characteristically gave himself, communicated himself, to the world. The Trinity is the prime instance of what this might mean in terms of the Christian doctrine of God.

time as a sign that something may be happening. My own limited sense since those innocent days of first arriving in America is that the movement may in fact be in the opposite direction: a turning away from trinitarian theological language as not having much, other than formalist, relevance in the life of the Protestant churches. I do not exempt the Pentecostal movement from this observation, despite their lively interest in pneumatology, on the grounds that the Spirit devotion there so often hearkens back (in historico-theological discussions at least) to archetypes from the Montanist movement, rarely to the fourth-century trinitarian fathers, and thus perhaps to an implicit monism inherent in the very notion of particular devotional focus on one of the three persons as a primary vehicle of faith. This mono-optic focus has often been diagnosed as operative in, for example, the "Sacred Heart" devotion of eighteenth- and nineteenth-century Catholicism, or the "Spirit devotion" of the charismatic movement.

In an exchange a few years ago I was advised by a Protestant contemporary theologian that the Orthodox Church needed to reform. Always eager for reform, I asked how. "Remove the sexist patriarchal language of its prayer" was the answer. When I pressed for details, it seemed that the person, who was a pastor as well as a theologian, had led the way in her own tradition by replacing the doxological invocation of Father, Son, and Holy Spirit with the titles of Parent, Child, and Nurturer. When I suggested that this might be more viable in her context than ours since we were a trinitarian church, and hers might not be, she took umbrage.[2] When I pressed the point and went on to ask how this liturgical change had actually been received over time by the people of God in her assembly, she did admit that it was only with a lukewarm response, and it eventually dropped off altogether after a year or so, and God was thereafter customarily referred to genderlessly. I suppose that meant generically—without mentioning the Trinity, without ever using the holy names. Most recently, one professional, professorial theologian said to me at a very high-level ecumenical discussion, on an occasion when I had said that Christian discourse really had to begin in a shared understanding of the Trinity: "Who cares about that? It is elitist theology, not rooted in the real lifestyles of the people of God." Well, this is a major issue.

2. Orthodoxy holds strongly to the belief that the "names" of the hypostases of God are part of the deposit of divine revelation. For this reason it regards the titles as more than merely formalist and socially constructed. The titles Father, Son, and Spirit, since they are the revealed names of the hypostases of the divine, are, as such, worthy of adoration. The Name carries the power of God within it, as the Scriptures of the old covenant rightly sensed, and its invocation endows prayer with the power of holiness. The Orthodox of both sexes will thus never cease to use the threefold and correct Name of God in all their prayer and invocation.

Trinitarianism in the Church's Confession

The initial approach to trinitarian theology can cause problems, perhaps. But consider these words of one of the great systematicians of the church:

> There is one essence, one divinity, one power, one will, one energy, one beginning, one authority, one dominion, one sovereignty, made known in three perfect subsistences [hypostases] and adored with one single adoration; believed in and worshipped by all rational creation; united without confusion and divided without separation, a thing which surely transcends thought.[3]

Now, as a catechesis this is clearly not of the same order as the Islamic theology of monism. Here in the Damascene is the careful setting of boundaries, so necessary to the intellectual tradition but not all-inclusive of Christian experience and passion, and one that ends by appealing to the need for caution, for silence; for the very thought itself eludes thought, and not only by quintessentially transcending the power of thought, but even by its fundamentally paradoxical nature as kataphatic statement. His debt is primarily to St. Gregory the Theologian and to St. Maximus the Confessor, with clear resonances of context additionally supplied by the Chalcedonian settlement and its famous adverbial way of depicting complex conjunction. The patristic doctrine of the Trinity that St. John articulates here, in other words, is not really a straightforward catechesis at all, although it is a synopsis of catechetical utterances carefully assembled into a reference compendium. Whether most trinitarian confession has the required force and energy of a truly catechetical statement of faith is an important question. One of the elements that I would always identify as the true mark of the genre, proving its capacity to bear the weight of a truly central dogmatic statement of the faith, is that it can demonstrate its liturgical origin. Take, for example, the manner in which the great Creed of Nicaea, however it was catechetically extended and developed through the Arian and Macedonian crises, still retained its fundamental character as a baptismal confession and still fulfills that role in the approach to the holy anaphora of the contemporary liturgy.

What *would* stand as Orthodoxy's direct antithesis to the Islamic confession of monist theology is our liturgy's doxology itself: + "Glory to the Father, and to the Son, and to the Holy Spirit." And it is no accident that this confession of praise, by using the prefatory word *Doxa*, is meant to evoke the simultaneous prayer of the angels, who afford God heavenly *doxa* in a manner completing that of the earthly church. It is also no coincidence at all

---

3. John of Damascus, *Exposition of the Orthodox Faith* 1.8.

that the doxology is traditionally accompanied, always, by the physical making of the sign of the cross over the body of the believer who utters it. These
three things describe the profession of the Trinity in the life of the church:
first, the knowledge that calls upon the true triadic Name of God, for the
power that is within the Name itself—not the "names," but the Name of
Father, Son, and Holy Spirit. Second, the life-giving grace that is within the
confession of praise of God and which elevates us to the *taxis* (order or rank)
of the angels in our worship. Third, the embodiment of all that this means
in the victory of the cross, an embodiment that sums up all that is meant by
the utterly transcendent Father, and the mysteriously indefinable Spirit, by
reference to the perfect articulation of who both are in the crucified Lord of
Glory, Jesus. These three dynamic characteristics, I would suggest, are at the
heart of the patristic theology of the divine triunity and mark this off from
what has often passed as "the patristic doctrine of the Trinity" as the latter
has been represented across several generations past in theological textbooks
of a historicist nature.

The Patristic Theology of Glory

In these three elements the patristic understanding of the Trinity emerges
as a dynamic mystery of salvation, a living theology of praise, not a set of
theological conundra that gather dust in the history books. We should note
first the claim to sing God's praises in a harmony of voice—not the monophonic tone of earthly believers stating theology, but the stereophonic voice
of a confession that rises to equal that of the angels, which is not available
as a mere insight of a generically religious nature[4] but is an essential mark of
the true church as the mystical bride of the Lamb. In other words, the praise
of God as Trinity cannot be uttered outside the marriage chamber of the
church as a fully functioning heavenly mystery and reality. The utterance of
God's praise is at once proof that the believer is illuminated. This illumination is all that allows the believer to utter it in praise. The ecstatic confession
is, itself, the understanding. The transcendent understanding gives wings of
fire to the praise.

We note second, the manner in which the confession is *doxa*, not simply
"praise," but the technical word of the New Testament for the very Shekinah
light itself. Such confession is not a descriptor of the *kabod* of God, that

---

4. In other words, the "religious" confession that all faiths speak of the same God cannot
possibly be true if confession of the Trinity, as Orthodoxy confesses its Living God, is a confession peculiar to the apostolic catholic Christian faith.

unapproachable power of holiness and presence from which Israel was always excluded (whether on Sinai or in the temple); it is, rather, entrance to the presence into which the New Israel has been admitted through the mercy of our triune salvation. As the apostle Paul put it: "It is through him, by faith, that we have obtained access [*prosagōgē*] to this grace in which we stand, and are confident of the Glory of God" (Rom. 5:2).[5]

Third, we note the enfleshment of this in the sign of the embodied cross; not just in the life of the enhominated Logos of God, Jesus, but precisely in the embodiment of the crucifixion, whereby he allowed his glory to be seen on the earth; in that moment of dissonance and failure, typified by the betrayal of Judas at the very heart of the new-covenantal gift of the Eucharist, whereupon we note how Jesus himself proclaimed the trinitarian doxology: "And having received the piece of bread, Judas immediately went out. It was dark. When he had departed Jesus said: 'At this moment is the Son of Man glorified. And in Him God is glorified'" (John 13:30–31). The awe-inspiring initiations of the Lord into the nature of the Triunity are given to the apostles in the context of the failure (in a certain sense) of the reconciling power of the sacrament of love. They are given in the very next breath after the departure of Judas to deliver Jesus's address in Bethany to the police of the high priest, a tactic meant to ensure that all the disciples could be surrounded and arrested in the early hours of that morning, but one that was foiled by the agonized compassion of the Christ, who prayed through the night in the garden to his Father precisely because he did not want to go home to his lodgings in Bethany and was determined to see the liturgy of his sacrifice through to its envisioned end. This solitary end, we note, not accidentally secured the literal salvation of all his disciples, for not one was arrested, not one executed alongside Jesus—a most peculiar phenomenon that has often escaped the notice of historians but that may help us, as theologians, to begin to understand the seed of what germinated in them in the light of the resurrection, as a theology of the cross that recognized that same cross as their liberation and forgiveness.

This context of the triunity of God as experience, within the illuminated church, of glory given through the cross, makes steady our claim as Orthodox that the theology of the Holy Trinity remains among us as a living force, a dynamic way of understanding and proclaiming our confession of God's salvation, not merely a theological formulation that has little grounding in practice, or small basis in the contemporary understanding of the body of present-day believers. It is not to say that the average Eastern Orthodox believer

---

5. Also Eph. 2:18: "Through him we have access in one Spirit to the Father." See also Eph. 3:8–18.

could articulate high patristic theology of the Trinity any better than his or her Western counterparts, but it is to claim that the manner in which the faith of the Trinity functions in the Orthodox world is significantly different, eschatologically charged and mystically dynamic in character, and that this is preserved to be witnessed in every page and prayer of its worship tradition, and thus of its authentically articulated theology. Trinitarian *orthopraxis* is thus critical for the Orthodox as they exegete the patristic tradition. We may not fully comprehend the greatness of the God who has revealed his own life and demonstrated his great love by offering to share it with humanity, but we can certainly celebrate it. By doxology the individual Christian grows slowly in the power of the Name and in the comprehension of its saving power. This *orthopraxis* is critical and is why, within the church, the tree of trinitarian doctrine is both massive and alive with green leaf. It shall always be so. It is one of the supreme marks of the living church. Where faith in the Trinity is static, dead, or formalist, doxology of the true Name of God cannot occur, and the gifts of power and grace begin to wither.

A Call to Reorientation

This context of the triunity of God as lived experience also makes another specific claim, on which I will focus for the rest of this essay: that, this being so, as I would argue it is, it follows that we may have been reading the fathers wrongly about the theology of the Trinity, because we have been reading them in piecemeal fashion as cut up and atomized in handbooks of patristic dogma, with the latter understood as a scholastic branch of the *Religionsgeschichte* school, which has held such a sway over late modern intellectual life, especially from the eighteenth century to the present in the academy. I am not here speaking against the historico-critical method. I have used it extensively in my own career and value its rigor and its richness. But I am issuing a warning that it is not the be-all and end-all. Mircea Eliade, when at Chicago, was renowned for issuing a warning that, perhaps, has been too much forgotten in Christian analytical circles: that when steeped in *Religionswissenschaft* (that fevered attempt to persuade ourselves and other academic colleagues that religion is a pure science), the practitioner must take great care to ensure regular periods of "de-provincialization," so as to restore a balanced perspective. What he meant by that was to remind his advanced students that the often-unspoken premises of scholarship tended to blind as much as they illuminated. He wanted his researchers to step outside their Euro-centric hierarchies of judgment over what constituted religious significance—such as the way we so often presumed that European philosophy of history ought to be the standard mode for analytical discourse. Not much of a help, Eliade thought, when dealing with nontextualized Mayan ritual. Maybe not a profound help, either, in our mapping of the transcendent.

The history-of-dogma approach has not been uncritically swallowed in every hallway of the intellectual patristic tradition, of course; far from it. It came into the academic world as a child of liberal Protestantism of the nineteenth-century type. But into the wider and generally more Catholic culture of patristic circles there came the other shining meteorite of nineteenth-century theory about Christian origins, exemplified most succinctly by John Henry Newman's *Essay on the Development of Christian Doctrine*. And in this schema of approach, which had achieved a high level of acceptance by the mid-twentieth century in the Catholic world, the history-of-religions approach was nuanced by a tendency to "read" the doctrine of the Trinity in terms of how it "developed" toward its high-water statement: namely, in terms of the fourth-century patristic dogmas of Athanasius and the Cappadocians. This is an unfortunate way of proceeding, however, if the high-water statements of the church's trinitarian initiation happen to be the Johannine and Pauline apostolic catechesis (as Origen and others had intimated several times) and if the generic variform patristic tradition of the Trinity is merely an extended exegetical commentary on it. Whether or not the method is problematic, however, it has certainly dominated the field for more than a century now.

Taking a typical trajectory to study the doctrine of the Trinity in this environment means, more or less, to begin with New Testament Trinity examples of Christology and pneumatology, move on to the apologists' embryonic models of Trinity, and resolve the matter in the high patristic age when the fully developed model of trinitarian confession is alleged to have been fashioned as a response to the Arian and Macedonian controversies. It follows as a certain form of postlude to this model of thinking that, because the Trinity appears to have been an emergency reaction to high Arianism, then once it had been stated, the need to restate it accordingly diminished; and this might explain why the notion was elaborated (albeit with such opacity) in the patristic age and was then left without much further comment throughout the medieval, Reformation, and modern periods.

This is a rapid pen sketch, perhaps too much of a caricature, though I could defend its substance by reference to more or less any curriculum (of those that do exist) dealing with the Trinity in Christian tradition.[6] It stands duty here

---

6. For a slower and historically more elaborated account of the trinitarian doctrine in the writings of the Greek fathers, see J. A. McGuckin, "The Trinity in the Greek Fathers," in *The*

to raise for us the question: "If we have been reading the fathers wrongly on the doctrine of the Trinity, how might we stand to correct our reading?" If we take St. Augustine's monumental *De Trinitate* as an example of a high-level discussion of the Trinity that was not actually precipitated by a crisis, it may serve to underline the point that "problematic" has been falsely elevated as the chief key of interpretation. For although the *De Trinitate* stood in for some of the highest level of thinking on the subject that the later church engaged in, it is nevertheless, in its original context, clearly the attempt of an African provincial bishop to make sense of a received and, for him, problematized understanding of a central matter of the faith. That in this great treatise Augustine makes so much use of Late Antique logic and rhetoric, psychology and imagination, to retell the trinitarian story of the church, and so little use of the prior theological heritage he has received, indicates how a powerful intellect could overcome a difficult narrowness of base when seeking a deeper self-education without recourse to a significant Christian library. In passing on his solutions to the Latin world that came after him, in all innocence Augustine also passed on the peculiar method he had adopted in the relative isolation of his North African see. As well as his solution, he thus passed along too his fixing of the Trinity as this certain domain of problematic.

St. Photios, among others in the Eastern tradition, would point the finger of blame at that part of the great African's system where he clouded the waters over the fundamental term of the procession of all being from the Father alone: the *monarchia* of the Father understood as triunity by seeing him as the single *Aitios* (cause) of the Godhead. And Photios would, further, point to what that really meant in practice: that the being that is expressed by the Son and Spirit equally is not "divine being" as such, some form of a common set of attributes or properties that they command or possess as coequal deities, but is rather, and by contrast, the very being of the Father in particularity. The Son and Spirit have no other being than the Father's own, and singular, being; and this is exactly why the Greek church professes that there is but one God, not three gods.

The bond of the triunity is, in the Greek church, identity of essence, not commonality of substance. The particular diffractions of the triunity are hypostatic, or distinct personal expressions of that being of the Father in the manner in which the Father's life-creating presence is celebrated. This is true both within the deity and without; or, to put it better, it is true both to God himself as Father, Son, and Spirit (more than which I cannot say, without saying

Cambridge Companion to the Christian Trinity, ed. Peter C. Phan (Cambridge: Cambridge University Press, 2011), 49–69.

what cannot be said) and to God's beloved creation, wherein the Triune God stands both as the fundamental celebration of life at the root structure of all created being and as the fundamental energy of therapeutic healing, for all that part of the creation (the sentient or noetic part of it) that needs remedy and rescue. In short, the triunity is, for God, pure celebration of being, the vitality of which we cannot imagine, yet we sense the conflagration of the light as we are drawn to it in the patterning of our existences; and for us, the angelic and human church of the Elect, it is the celebration of reconciliation. In a word, the Trinity is the dynamic of our salvation. Metropolitan John of Pergamon expressed it in the following way, which brings out the uniqueness and radicality of the high patristic doctrine as stated (for example) by St. Gregory the Theologian: "Outside the Trinity there is no God, no divine substance, because the ontological 'principle' of God is the Father. The personal existence of God (Father) constitutes His substance, makes it *hypostasis*. The being of God is identified with the person."[7] Most recently Christopher Beeley has done a marvelous job in demonstrating how this dynamic, in the hands of Gregory the Theologian, makes sense of his passion for the Trinity: "My Trinity," as he so often called his God.[8]

To read the Greek fathers rightly on the Trinity, therefore, I would suggest we scale back the apologetic context of our analysis, reduce the urgency of our need to see patterns of development, and become more ready to accept eschatological utterance on this theme for what it was, a commentary on the glory of the living God manifested in the creation or in the act of salvation (the song of the angels, or the song of the cross). It was this, far more than ever it was "this or that apologia"; for the apologetic element was merely its occasion, not its cause. It is only by approaching the mystery of the Trinity in this way, as the mystery of our salvation and God's life-giving outreach to humanity, that it can be saved from becoming, for us, a mere conundrum, of the type where all the facts of the Trinity can be rehearsed as if they were mathematical formulae: three persons in one God, each person wholly divine, making not three gods or three parts of one God, but all who are one God, possessed of the selfsame nature in three coequal hypostases and expressing a single power, glory, and will. This, the solemn high patristic doctrine of the Trinity, is a mystery full of significance and symbolism. It is not a schoolroom problem but the song of the church. But the words of the verses are not entirely exhausted by the fourth-century patristic consensus. It is this element of the Trinity as canticle

7. John D. Zizioulas, *Being as Communion* (Crestwood, NY: St. Vladimir's Seminary Press, 1985), 41.

8. Christopher Beeley, *Gregory of Nazianzus on the Trinity and the Knowledge of God* (Oxford: Oxford University Press, 2008).

of glory that I suggest should be restored to our global reading of the Greek fathers, and not least on the grounds that they were often pastorally rooted saints before they were subtle theoreticians. If it cannot be rescued from its presentation among the schools as merely a problematic, the concept of Trinity will not simply be a conundrum for Islam or Judaism, and *de facto* even more so for other religious systems, but will increasingly become a matter of profound difficulties of future communication with Western Christendom.

This perspective also suggests that the doctrine of the Trinity from all parts of the patristic era matters—that the Irenaean nonformulaic trinitarian conceptions, for example, are in no sense merely embryonic because they are pre-Nicene, and that the imagery of the apologists is not necessarily defectively drawn because it is not logically watertight. Nothing, in fact, could be purer to take as a final example than that earliest of theologians, who is so rarely cited as a trinitarian teacher, Polycarp, the martyr and bishop of Smyrna who prophetically uttered at his execution in 156:

> O Lord, Pantocrator, Father of your Beloved and Blessed Son Jesus Christ, through whom we have received the perfect knowledge of You, . . . I bless and glorify You through the eternal and heavenly High Priest, Jesus Christ your Beloved Son, through whom be glory to You, with Him and the Holy Spirit, both now and for the ages to come. Amen.[9]

If I had time—and it would certainly be a fruitful exercise for someone to do this systematically—all the major patristic statements about the trinitarian relations could, and should, be reexegeted as liturgical doxologies. It will have to suffice simply to draw attention to a few of the major thinkers who never depart from the liturgical matrix, the poetic élan that always characterizes even the most abstruse defenses of trinitarian thought in the fathers. We can begin with Athanasius, who, exegeting the Johannine Discourse,[10] lifts up the powerful, and beautiful, image of radiance: life-giving illumination as what the Trinity essentially means, the invisible Father given in the features of Christ's face:

> The whole being of the Son belongs to the Father's substance, as radiance from light, and stream from spring; so that he who sees the Son sees what belongs to the Father; and knows that the Son's being is in the Father just as it is from the Father. For the Father is in the Son as the sun is in its radiance, the thought in the word, the spring in the stream.[11]

9. *Mart. Pol.* 14 (PG 5:11040).
10. John 14:6–11.
11. Athanasius of Alexandria, *Against the Arians* 3.1–3.

Or we may take the two beautiful prayers in St. Basil's *De Spiritu Sancto*, which many have seen to be an imagistic core of the work. In the first, he speaks of the illumination that is the Trinity as given by the enlightenment of the Spirit of God, like a light falling onto a transparent vessel. It is a supreme example of what Gregory the Theologian would articulate, almost simultaneously, when defining the scope of *Theologia* as akin to that of poetry. St. Basil says:

> Shining upon those that are cleansed from every spot, [the Spirit] makes them spiritual by fellowship with Himself. Just as when a sunbeam falls on bright and transparent things, they themselves become brilliant too, and shine out a fresh brightness from themselves; so it is with souls in which the Spirit dwells. Being illuminated by the Spirit, they themselves become spiritual, and then send forth their grace onto others.

In the second prayer, Basil approaches the deity of the Spirit by means of an extended commentary on 2 Corinthians 3:18, using the image of sunlight spreading color cast in a room to represent the lucent character of the soul of a saint. This passage comes after chapter 19 of the treatise, which makes its major dogmatic statement on the basis that the church's experience of God demands we give a doxology that triadically includes the divine Spirit. Here he says:

> Just as objects which lie adjacent to brilliant colours are themselves tinted by the brightness which is lucent around them, so is the person who fixes his gaze firmly on the Spirit transfigured by the Spirit's glory somehow into even greater splendour. For such a person's heart is lighted up, as it were, by a kind of light that streams from the truth of the Spirit. And, this is what is meant by being changed from "glory into glory," that is, by the glory of the Spirit into His very own glory, not in any partial degree, or as it were dimly and indistinctly, but rather in the fashion we might expect of any one who has been enlightened by the Spirit.[12]

Gregory the Theologian, an exegesis of whose trinitarian theology ought not to be attempted by those who do not have years on their hands, also shows himself never to have lost the doxological context of what he has been so able to expound metaphysically when necessary. The following short words from his *Orations* have the force of poetic imagery that rises into prayer; however complicated the thought, the sense of it communicates easily and rises like incense at the time of worship. The same point could be made more forcefully, and more extensively, by expounding his trinitarian theology from out of his corpus of poetry:

12. St. Basil, *On the Holy Spirit* 21.

> Adorable unity in trinity,
> trinity recapitulated in unity;
> entirely venerable, entirely regal,
> of the same throne and glory,
> transcendent and timeless,
> uncreated, indivisible,
> untouchable, uncircumscribable.[13]

Or consider the deftness and richness of this exposition of perichoresis: "That single radiance of the single Godhead, personally distinct in a way that unites, and united together in a way that keeps its distinctions: all of which is a paradox."[14]

I will conclude with the whole richness of the Orthodox patristic trinitarian theology as expressed in this prayer, from the Vespers of Pentecost Sunday, attributed to the Emperor Leo, whom no textbook would even list as a theologian. This troparion begins with a liturgical catechesis and ends with a skillful set of variations on the Trisagion. I shall use it to bring full circle this consideration of how we conceive of what the patristic tradition of Trinity is and how we always need to contextualize it in Christian doxology:

Come all you peoples and let us worship the Divinity in three hypostases:

> The Son in the Father with the Holy Spirit.
> For the Father timelessly begot the Son,
> who is coeternal, sharing the same throne as he;
> And the Holy Spirit who is in the Father, glorified with the Son.
> There is one power, one essence, one deity,
> Which we all worship in words such as these:
> Holy God,
> who created all things through the Son,
> with the co-operation of the Holy Spirit;
> Holy Mighty,
> through whom we have known the Father,
> and through whom the Holy Spirit came into this world;
> Holy Immortal,
> the Comforting Spirit, who proceeds from the Father,
> and abides in the Son;
> O Holy Trinity, glory to you. *Doxa soi.*

13. St. Gregory the Theologian, *Oration* 6.22.
14. St. Gregory the Theologian, *Oration* 28.1.

6

MAXIMUS THE CONFESSOR AND JOHN OF DAMASCUS ON THE TRINITY

BRIAN E. DALEY, SJ

We are probably not inclined to think of the centuries that followed the Council of Chalcedon, especially in the Christian East, as a time of intense speculation on the threefold mystery of God. The harvest of theology, in every age, seems to seek out new fields in which to apply its cutting edge. If the church's theological energies in the second century were mainly engaged, against the challenges of what we call gnosis, in reflecting on the importance of the ordinary reality we live in—the body, the institutional church, the world around us—as the place of salvation in Christ; and if the principal focus of theological argument in the fourth century lay more with the relationship of Jesus, and eventually also of the Spirit he gives, to the God Jesus calls Father— the God of Israel and of the philosophers; then it seems equally clear that the main theological battleground of the sixth, seventh, and eighth centuries, at least in the Greek-speaking church, was the formulation of Christology: the reception and assimilation of the portrait of Christ's person and being that had been so fatefully formulated at Chalcedon in 451. Theologians, pro and contra, struggled to make sense of the council's explicit confession that "one and the same Lord Jesus Christ, the only-begotten Son, must be acknowledged in two natures, without confusion or change, without division or separation," as "one *persona* and one hypostasis."[1]

For almost exactly a century after Chalcedon, pro- and anti-Chalcedonian writers in the eastern part of the Roman Empire—those who saw the council's decree as crypto-Nestorian, inspired by theologians of the Antiochene tradition and encouraged by secular-minded bishops from the Latin West, and who sought to replace it with a more clearly divine conception of the Savior; and those who accepted Chalcedon as a binding, official expression of traditional orthodox faith and who continued to try and reinterpret its language in terms that might be more appealing to its critics—argued tirelessly about the real meaning of Chalcedon's terms. Debate swirled, in the late fifth and early sixth centuries, about the propriety of using "nature" as a way of speaking both of the individual, concrete reality of a thing and the universal, identifying reality in which it shares, to be what it is; about the admissibility of speaking of "one composite hypostasis" in Christ, human and divine, as opposed to "one composite nature" or natural unit; and more important, perhaps, about the soteriological implications of such technicalities—about the difference they make for our relationship to God and our participation in the life of the church.

Much of the language used in post-Chalcedonian controversy, as well as the dominant style of argument in debates about the unity and plurality in Christ—amply furnished with definitions, theses, chains of syllogisms, and corroborative anthologies of testimonies from the earlier voices of orthodoxy—seems to have come from the classroom rather than the pulpit and was clearly influenced by the school philosophy of the day: the great Neoplatonic commentaries on Plato and Aristotle by such authors as Simplicius, Ammonius Hermeiou, and the anti-Chalcedonian Christian John Philoponus.[2] Even after the Second Council of Constantinople, in 553, formally confirmed the Chalcedonian formulation of the saving mystery of Christ as the norm of orthodoxy, debate over that formulation's implications and attempts to reinterpret or even modify controversial aspects of its language continued, with unabated scholastic rigor. In the seventh century, suggestions by the Byzantine emperor Heraclius and his theological advisors that the two distinct natures of Christ still revealed the operation of a single, divine energy and a single, divine will were doggedly opposed by the aged patriarch Sophronius of Jerusalem and the

1. Council of Chalcedon, Definition, trans. J. Neuner and J. Dupuis, in *The Christian Faith in the Doctrinal Documents of the Catholic Church* (New York: Alba House, 1981), 154–55, no. 615 (modified).

2. See Brian E. Daley, "Boethius' Theological Tracts and Early Byzantine Scholasticism," *MS* 46 (1984): 158–91, for a full discussion of the intellectual style of fifth- and sixth-century Greek theology.

monk Maximus the Confessor, whose defense of the paradox of Chalcedon, and of the continued operation of Christ's two natural wills that Chalcedon implied, was eventually adopted by the Third Council of Constantinople in 680/81. Even the eighth- and ninth-century debates about the propriety of offering religious veneration to humanly made images of Christ and the saints—a tradition defended staunchly by mainstream theologians such as John of Damascus—became heated and focused precisely as a particular application of faith in the one transcendent Word of God, who has truly made our human nature and our material shape his own. So the dogmatic decision of the Second Council of Nicaea, in 787, approving the use of icons in Christian worship, presented itself not simply as a disciplinary regulation but as a reaffirmation of the faith of Chalcedon: such images, like the narratives of Scripture, "confirm the truth—which is not simply in our imaginations—that the Word of God has become human."[3]

Still, even though the central focus of sixth- and seventh-century theological debate was, in our modern parlance, christological, major religious thinkers of the period remained acutely aware that what we say and think of Christ is never entirely separable from what we say and think of God—that our language and concepts for the mystery of Christ's person are, in a way, an inverted image of our language and concepts for the three distinct yet inseparably related persons we call Father, Son, and Holy Spirit, who are, as Augustine constantly reminds us, "what God is."[4] The first anathema, for instance, promulgated by the Second Council of Constantinople in 553, against the "three chapters"—the classical representatives, for Chalcedon's opponents, of an excessively divided Christology—is a recapitulation of the by-now classic trinitarian conception of God: "If anyone does not confess the one nature or substance of Father and Son and Holy Spirit, and their one power and authority, as a Triad of the same substance, one divinity which is adored in three hypostases or *personae*, let such a one be anathema. For [it adds, expanding on 1 Cor. 8:6] there is one God and Father, from whom are all things, and one Lord Jesus Christ, through whom are all things, and one Holy Spirit, in whom are all things."[5] The canons of Constantinople II then

---

3. Definition of the Second Council of Nicaea (787), in *Decrees of the Ecumenical Councils*, ed. Norman P. Tanner (London: Sheed and Ward; Washington, DC: Georgetown University Press, 1990), 135 (translation mine).

4. For this characteristically Augustinian phrase, "Trinitas, quae Deus est," see, for example, *De Trinitate* 1.4.7. For a sustained attempt to argue that the way we conceive of God as one or three is inextricably related to our conceptions of the unity or duality of Jesus as God and human, see Brian E. Daley, "'One Thing and Another': The Persons in God and the Person of Christ in Patristic Theology," *ProEccl* 15 (2006): 17–46.

5. *Decrees of the Ecumenical Councils*, 114 (translation mine).

go on to develop a carefully phrased and detailed outline of the church's normative faith in the incarnate hypostasis of the Word, attempting to put the Chalcedonian understanding of who Christ is—God the Son in his fully human form—with a clarity beyond dispute; that, after all, is what the council of 553 was summoned by the emperor Justinian to do. But the implication is clearly that the foundation of this understanding of Christ, as one person who is fully human and fully divine, lies in a corresponding understanding of the divine mystery as a single, transcendent reality, constituted by the three inseparably related hypostases or "persons" of Father, Son, and Spirit—an understanding that functions for the church, as the passage from 1 Corinthians suggests, in the same way that the Shema provided the foundation of the faith of ancient Israel. In fact, one of the main concerns of the defenders of Chalcedonian Christology in the sixth and seventh centuries was to insist that the way we conceptualize the single, unique Christ, as the individual who gives concrete existence both to God's form of being and to ours, must be the same as the way we conceptualize the three "individuals" or "persons" who together are what God is and do what God does. As Gregory of Nazianzus had observed in his famous *First Letter to Cledonius* (Ep. 101), the way that humanity and divinity are united and distinguished in the one Christ is "the opposite of how it is in the Trinity."[6] The reciprocity and distinctions we necessarily observe in Christ—two substances or realities, one hypostasis or individual agent—provide us with an inverse image of what we see as one (substance), and what as three (hypostasis), in the mystery of God.

In this essay, I cannot hope to offer a complete survey of the way classical Christian understanding of the triune reality of God was received and developed by later Greek theologians such as Maximus, writing in the mid-seventh century, or John of Damascus, who flourished a century later. Still, even a brief summary of their trinitarian thought sheds clear and, I think, significant light on how this sense of the relatedness of individual existence and universal nature in the Chalcedonian understanding of Christ, for these major late patristic thinkers, had come to be embedded in the church's universally accepted trinitarian confession, with all its paradoxes and linguistic anomalies, and how the by-now normative Christian confession of a single, simple God who *is* three related hypostases—eternally underlying the flow of created history—continued, in turn, to shape Orthodox concerns in confessing Jesus Christ as Savior.

6. Gregory of Nazianzus, Ep. 101, *First Letter to Cledonius*, in *Lettres théologiques*, SC 208, ed. Paul Gallay (Paris: Cerf, 1998), 44. For explicit development of this principle of Gregory's, see especially the mid-sixth-century writer Leontius of Byzantium, *Contra Nestorianos et Eutychianos* 4 (PG 86:1288c–1289a); *Epilyseis* 3 (PG 86:1921b–1925b).

Maximus and John, for all their differences of style and agenda, were similar theologians in a number of ways. Neither was a bishop, although bishops consulted them and were their frequent correspondents. Both were monks, committed since a "conversion" in early adulthood to the prayer and ascetical discipline of established Greek coenobitic life. Maximus—born probably around 580—is said by his Greek biographer to have started his adult life as a court official in the imperial capital, but entered monastic life in his early thirties: first at Chrysopolis, across the Bosporus from Constantinople, around 613, and a few years later moving to a new community at Cyzicus, further west on the Sea of Marmara. Ten years later, probably in the face of a massive Persian invasion of Asia Minor in 626, he moved westward again: to Cyprus, then perhaps to Alexandria, and eventually to the outskirts of Carthage in North Africa, where he remained for some twenty years, actively promoting, in his correspondence, both Chalcedonian orthodoxy and the contemplative and ascetical core of the Eastern monastic tradition.[7] John was born to a Syrian Christian family in Damascus, probably in the third quarter of the seventh century, around the time of Maximus's heroic trial and martyrdom. Like his father and Maximus, he too apparently began adult life as a bureaucrat, working as an administrator in the Muslim caliph's treasury in Damascus. But he too eventually left the secular world and migrated west, entering one of the monasteries in the Judean desert near Jerusalem. There he spent the rest of his life, until his death around 750, as a scholar, poet, controversialist, and contemplative.[8]

Both Maximus and John were obviously well trained in Greek literature as well as in the often abstruse subtleties of late antique philosophical discourse and dialectics. Both were Aristotelians in language and analytical habit of mind, although their Aristotle was—typically for their age—filtered through a clearly Neoplatonic understanding of the world and the self. Both were steeped in earlier Greek theology, especially in the now-classical trinitarian thought of the Cappadocian fathers and the mystical, hymnodic speculation of the anonymous writer we call Dionysius the Areopagite. And although they rarely acknowledge their sixth-century sources, both were also reflective, committed "neo-Chalcedonians," deeply indebted to the christological controversialists who

7. For a discussion of the sources and problems involved in reconstructing Maximus's life, see Brian E. Daley, "Making a Human Will Divine: Augustine and Maximus on Christ and Human Salvation," in *Orthodox Readings of Augustine*, ed. Aristotle Papanikolaou and George Demacopoulos (Crestwood, NY: St. Vladimir's Seminary Press, 2008), 101–26, esp. 106–11.

8. For a discussion of the few details we know about John's life, see Andrew Louth, *St. John Damascene: Tradition and Originality in Byzantine Theology* (Oxford: Oxford University Press, 2002), 3–14, esp. 5–8.

prevented imperial theology from abandoning the Chalcedonian formula and paved the way to the Second Council of Constantinople. Although they almost never mention him by name, both were also particularly indebted to the mid-sixth-century defender of Chalcedonian Christology, Leontius of Byzantium.

But did either Maximus or John add anything new to the church's by-now-traditional understanding of God? How did they receive it and integrate it into the theological concerns of their day? In his influential study of Maximus, *Cosmic Liturgy*, Hans Urs von Balthasar argues that the center of Maximus's thought lay elsewhere and that the Confessor's approach to the Trinity simply shows he is "heir to his past":

> He is heir to the Cappadocians, to Evagrius, to Pseudo-Dionysius; reaching back on his own beyond them all, he is heir also to Origen. A love for a theology that celebrates the inscrutable mystery liturgically is just as noticeable in his thought as in that of Pseudo-Dionysius, so it is not surprising to find in his work traces of the same tendency to remove the triune life of God from any sort of rational speculation.[9]

For Maximus, Balthasar adds, discussion of the Trinity takes place principally through "negative theology," while "positive" theology is focused on "the God of 'salvation history.'"[10] Balthasar is surely right in seeing Maximus's treatment of the Trinity as deeply rooted in the earlier Greek traditions he mentions. Still, this judgment seems to me an oversimplification: first, in that it assumes that speculation on the reality and the inner, hypostatic life of God can be separated from reflection on the events of the sacred history that culminates in Christ; and second, in that it restricts Maximus's assimilation of earlier language about God to simply receiving and repeating earlier tradition.

John of Damascus, too, is rightly regarded by most modern scholars as a discerning synthesizer of the best products of earlier Greek theology, one who deliberately shunned any attempt at innovation. Yet as Andrew Louth observes, John's very activity as an interpreter of earlier theology was itself an active and original contribution to its lasting shape:

> For the theological tradition to which he belonged, in the narrower sense, may be said to have culminated in John, and it is John who represents this tradition in later theology. This later role, as pre-eminent bearer of accumulated tradition and the source of later influence, took some time to develop. . . . But by the

---

9. Hans Urs von Balthasar, *Cosmic Liturgy: The Universe according to Maximus the Confessor*, trans. Brian E. Daley (San Francisco: Ignatius Press, 2003), 98–99.

10. Ibid., 99.

eleven century John's role as the pre-eminent representative of the Byzantine theological tradition had become evident, and in the twelfth century and thereafter it made itself felt in the West.[11]

In the way they integrate and refine earlier, mainstream Greek tradition on the mystery of God and the saving work of Jesus Christ, using it as a guide to dealing with the urgent theological debates of their own times—in the way they draw out the implications of what was by then classically formulated dogma—both Maximus and John do, I think, move the church's thinking deeper into a participative awareness of the fullness of faith's mysteries. Here we shall have to be content with simply observing a few high points of their contributions to the Christian way of thinking and speaking about God.

Celebrating the Mystery

In several passages from his "middle" works—written in the late 620s and early 630s, shortly after his migration to the West[12]—Maximus reflects on the comprehensive mystery of God in the solemn, doxological style of a creed or a litany. In one striking text, for instance, from chapter 23 of his *Mystagogy*—a heavily typological meditation on the drama of the sacred liturgy, its space, and its actors—Maximus describes the effect of the Word's inner instruction on the purified soul:

> The Word then leads it to the knowledge of theology (i.e., knowledge of the inner reality of God) made manifest after its journey through all things, granting it an understanding equal to the angels as far as this is possible for it. He will teach it with such wisdom that it will comprehend the one God, one nature and three hypostases, a substantial Monad in three hypostases and a consubstantial Triad of hypostases, a Monad in a Triad and a Triad in a Monad; not one and the other, or one alongside the other, or one through the other, or one in the other, or one from the other, but the same in itself and by itself and alongside itself, the same with itself.[13]

11. Louth, *St. John Damascene*, 16.

12. For the dating of Maximus's works, the standard study remains Polycarp Sherwood, *An Annotated Date-List of the Works of Maximus the Confessor*, SA 30 (Rome: Herder, 1952). Sherwood dates Maximus's *Mystagogy* to 626–30, just after his flight from Cyzicus. He places the *Commentary on the Lord's Prayer* at 628–30, and the *Chapters on Theology and the Economy*, also known as the *Chapters on Knowledge*, at 630–34. This would situate both the latter works in the early years of Maximus's residency in a Greek monastic community near Carthage.

13. Maximus, *The Church's Mystagogy* 23, trans. George C. Berthold (New York: Paulist Press, 1985), 205 (modified). Maximus's *Mystagogy* is now available in a critical edition by

Maximus then goes on to reflect on how this mystery of divine unity and multiplicity, revealed in the church's Scriptures and in its consciousness of its own life, can be articulated in human terms, drawing unambiguously (as we shall see again later) on the language of sixth-century discussions of the Christology of Chalcedon:

> The same Monad and Triad has unity without composition or confusion, and distinction without separation or division. It is a Monad by reason of essence or of being, but not by any composition or joining together or confusion; it is a Triad by reason of how it exists and subsists [*kata tēn tou pōs hyparchein kai hyphestanai logon*], but not by any separation or diversity or division. For the Monad is not divided in the hypostases, nor is it in them or recognized in them in the way of an external relationship [*schetikōs*]. Nor are the hypostases put together to form a Monad, nor do they make it up by contraction, but it is by itself the same reality, sometimes recognized in one way, sometimes in the other. For the holy Triad of hypostases is an unconfused Monad in essence and in its simple structure [*logō*]; and the holy Monad is a Triad in its hypostases and in its mode of existence [*tō tropō tēs hyparxeōs*].[14]

In chapter 8 of his great synthesis of classical Greek dogma, *An Exposition of the Orthodox Faith*, written a little more than a century later (probably in the 640s), John of Damascus begins with a similar summary of the traditional understanding of the reality of God as revealed in the experience of Israel and the church and as refined by philosophical reflection:

> We believe, then, in one God: one principle without source [*archē anarchos*], uncreated, unbegotten, indestructible and immortal, eternal, unlimited, uncircumscribed, unbounded, infinite in power, simple, uncompounded, incorporeal, never diminishing, unaffected from without [*apathēs*], unchangeable, unalterable, invisible, source of goodness and justice, light intellectual and inaccessible . . . ; one substance, one godhead, one power, one will, one operation, one principality, one power, one domination, one kingdom; known in three perfect hypostases and adored with one adoration, believed in and worshiped by every rational creature, united without confusion and distinct without separation—which is a

---

Charalambos G. Sotiropoulos (diss., University of Athens, 1978); for this passage, see Sotiropoulos, 239–40.

14. Ibid (Sotiropoulos, 240; Berthold, *Church's Mystagogy*, 205 [modified]). For a discussion of Maximus's language on God as "Monad" and "Triad," see J. M. Garrigues, "Théologie et monarchie," *Istina* 4 (1970): 435–46, 458–62. For similarly dense, quasi-liturgical meditations on the church's trinitarian confession, see Maximus, *On the Lord's Prayer* (PG 90:876d–877a, 884a–c; Berthold, *Church's Mystagogy*, 110–11); *Chapters on Theology and the Economy* 2.1 (PG 90:1124d–1125c; Berthold, *Church's Mystagogy*, 147–48).

paradox! We believe in Father and Son and Holy Spirit, in whom we have been baptized; for so the Lord taught the apostles to baptize.[15]

Later on, in chapter 49 of the same work, where he is explaining the traditional Greek understanding of the incarnation of the Word, John returns to the mystery of the three hypostases in God, which the incarnation, in its formal structure, both reverses and reveals:

> And we confess one nature in the godhead, but say that there are in truth three hypostases; and we say that everything natural and substantial [in God] is simple, but recognize that the difference in hypostases lies only in the three characteristics they have—the characteristics of being uncaused and Father, of being caused and Son, and of being the one who proceeds. And we understand them to be inseparable and without interval from one another, united and interchanging their being [perichōrousas] in each other without confusion—united without confusion (for they are three, even if they are united) but distinguished without separation. For even if each exists for himself, or (to put it another way) is a perfect hypostasis and possesses his own characteristics or different manner of existence [tēs hyparxeōs tropon diaphoron kektētai], still they are united in substance and in natural characteristics, and are called one God because they are not separate from the Father's hypostasis nor do they depart from it.[16] And in the same way we also confess, in the divine and ineffable economy of God the Word, our Lord Jesus Christ, one of the holy Trinity—something that goes beyond all understanding and comprehension—two natures . . . , but one composite hypostasis perfectly formed from the two natures.[17]

The Being of God and the Being of Christ

These passages, like others in the work of both writers, sound more like celebrations of a generally accepted linguistic and theological tradition than

---

15. John of Damascus, *Exposition of the Orthodox Faith* 8, in *Die Schriften des Johannes von Damaskos*, ed. Bonifatius Kotter (Berlin: de Gruyter, 1973), 2:18–19, translation in Frederic H. Chase Jr., *Saint John of Damascus: Writings*, FC 37 (New York: Fathers of the Church, 1958), 176–77 (modified). Andrew Louth observes about this passage: "This carefully constructed confession of faith recapitulates the teaching about God found earlier in *On the Orthodox Faith*, casting it now in the form of a confession, rather than an argument, so that it almost takes the form of an aretalogy" (Louth, *St. John Damascene*, 105).

16. Like Gregory of Nazianzus in a number of passages, John makes it clear that the foundation of the divine unity of substance is not the generic divine being considered somehow in itself, but the concrete, infinite, primordial being of the Father. It is the Father who is "principle without principle," not the divinity.

17. John of Damascus, *Exposition of the Orthodox Faith* 49 (in Kotter, *Die Schriften des Johannes von Damaskos*, 2:118; translation mine).

like argument or speculation. What is most striking, perhaps, in both these authors' development of the classical trinitarian theology of the East is not so much its use of the language of substance and individual, universal and particular, as the carefully constructed parallels both of them make between this structure of God's being and the structure of Christ's incarnate person. Chalcedonian Christology, it seems, had inevitably become the unifying matrix for their whole assimilation of earlier theological tradition. Let us make at least a few observations on these dense passages, and others like them, that might shed some light on the relationship of these two theologians to the tradition they received and interpreted.

First, both Maximus and John treat the mystery of God's being as at once both Monad and Triad, radical unity and irreducible trinity, as a conception simply central and fundamental to the church's life as a eucharistic community. In the doxological or confessional passages we have referred to, they do not speak of it as a theory, or an explanation that adds to our knowledge of what God is, but rather proclaim it solemnly in a quasi-creedal formula, which John explicitly links to Jesus's commission to baptize in Matthew 28.[18] John also treats the church's classical way of speaking about the divine Triad, in terms of single substance or nature existing in and as three distinct but interrelated hypostases, as *similar* to the way the church speaks of Christ, the Word made flesh, as one hypostasis subsisting in and as two complete natures: similar, as he goes on to explain, not in its inner structure (which in fact is the exact opposite), but in the fact that number does not divide, nor sameness confuse. So John concludes chapter 49 of his *Exposition* by commenting on this similarity:

> As then it is impossible to say that the three hypostases of the Godhead are one hypostasis, even if they are united with each other, because this does not bring about any confusion or abolition of the difference between the hypostases, so also it is impossible to say that the two natures of Christ, hypostatically united, are one nature, lest we bring about an abolition and confusion of the difference between them, and make it nonexistent.[19]

Both the structure of God's being as a whole and that of Christ the Son in particular are prime, if inexplicable, examples of radical, substantial unity within radical differentiation; that unity is simply realized on opposite ontological levels.

18. See the passage of *Exposition of the Orthodox Faith* 8 quoted above.
19. *Exposition of the Orthodox Faith* 49 (in Kotter, *Die Schriften des Johannes von Damaskos*, 2:118; translation mine).

Second, clearly this relationship of unity and difference is, in both cases, a *paradox*, as John of Damascus observes with a certain understatement—not something we ordinarily encounter, or can fully rationalize. John insists, for instance, in chapter 9 of his *Exposition*, that "one should not suppose that any one of those things which are affirmed of God is indicative of what He is in essence. Rather, they show either what He is not, or some relation to one of those things that are contrasted with Him, or some thing or operation that follows on His nature."[20]

Maximus, like John, is willing to apply the language of essence and hypostasis to the divine mystery of Father, Son, and Holy Spirit, presumably because this was sanctioned by the long orthodox tradition reaching back to the Cappadocians and had been applied in a consistent way by sixth-century theologians like Leontius to the terms of the Chalcedonian definition, as laying the groundwork for an orthodox conception of Christ.[21] Yet Maximus is fully aware that even language of substance and hypostasis is to be used of God in a cautious, self-consciously adapted or (as the medieval West would say) analogous way. He writes, in a burst of Dionysian apophaticism, in *Ambiguum* 10, probably written in the late 620s, after his journey west:

> The Godhead is beyond all division and composition and part and whole, because it is without quantity, and removed from all arbitrary categories of existence and from the kind of consideration that defines how it is; for it is without quality, free from any relation to anything else, unbounded. It exists without relations, in fact, with nothing before or after or alongside it, since it is beyond everything, and ranked with none of the things that exist, by way of structure or mode of being.[22]

Still, as Maximus suggests in other, somewhat earlier, works, the particular characteristics we attribute to Father, Son, and Holy Spirit that constitute

20. *Exposition of the Orthodox Faith* 9 (in Chase, *Saint John*, 189; translation modified).

21. In Epistle 15, for instance, to the Alexandrian deacon Cosmas, which Sherwood dates between 634 and 640, Maximus gives a classical exposition of the meaning and proper use of these terms, principally their application in a christological context. His starting point, however, is the accepted propriety of speaking of God as a single substance or nature subsisting "in three distinct hypostases," which makes clear that the terms "substance" and "hypostasis" are not to be used as synonyms but are to be related as general to particular, common to proper. "Unbegottenness and begottenness and procession do not divide the one nature and power of the ineffable divinity into three substances and natures, unequal or equal," he adds. "But those things in which—or which—the one divinity (that is, the substance or nature) is, mark out persons [*prosōpa*], that is, hypostases." See Ep. 15 (PG 91:549d–552a).

22. Maximus, *Ambiguum ad Joannem* 10 (PG 91:1185d; translation mine). Maximus's *Ambigua to John*, a collection of comments explaining difficult or disputed passages in the classical theological tradition, mainly passages from Gregory of Nazianzus, is dated by Sherwood to 628–30.

their relations to each other are present, at least analogously, in the world around us. Substance, formal differentiation, and life are features of every intellectual creature and are, he suggests in one of his *Quaestiones et Dubia*, simply hypostatized or personally concretized in God as their first cause.[23] God's mysterious being, then, is not totally beyond our knowing; but the created mind has to be laboriously purified to contemplate him and relies on his revelation in history to identify what it knows as even distantly indicative of the being of God. To know experientially and to be united with the living mystery of God is the goal of the intellectual creature's existence, Maximus eloquently asserts in *Quaestiones ad Thalassium* 60; this knowledge has been revealed through time in Scripture, in order to make possible our participation in Christ.[24] But if the human mind is to come to know God as he has revealed himself, it must go through a strenuous process of cleansing, just as Abraham recognized God in his conversation with his three visitors only because Abraham had "left behind the appearances" of the material world.[25] So Maximus writes of the sanctified human person, a little further on in *Ambiguum* 10:

> Realizing that the soul is situated at the midpoint between God and matter, and that it has the potential to bring both of them together—I am speaking of the mind's potential towards God and sense-perception's potential towards matter—[holy human beings] shake off sense-perception, along with sensible objects, with respect to its habitual activity of relating, and in mind alone become ineffably associated with God. As the soul is made one with God in his fullness, in a way beyond knowing, they contemplate it [i.e., the soul] in its fullness, as image of the archetype: containing by likeness in mind, reason, and spirit a resemblance to God, as much as this is possible. Thus they learn, in a mystical way, the unity that is recognized in the Trinity.[26]

23. Maximus, *Quaestiones et Dubia* 136, ed. José Declerck, CCSG 10 (Turnhout: Brepols, 1982), 97. Sherwood and Balthasar date this collection of brief responses to theological and scriptural questions before Maximus's departure from Cyzicus in 626. See also *Quaestiones ad Thalassium* 13 (dated between 630 and 633), which suggests that the *being* of the world reveals the existence of God, its orderly arrangement or *differentiation* his wisdom, and its *motion* his life, all of which reflect the divine hypostases of Father, Son, and Holy Spirit.

24. Maximus, *Quaestiones ad Thalassium* 60, ed. Carl Laga and Carlos Steel, CCSG 22 (Turnhout: Brepols, 1990), 73–79, translation in Paul Blowers and Robert Wilken, *On the Cosmic Mystery of Jesus Christ* (Crestwood, NY: St. Vladimir's Seminary Press, 2003), 125–27.

25. Maximus, *Quaestiones et Dubia* 39 (ed. Declerck, p. 32).

26. Maximus, *Ambiguum* 10 (PG 91:1193d–1196a; translation mine). Andrew Louth remarks, in a note on his own translation of this passage (*Maximus the Confessor* [London: Routledge, 1996], 147), that Maximus's comparison of the structure of the self-conscious mind to the trinitarian mystery reminds one of Augustine's *De Trinitate* 9–10, but that this analogy is found less frequently in the Byzantine tradition than in the West.

God, he argues in this dense, metaphysical passage, is the only utterly simple reality. Unlike matter, which is always capable of division and extension, always ready to be shaped into unitary, intelligible forms, God simply *is*, without motion or change: to use traditional Platonic language, God is the only genuine *monad*, in contrast to whom all other reality is somehow multiple, a *dyad* at least in potency, waiting for limitation or division.[27] Yet because God is present actively and lovingly to creation, containing in his providence the *logos* or intended shape and character of every individual creature,[28] the created mind is able to come to at least a limited understanding of God's simplicity and unity through the discipline of ascetical self-control and the practice of contemplation. This process begins in what the ascetical tradition called *praktikē*: the gradual detachment of knowledge and choice from passionate attachment to the material world; it continues in *theoria physikē*: the attentive contemplation of the natural world in order to see beyond its simply sensible dimensions and find its deeper significance. Eventually, the contemplating mind is overcome with love and desire not for material satisfaction but for God himself, perceived now not simply in his historical works but in the unity and simplicity that forms Father, Son, and Holy Spirit in their common, transcendent identity. So Maximus writes of the contemplative process, a little further on in the same essay:

> If anyone can get control of [attractions to sensible objects] and persuade them to be directed where they should be, in an appropriate way, and leaves them subjected as servant-powers to the rule of reason or even abandons them completely, and holds on simply to the unwavering enchantment of loving knowledge through reason and contemplation; and if that person is focused on one single motion from many—pure and simple, inseparable from the manly power of yearning—and in this movement has firmly planted its stability within himself, by the philosophic movement towards God; he is truly blessed, and shares not only in true and blessed union with the holy Trinity, but in the oneness which is recognized in the holy Trinity, having become simple and indivisible and uniform in his own potential for being, in relation to the one who is simple and indivisible by nature.[29]

The contemplative Christian has become formed in the image of the transcendent, differentiated unity of God. He has become simple himself, by contemplating God's simplicity.

27. Maximus, *Ambiguum* 10.40–41 (PG 91:1184b–1188c).
28. Ibid., 42 (PG 91:1192ab).
29. Ibid., 43 (PG 91:1196ab; translation mine).

Third, an important part of the way these two Greek theologians use the language of substance and hypostasis, as we have already seen, is their identification of the latter with the concrete *mode* of a substance's being, the *way* (*tropos*) in which a thing is what it is. Conceiving of "hypostatic" being—the being of the concrete, individually nameable and countable human, for instance, rather than of humanity as such—as a "manner" or *tropos* in which the common, intelligibly identifiable reality (substance or essence) exists, goes back, among Christian authors, at least to Gregory of Nyssa. Gregory, like most of those influenced by his work, conceives of this peculiar, hypostatic "manner of being" of any individual as determined principally by his or her unique origins: by parentage and ancestry, the circumstances and family relationships in which the human individual comes to be who and what he or she is.[30] So Maximus, commenting on a famous passage in Gregory of Nazianzus's *Christmas Oration* (*Or.* 38) that speaks of a "second communion" of God and the human creature more splendid than that of Adam with his creator in Eden, points to the new relationship realized for us all in the incarnation:

> Now it [human nature] has received a union in hypostasis with him [i.e., the Logos], through the ineffable union, preserving unchanged—through the union—its own different structure of substance [*logon tēs ousias*] in relation to the divine substance, towards which it is hypostatically one and yet different. As a result, in the structure of its being [*tō tou einai logō*], according to which it has come into existence and continues to be, it [Christ's humanity] remains in unquestionable possession of its own being, preserving it undiminished in every way; but in the structure of *how it is* [*tō tou pōs einai logō*], it receives existence in a divine way, and neither knows nor accepts at all the urge towards movement centered on any other thing.[31]

The first element determining the "mode of being" of any concrete reality is its origin, its parentage and the concrete details of its birth; so the mode of being of the Son within the mystery of God is his generation by the Father, that eternal, unique relationship of dependence and total receptivity by which he exists in substantial fullness as God. But as Word made flesh, as personified

30. For a full discussion of the philosophical background of this kind of language and of its use in Christian theological and christological discussion, see Brian E. Daley, "Nature and the 'Mode of Union': Late Patristic Models for the Personal Unity of Christ," in *The Incarnation*, ed. Stephen T. Davis, Daniel Kendall, and Gerald O'Collins (Oxford: Oxford University Press, 2002), 164–96. For Gregory of Nyssa, see 173–77.

31. Maximus, *Ambiguum* 36 (PG 91:1289c–d). Maximus, in the last phrase of this text, is clearly referring to worldly passion, which is not part of the actual structure of human nature but represents a modification in the "manner" in which nature is realized: in this case, a self-induced departure from the ideal "manner of existing" intended by God for his creatures.

in Jesus, the Son has yet another origin: he is born without sexual passion from Mary, in full possession of human reality, yet by the miraculous, genuinely divine "mode" of virginal conception. This gives to his unique human reality a distinctive character, a "personality," which does not alter his divine subjective identity: "The structure of human nature [in Jesus] is the fact that it is soul and body, and that its nature is constituted by soul and body; but its mode is the order found in this natural give-and-take of activity, something often varied and altered, yet not altering the nature at all along with itself."[32] Because nature can come into concrete existence and live out that existence in different "modes," then, without becoming another natural thing, Maximus argues that humanity as a whole can remain *what* it essentially is, and yet be renewed in its *way* of being, by taking on Jesus's mode of being through the "new birth" of baptism and the new filial relationship with God as Father that follows upon it.[33]

John of Damascus retains this traditional habit of seeing the distinguishing mark of any hypostasis not in its general, defining features but in its "mode of being." So he remarks, with reference to God, in his treatise *Against the Jacobites*, that "everything is common among the Father and the Son and the Holy Spirit except for the mode of their existence."[34] As Gregory of Nyssa had argued in *To Ablabius* almost four centuries earlier, the only marks that distinguish the hypostases in God from one another are the ways in which they do or do not give and receive the infinite, inconceivable divine being—the ways they are or are not "caused" to be. So in the case of the Word incarnate, John observes, one must not speak generally of an incarnation of any divine hypostasis, "because not all the hypostases have received it [human nature], but only the manner of existence [of the Son]. Incarnation, then, has come to be a second mode of existence for the only-begotten Son alone, and is fitted to the Word in such a way that his proper characteristic [i.e., as Word] remains unshaken."[35]

Fourth, hypostatic existence, then—as a "mode of being" in which a universal, definable essence is given concrete reality—fits conveniently, in the post-Chalcedonian tradition, both with the way Father, Son, and Holy Spirit are (albeit analogously) thought of within the mystery of God, as distinguished solely by their causal origins—the way in which they share the divine

---

32. Ibid., 42 (PG 91:1341d10–14).

33. Maximus, *Opusculum 4*, to the Hegumen George (PG 91:60a). Sherwood dates this essay also somewhere between 634 and 640.

34. *Contra Jacobitas 52*, in *Die Schriften des Johannes von Damaskos*, ed. Bonifatius Kotter (Berlin: de Gruyter, 1981), 4:126.

35. Ibid (in Kotter, *Die Schriften des Johannes von Damaskos*, 4:127).

reality—and with the existence of Jesus, who lives out both in human and in divine terms, infinitely different though they are, what it is to be the only Son of God. Christ, as Maximus observes several times, is "divine in a human way, and human in a divine way." For John of Damascus, the hypostatic "mode," at least in the realm of human beings, is not simply determined by ancestry and "family relationships," but by "a particular mode of motion, particularly chosen by the individual"[36]—by a person's will and free action, in other words. We recognize ourselves as particular individuals because, by using our common natural freedom, we choose to act in different ways; the will and the other operations of our nature have a different manner of realization in each of us. For this reason, he immediately goes on to observe, our technical language limps when applied to the Trinity: we cannot speak of Father, Son, and Spirit as "three gods" in the way we speak of three human hypostases as "three human beings," simply because the divine hypostases will and act always as one—their hypostases, unlike ours, realize the same nature in infinite perfection and are distinct in origin alone.[37] Nevertheless, the language of "hypostasis," even when applied to Father, Son, and Spirit, inevitably brings with it a hint of independent activity and self-determination that is hard to eradicate and raises further questions these late Greek theologians felt compelled to confront.

In a famous passage of his *Third Theological Oration*, for instance, Gregory of Nazianzus had spoken of the multiplicity of "faces" in God not as a source of potential inner conflict but as marked by "like dignity of nature, agreement in will, sameness of movement, so that even if [the divine being] should be differentiated numerically, it is not divided substantially." Gregory adds: "For this reason the Monad, from the beginning, being in movement towards a Dyad, comes to rest at a Triad. And this is, in our terms, the Father and the Son and the Holy Spirit."[38]

Maximus, whose two sets of *Ambigua* are mainly short explanatory notes on difficult passages in Gregory of Nazianzus—by his time, "the Theologian," the classic representative of mainstream tradition—struggles in several texts to explain what Gregory might mean by such hypostatic "motion" within God. In *Quaestiones ad Thalassium* 60, Maximus concedes what has been a principle of Christian thought since at least the Cappadocians: that "naturally we must not consider *change* at all in God, nor consider any *movement* in him. Being changed properly pertains to moveable creatures."[39] So he is forced to

36. *On the Two Wills in Christ* 7 (in Kotter, *Die Schriften des Johannes von Damaskos*, 4:184).
37. Ibid. See also Daley, "Nature and the 'Mode of Union,'" 191.
38. Gregory of Nazianzus, *Oration* 29.2.
39. Maximus, *Quaestiones ad Thalassium* 60 (Laga and Steel, 75.1–4; trans. in Blowers and Wilken, *Cosmic Mystery*, 124).

reflect more deeply on what Gregory might really have meant in speaking of this movement or *kinēsis* within the divine being.

In the first of his *Ambigua to Thomas*, composed in the mid-630s, Maximus explains the passage in Gregory's *Third Theological Oration* this way:

> If, having heard the word "movement," you wonder how the divinity that is beyond eternity is moved, understand that the passivity belongs not to the divinity, but to us, who first are illumined with respect to the rational principle of its being, and thus are enlightened with respect to the mode of its subsistence, for it is obvious that being is observed before the manner of being. And so, movement of divinity, which comes about through the elucidation concerning its being and its manner of subsistence, is established, for those who are able to receive it, as knowledge.[40]

God is "in motion," in other words, not so much in terms of God's own being as in terms of his relationship to us: in terms of our gradual growth to know his being as triune and to participate in it. In this same brief explanatory essay, just before the comment we have quoted, Maximus seems to go out of his way to draw on the dense, philosophical language of the defenders of Chalcedon—Leontius of Byzantium, especially—to characterize this paradoxical relationship of simplicity and timelessness to the three distinct "persons" the church recognizes as God, in a way that avoids ascribing to God any temporal development.

> We revere this unified sovereignty as "that which is constituted" by the Triad, which is by nature equal in honor, that is, Father, Son and Holy Spirit. "Their wealth is sameness of nature and the one effulgence of radiance";[41] "divinity is not diffused beyond them, lest we introduce a community of gods, nor is it limited to one of them, lest we be deemed worthy of condemnation because of the poverty of divinity."[42]
>
> This is not a causal explanation of the cause of beings, which is itself beyond being, but a demonstration of how one is piously to think about it. The Divinity is monad, but not dyad, and triad, but not plurality, since it is without beginning, without body, and without conflict. The monad is truly monad. It

---

40. Maximus, *Ambiguum ad Thomam 1*, in *Ambigua ad Thomam una cum Epistula secunda ad Eundem*, ed. Bart Janssens, CCSG 48 (Turnhout: Brepols, 2002), translated in Joshua Lollar, *Maximus the Confessor: Ambigua to Thomas; Second Letter to Thomas* (Turnhout: Brepols, 2009), 51. In his incompletely preserved *Second Letter to Thomas*, Maximus revises this interpretation to include the idea that the Trinity of God is not so much a sign of plurality as of fullness and perfection (Janssens, p. 80).

41. A quotation from Gregory of Nazianzus, *Oration* 40.5 (*On Holy Baptism*).

42. A quotation from Gregory of Nazianzus, *Oration* 38.8 (*On the Theophany*).

is not the principle of things that come after it in a sort of condensation deriv-ing from its self-differentiation, as though, making its way to plurality, it were naturally poured out. Rather, it is the concretely existing essential reality of the consubstantial triad [*enhypostatos ontotēs homoousiou Triados*]. And 'the triad is truly a triad; it is not composed of individual numbers.'[43] It is not a synthesis of monads, that it should experience division; rather, it is the essential existence of the tri-hypostatic monad [*enousios hyparxis trishypostatou monados*]. The triad is truly monad, since thus it is [*esti*]; and the monad is truly triad, since thus it subsists [*hyphistatai*]. Indeed, the divinity is one, existing monadically and subsisting triadically.[44]

By subtly interweaving the language of intelligible being or substance (*einai, ousia*; the being of the universal forms, which give shape and identity to all things, even to God, who is by definition "beyond being") and concrete exis-tence (*hyphestēnai, hypostasis*; the being of the individual realities that enable these universal forms to be actually realized and given proper names, to "be in themselves"), Maximus here suggests that the same mutual implication of universal and individual planes of reality that we find in the incarnate Word is the key to understanding how the utterly simple, transcendent God simply *is* the three ordered, distinct, interrelated "persons" we call Father, Son, and Holy Spirit. The language of *ousia* and *hypostasis*, central to the controver-sies over the person of Christ for two centuries, is offered here as not simply Chalcedon's solution to difficulties in understanding the Savior as God and a human being, but as the foundation to all right Christian speech about the simplicity and multiplicity of God.

A different way of approaching the inner dynamism of the divine hyposta-ses—not explicitly connected with this passage from Gregory Nazianzen, but seemingly dealing with the same basic question: the relation of the hypostases as a kind of divine "give and take"—is John of Damascus's use of the term "interpenetration" (*perichōrēsis*). This term, suggesting spatial circulation or the exchange of places, had been used by Maximus in a number of texts[45] to refer to the mutually formative relationship of the divine and the human in Christ; in its verbal form, the term had already been used by Gregory of Na-

---

43. A quotation from Gregory of Nazianzus, *Oration* 23 (*On the Peace III*) 10.

44. Maximus, *Ambiguum ad Thomam* 1 (in Janssens, *Ambigua ad Thomam*, 6–7; trans. Lollar, *Maximus the Confessor*, 50–51). In this dense passage, Maximus draws from the clas-sical terminology of Chalcedonian Christology the distinction between "being" (*einai*), which is proper to universal, intelligible reality, and "subsisting" (*hyphistanai*), which is proper to the concrete individual that makes that universal reality immediately available to experience.

45. See, for example, Maximus, *Opuscula* 8 (PG 91:88a) and 17 (PG 91:189b); *Dialogue with Pyrrhus* 337C, 345D.

zianzus for the interpenetration of Christ's divine and human realities,[46] and the noun was used also in Maximus's sense by the Damascene. In his *Contra Jacobitas*, for instance, John writes of the hypostatic union: "Interpenetration [*perichōrēsis*] is set in motion by the divinity; for this is what gives to the flesh a share of its [i.e., God's] own glory and brilliance, without [the divine nature's] sharing the sufferings of the flesh. Therefore the nature of the flesh is divinized, but does not change into flesh the nature of the Word."[47]

But in the same chapter of the *Exposition of the Orthodox Faith* where he deals most fully with the relationships within the divine Triad, John uses this same term in a bold new way, to refer to the very life of God:

> We do not call the Father and the Son and the Holy Spirit three gods, but rather one God, the holy Triad; we refer this to the one cause of the Son and the Spirit, but do not compound them or blend them together by a Sabellian contraction. For they are unified, as we have said already, not in such a way as to be confused, but so as to cling to each other, and they have this interpenetration [*perichōrēsis*] with each other without any trace of compounding or blending. Yet they are not projected away from each other, or cut apart in their substance, as they are by Arius's division.[48]

To be able to speak of the hypostases in God as bound together in the relationship of a shared single life, and yet as eternally distinguished by the ways in which that life is given and received, requires us to grope for new language, to reach beyond our ordinary experiences of the one and the many. But as John realized, the orthodox tradition of speaking about God, founded on faith in Christ, requires of us nothing less.

Conclusion: The Way of Christ

In all the ways I have mentioned, John and Maximus are really talking about the Trinity in what we might, from our modern perspective, call christological as well as strictly theological language. Sixth-century defenders of the Chalcedonian formula, such as Leontius of Byzantium, had insisted on the importance of using the canonized trinitarian language of substance and hypostasis, nature and *persona*, in a consistent way also for the person of Christ;

---

46. See Ep. 101 (*To Cledonius* 1).

47. John of Damascus, *Contra Jacobitas* 52 (in Kotter, *Die Schriften des Johannes von Damaskos*, 4:127).

48. *Exposition of the Orthodox Faith* 8 (in Kotter, *Die Schriften des Johannes von Damaskos*, 2:29.259–65); see also *Exposition of the Orthodox Faith* 49, quoted above.

only in that way could the reciprocity and intimate link between what we understand of God and what we profess in Christ stand out clearly. For both Maximus and John, it seems, the influence flowed in the opposite direction, too. It was the Chalcedonian conception of the person of Christ, yoking two utterly different and incommensurable realms of reality into the unique story of a single living and active person, that opened a new window of clarity—or at least of clarifying analogy—for looking toward the mystery of God. God is always beyond concepts and technical language, beyond both knowledge and ignorance, as Dionysius had stressed—beyond being itself. Yet in the complex, yet humanly perceptible, mystery of the person of Christ, "God with us," all that we humans can say about God, and all that we can hope to share of God's life, is given to us.

For John of Damascus, the great synthesizer and systematizer of the patristic tradition, the main goal seems to have been to bring out the unity and inner coherence of the Christian understanding of God, the world, and human hope for salvation. His main innovation in speaking of God as Trinity seems to have been to use for this mystery the language of mutual interchange (*perichōrēsis*), which Gregory of Nazianzus had applied in its verbal form to the relationship of the divine and the human in Jesus and to which Maximus had given technical precision as a noun. John's predecessor Maximus, the contemplative monastic steeped in the ecstatic thought of the Pseudo-Dionysius, often emphasizes, in addition, the movement of the human mind from hypostatic threeness to substantial oneness, from Triad to Monad, in meditating on the mystery of God, a process that he identifies with a gradual, saving unification and simplification of the mind itself, as it reaches for God. He points out, too, that in the concrete, active love of self and neighbor that is the "way" of Jesus, the disciple finds access to a contemplative unity with God as Trinity that is otherwise simply beyond us.

In one of his letters to his friend, the courtier John the Cubicularius, for instance, written during the early years of his monastic life, Maximus insists that it is not speculative knowledge or ascetic practice but only love that draws human beings into unity with each other and with God, who has become human for us.

> Love is a great good, the first and most outstanding of goods, because it brings God and human beings together, by its own power, around the person who possesses it; it paves the way for the creator of human beings to reveal himself as human, so that the deified person has become indistinguishable from God, with regard to the goodness that is humanly attainable. As I understand it, this enables us to love the Lord our God with our whole heart and soul and strength, and our

neighbor as ourselves. If I were to sum this up and say it in one sentence, love is a general, inner relationship towards the First Good, with all its providential care for our natural race. It is impossible for the human being who loves God to be drawn up to anything higher than this, once all the ways of piety that one can take have been traversed. We recognize this and call it love, not in a way that directs one kind of love to God and another to our neighbor, but see all love as one and the same: owed to God, and in addition, binding humans to each other. The realization [*energeia*] and clear demonstration of perfect love for God is this: a genuine attitude of willing benevolence towards one's neighbor. "For the one who does not love his brother or sister, whom he sees," says the divine Apostle John, "cannot love God, whom he does not see."[49] This is the way of Truth, which the Word of God identifies with himself; those who walk on it he presents to God the Father, purified from every kind of unhealthy attachment. This is the door through which a person gains entrance to the Holy of Holies, and is enabled to become a worthy contemplator of the inaccessible beauty of the Holy and royal Trinity.[50]

To love as Christ loved, to walk in the way laid out for disciples in the gospel, is to enter into the dynamic giving and receiving of infinite love that are the very core of God's being, revealed to us in Christ and shared with us in the gift of the Spirit. It is to walk toward the Father with Christ, as sons and daughters, and to be part of the community of love his Spirit has formed in the church. For that reason, it is only in Christlike love that the mystery of God's transcendent being is made open to us, as goal and as invitation.

Perhaps the real contribution of these two late patristic synthesizers was to show that these two focal points of the one Christian faith—the being of God, as revealed humanly in the person of Christ, and the saving reality of Christ, as the human presence of God with us—are really two faces of a single mystery.

---

49. 1 John 4:20.

50. Maximus, Letter 2, *To John the Cubicularius* (PG 91:401c–404a; translation mine). This letter was apparently written while Maximus was a member of the monastic community of St. George at Cyzicus, across the Sea of Marmara from Constantinople, before he left for the West in 626.

7

DEIFICATION IN AUGUSTINE: PLOTINIAN OR TRINITARIAN?

MATTHEW DREVER

John McGuckin has again called on the Eastern church to maintain and the Western church to acknowledge more clearly the place of the Trinity in its ecclesiology.[1] McGuckin's call resonates not only within the context of contemporary Orthodox theology but also within a wider historiographical and theological resurgence of interest in the Trinity in Western theology, a resurgence that has continued to reverse a late nineteenth- and early twentieth-century trend that Claude Welch described as the quiet funeral of trinitarian thought.[2] It is by no means obvious that Augustine has a constructive role to play in contemporary discussions, which is something of an oddity considering his influence in the history of Western thought. One of the reasons for this is the place his trinitarianism accords to Neoplatonism, which critics contend leads to a doctrine of God either detached from or destructive to a Christian

---

1. See chap. 5 of this book, John McGuckin, "The Holy Trinity as the Dynamic of the World's Salvation in the Greek Fathers."
2. Claude Welch, *In This Name: The Doctrine of the Trinity in Contemporary Theology* (New York: Scribner, 1952). Welch was primarily concerned with the demise of trinitarian thought in liberal Protestant theology from Schleiermacher onward.

concept of salvation rooted in the church and open toward the world. These critics argue that Augustine's doctrine of God weights more on the side of a Neoplatonist monism that moves away from engagement with the church and world than on the side of a trinitarian theism closely engaged with them.[3] Related to this, Augustine's understanding of human salvation and reunion with God has come under scrutiny for relying on a method of inward, rational contemplation that moves through the soul and up to God. Scholars question whether it is an exercise in Christian piety or a form of Neoplatonist contemplation incompatible with Christian views of salvation.[4]

Recent historical scholarship has begun to raise serious questions about such criticisms. Michel Barnes has taken contemporary scholarship to task for accepting a Platonist framework as the basis of Augustine's trinitarianism while ignoring the influence of the wider Latin and Greek trinitarian tradition, and then assuming this falsely construed framework runs afoul of his wider Christian commitments.[5] Barnes's critique belongs to a growing body of recent patristic scholarship that argues for the coherency of a "pro-Nicene" tradition that is rooted in the biblical tradition and religious controversies of the early church, that spans the East and West, and that influences the development of Augustine's trinitarianism.[6] As part of this project, scholars have traced the complex doctrinal, philosophical, rhetorical, and polemical issues that shape

3. John Zizioulas maintains that Augustine's doctrine of God, anthropology, and ecclesiology has an abstract, intellectualist, otherworldly character due in no small part to his Neoplatonist heritage; see Zizioulas's *Being as Communion: Studies in Personhood and the Church* (New York: St. Vladimir's Seminary Press, 1985), 25, 41n35, 88, 95, 100, 104n98. Catherine LaCugna echoes this in a critique of Augustine's place in the historical development of the Latin doctrine of the Trinity; see *God for Us: The Trinity and Christian Life* (San Francisco: Harper, 1991), 81–109. Colin Gunton joins this interpretation as well when he argues that Augustine's famous analogy between the triadic structure of the mind and the Trinity derives from a Neoplatonist philosophy of mind, with the result that his trinitarianism becomes rooted in an abstract individualism and intellectualism that undermines its ecclesiological and soteriological context. See Gunton, *The Promise of Trinitarian Theology* (Edinburgh: T&T Clark, 1997), 42–45.

4. Olivier Du Roy is one of the leading voices of the Neoplatonist interpretation of Augustine's trinitarianism. See his *L'Intelligence de la foi en la Trinité selon saint Augustin: Genèse de sa théologie trinitaire jusqe'en 391* (Paris: Études Augustiniennes, 1966). For a critique of this interpretation, see Luigi Gioia, *The Theological Epistemology of Augustine's De Trinitate* (Oxford: Oxford University Press, 2008). There is also a recent debate between John Cavadini and Lewis Ayres on this issue. Cavadini argues that Augustine's trinitarianism in *On the Trinity* develops a Neoplatonist model that intentionally fails in order to point the way to faith in Christ, while Ayres argues that Augustine's model has a basic trinitarian and christological core. See John C. Cavadini, "The Structure and Intention of Augustine's De Trinitate," *AugStud* 23 (1992): 102–23; Lewis Ayres, "The Christological Context of *De Trinitate* XIII: Toward Relocating Books VIII–XV," *AugStud* 29 (1998): 118–20.

5. Michel René Barnes, "Augustine in Contemporary Trinitarian Theology," *TS* 56 (1995): 244.

6. See also Rowan Williams, "*Sapientia* and the Trinity," in *Collectanea Augustiniana: Mélanges T. J. van Bavel*, ed. B. Bruning, M. Lamberigts, and J. van Houlin (Leuven: Leuven

trinitarian developments in Eastern and Western patristic authors. In turn, this has shown the complexity of issues intertwined in the trinitarian models of thinkers such as Augustine and demonstrated more broadly the inadequacy of facile contrasts between the East and West.

It is not just Augustine's trinitarianism that benefits from such reexaminations. Issues related to it stand to profit as well. This is particularly true of Augustine's sparsely studied account of deification.[7] Admittedly, he does not develop as explicit an account as is developed in the Greek tradition. Indeed, *deificari/deificatus* and their various forms appear only about eighteen times in Augustine's writings.[8] The paucity of such terminology in Augustine, as well as in the wider Latin tradition, has led Orthodox scholars such as Vladimir Lossky to argue that the West does not develop a doctrine of deification as in the East.[9] Similarly, Christos Yannaras argues that Western theology develops a rationalistic methodology in its understanding of the divine-human relation and lacks a concept of human participation (deification) in God.[10] Here as elsewhere, however, caution must be given to generalized contrasts between the Latin West and the Greek East.[11] In the case of Augustine, the lack of the

University Press, 1990), 317–22; Lewis Ayres, *Nicaea and Its Legacy: An Approach to Fourth-Century Trinitarian Theology* (New York: Oxford University Press, 2004).

7. Vernon Bourke pointed out some fifty years ago that this topic has not been well studied; see *Augustine's View of Reality*, The Saint Augustine Lecture 1963 (Villanova, PA: Villanova University Press, 1964), 24–25. The one recent and notable exception to this is David Meconi, *The One Christ: St. Augustine's Theology of Deification* (Washington, DC: Catholic University of America Press, 2013).

8. David Meconi, "Becoming One Christ: The Dynamics of Augustinian Deification," in *Tolle Lege: Essays on Augustine and on Medieval Philosophy in Honor of Roland J. Teske, SJ*, ed. Richard C. Taylor, David Twetten, and Michael Wreen (Milwaukee: Marquette University Press, 2011), 157–58. Meconi charts each of the eighteen references, dividing them into three categories: philosophical, textual, and explicitly Christian.

9. Lossky cites Anselm's supposed reduction of soteriology to a juridical ransom theory of the cross as one of the primary villains in the West's lack of a concept of deification and, more generally, in its loss of the rich and varied patristic christological and soteriological models. See Lossky, "Redemption and Deification," in *In the Image and Likeness of God* (Crestwood, NY: St. Vladimir's Seminary Press, 1985), 99. See also Jouko Martikainen, who traces this thesis in the Protestant (Lutheran) tradition, contrasting the Eastern focus on deification with the Protestant focus on justification, in "Man's Salvation: Deification or Justification?" *Sobornost* 7, no. 3 (1976): 180–92.

10. Christos Yannaras, "Orthodoxy and the West," *ECR* 3, no. 3 (1971): 287. Yannaras's contention of Western rationalism and its accompanying lack of a robust soteriology (deification) connects on a more general level to Zizioulas's and Gunton's argument that the rationalism in Western (Augustinian) trinitarianism also undermines a robust soteriology.

11. In his overview of Augustine's concept of deification, Gerald Bonner argues that the differences between the Greek East and the Latin West are overstated on this issue. Augustine may differ from the Greek fathers on issues such as predestination, but Augustine's model of deification has more similarities than differences with Greek thought. See Bonner, "Augustine's Concept of Deification," *JTS* 37, no. 2 (1986): 370.

terminology of deification does not indicate the absence of the idea, which often comes through alternate language.[12] This has been brought out recently in a couple of studies of Greek models of deification that have also shed light on notable similarities Augustine shares with that tradition.[13] Here I would like to offer a further examination of Augustine's views not only to further bridge East and West but also to allay some of the contemporary criticisms of his trinitarianism.

There is a long-standing and well-known debate surrounding Augustine's mystical ascents to God in *Confessions* 7.[14] I do not wish to comment here on the technical aspects of this debate, but rather to speak to the nascent model of deification that emerges as Augustine begins to read humanity's upward participation in God described in the ascent narratives through a trinitarian framework of the Son's downward participation in humanity.[15] Scholarship

12. Alternate ways Augustine develops the idea of deification come in the language of adoption and in phrases such as "I say: you are gods [*ego dixi: Dii estis*]" (*Expositions of the Psalms* 49.2) and "to make gods of those who were human [*Deos facturus qui homines erant*]" (Sermon 192.1). A variety of scholars have argued that the idea of deification, if not always the terminology, is fairly well established in Augustine. In addition to the works of Meconi and Bonner already cited, see also Patricia Wilson-Kastner, "Grace as Participation in the Divine Life in the Theology of Augustine of Hippo," *AugStud* 7 (1976): 135–52; Henry Chadwick, "Note sur la divinisation chez saint Augustin," *RevScRel* 76, no. 2 (2002): 246–48; A. Casiday, "St. Augustine on Deification: His Homily on Psalm 81," *Sobornost* 23 (2001): 23–44.

13. Daniel Keating offers a good comparison between Augustine and Cyril of Alexandria on the topics of Christology, deification, and the sacraments. Keating's overall conclusion is that though they may employ different terminology at points, the two thinkers are conceptually close in most areas, including Christology and deification. See Keating, *The Appropriation of Divine Life in Cyril of Alexandria* (Oxford: Oxford University Press, 2004), 231–51. Norman Russell offers a succinct overview of Augustine's account of deification within his wider study of the Greek tradition; see his *The Doctrine of Deification in the Greek Patristic Tradition* (Oxford: Oxford University Press, 2004), 329–32.

14. Pierre Courcelle argues that the ascents are the fruit of Augustine's encounter with the Platonist books and are a failed attempt at Plotinian ecstasy; see Courcelle, *Recherches sur les Confessions de saint Augustin* (Paris: E. de. Boccard, 1950), 157–67. James O'Donnell accepts the basic Plotinian structure of Augustine's mystical ascents, but argues that while Augustine fails in his first mystical ascent (*Confessions* 7.10.16), he is successful in his second ascent (7.17.23), at least on Plotinian grounds (see O'Donnell, *Augustine:* Confessions [Oxford: Oxford University Press, 2012], 2:435). Andrew Louth also argues for the strongly Plotinian character of the ascents, but contends that Augustine's search for a more permanent reunion with God leads him from a Plotinian model of ecstasy to a Christian model of the beatific vision. See Louth, *The Origins of the Christian Mystical Tradition: From Plato to Denys* (Oxford: Oxford University Press, 2007), 133.

15. The first explicit Christian use of the language of deification occurs in Sermon 23b, which dates to 404, about seven years after the completion of *Confessions*. However, David Meconi has charted the three references to *participatio* in *Confessions* 7 that move toward Augustine's model of deification. Two of the references are to the upward participation of humanity in God (7.9.14; 7.19.25), and one refers to God's downward participation in humanity (7.18.24). Meconi associates the two instances of upward participation with a Neoplatonist model, but contends that the third instance, referring to God's downward participation in humanity, indicates the

has often focused on the Platonist framework that structures Augustine's narration of his mystical ascents, a framework that, according to some, becomes a critical liability in current trinitarian discourse. In assessing such criticisms, however, it is important to understand the complicated way this framework develops in conjunction with his emerging understanding of the incarnation. Augustine begins the account of his first mystical ascent with the claim, "By the Platonic books I was admonished to return into myself. With you as my guide I entered into my innermost citadel, and was given power to do so because you had become my helper."[16] The admonition of the Platonist books is the immediate source of his turn inward, and this theme carries through as Augustine structures the ascent within a Platonist hierarchical model of inward and upward rational movement to God. But beneath and before this Augustine contends that God guides him.[17] The source of Augustine's ascent is God's act, an act Augustine is searching to understand in terms of the incarnation.[18] As he continues, this dynamic plays out in his discussion of the pinnacle of the ascent and its aftermath: "When I first came to know you, you raised me up to make me see that what I saw is Being [*esse*], and that I who saw am not yet Being [*esse*]."[19] The passage conveys a movement toward participation in God—Augustine has not yet, but will someday, become *esse* (God). His ensuing fall from God into a "region of dissimilarity" (*regione dissimilitudinis*) reiterates that he cannot join with God because he is not yet like God. This may in some sense point to a failed Platonist exercise (à la Courcelle and O'Donnell), but it is also an insight into the gap between Augustine and God that his inward ascent could not bridge.[20] Augustine's failure is part of his transformation from understanding reunion with God

beginning of Augustine's break with Neoplatonism. Meconi argues Augustine comes to this insight around 397 as he considers the basic differences between Christianity and Platonism that arise from the doctrine of the incarnation. See Meconi, "The Incarnation and the Role of Participation in St. Augustine's *Confessions*," *AugStud* 29, no. 2 (1998): 61–75. See also Louth, *Origins of the Christian Mystical Tradition*, 140.

16. *Confessions* 7.10.16. English citations are taken from Augustine, *Confessions*, trans. Henry Chadwick (Oxford: Oxford University Press, 1991).

17. James O'Donnell notes that "what is at stake is not strictly an 'ascent' but an 'assumption' ('*adsumpsisti*'). The notion of divine initiative is certainly more Christian than Platonic." O'Donnell continues by commenting that even though Courcelle finds Plotinian echoes in the passage, the language of "*duce te*" (you as my guide) that opens the ascent narrative, anchored as it is in divine initiative, moves in the opposite direction of Plotinus. See O'Donnell, *Augustine: Confessions*, 2:437–38.

18. *Confessions* 7.9.13.

19. *Confessions* 7.10.16. "*Et cum te primum cognovi, tu assumpsisti me, ut viderem esse, quod viderem, et nondum me esse, qui viderem.*"

20. Cavadini, "Structure and Intention of Augustine's *De Trinitate*," 107; John Quinn, "Mysticism in the *Confessiones*: Four Passages Reconsidered," in *Augustine: Mystic and Mystagogue*,

as momentary ecstasy, which never could satisfy him, to finding permanent reunion in the beatific vision, which requires likeness to God (i.e., deification). Augustine concludes the ascent narrative with the enigmatic statement: "[I] heard as it were your voice from on high; 'I am the food of the fully grown; grow and you will feed on me. And you will not change me into you like the food your flesh eats, but you will be changed into me.'"[21] Whether or not he is referring to the Eucharist, Augustine makes a strong claim on the need to be changed into Christ in order to achieve reunion with God.[22] In this way, Augustine's inward ascent shows his dissimilarity with God and beckons him toward becoming like God, not through the practices found in the Platonist books, but through Christ.

This leads into another noteworthy feature of the first ascent narrative, namely the way Augustine frames it in terms of his preceding discussion of sin and the incarnation.[23] Leading into the discussion of the ascent, Augustine draws on various passages in Scripture to highlight the resources Platonism does and does not provide for bringing about reunion with God. While Platonism offers a correct view of the eternal, spiritual, and immutable nature of God, it does not grasp the sinful nature of humanity or how the immutable God takes on mutable humanity in Christ to remedy sin. Citing Romans 1:18–23, Augustine contends that Platonism fails to realize that humans can no longer move through creation toward reunion with God.[24] Sin blocks this path not in undoing the order of God's creation but in the way it distorts the soul. Augustine describes this distortion as a type of idolatry that he associates with the divine image in the soul: in sin, humans exchange the image of the

---

ed. Frederick Van Fleteren, Joseph Schnaubelt, and Joseph Reino, Collectanea Augustiniana (New York: Peter Lang, 1994), 256.

21. *Confessions* 7.10.16.

22. Gerald Bonner tentatively suggests Augustine may be referring to the Eucharist; see Bonner, "Augustine's Concept of Deification," 384. John Quinn argues the eucharistic context is unlikely, noting that Augustine does not appear to use this or any other closely related phrase in a eucharistic context in his other writings. Quinn does acknowledge, however, a strong theme of deification present in the passage; see "Mysticism in the *Confessiones*," 279n19.

23. *Confessions* 7.9.13–15.

24. *Confessions* 7.9.14. Augustine's critique here may be anti-Porphyrian as often assumed, though this need not necessarily be the case. It is difficult to pinpoint exactly when Augustine becomes aware of Porphyry's anti-Christian claims that would occupy his attention in *De Civitate Dei*. Eugene TeSelle speculates it may have been as early as 390, but he posits this date cautiously. He goes on to note that Augustine's sharp shift in sentiment against Porphyry sometime after 405 does not necessarily signal that he has become aware of Porphyry's *Against the Christians* (Pépin's thesis), but may indicate a growing gap between basic Christian and Platonist doctrines in Augustine's understanding. See TeSelle, *Augustine the Theologian* (New York: Herder and Herder, 1970), 242–58; Jean Pépin, *Théologie cosmique et théologie chrétienne* (Paris: Presses universitaires de France, 1964), 418–61.

immortal God for images of corruptible (mortal) things.[25] The glory of God's creation leads wayward humanity not to worship God but to worship creation in a way that distorts the divine image. Any attempt, Platonist or otherwise, to ascend through the sinful soul to God must inevitably fail.

Against this backdrop, Augustine's own ascent, which comes in the next paragraph, serves as a warning. The problem Augustine encounters, which mirrors his reading of Romans 1:21–23, is not a failure to know God per se but a failure to know God in a manner that issues in the permanent worship and love of God.[26] This requires the reforming of the soul, which in this context Augustine associates with the humility of Christ. Citing passages such as Philippians 2:6–8, he argues that as Platonism fails in its diagnosis of sin (especially pride), it also fails to understand that the soul requires the remedy of Christ's humility.[27] Beyond the issue of humility, Augustine will come to realize by *Confessions* 10 that the reforming of sinful habits is a lifelong process of trying to reorient one's basic desires (loves).[28] Augustine's quest to understand the depth and origin of both sinful and divine love leads him in book 13 to explore the healing that must come through the Trinity and the church.[29] Thus, when Augustine takes up the admonition of the Platonist books to turn inward, he is not only narrating a failed attempt at reunion with God but also undertaking a profound transformation in his understanding of how humans must ascend to God through Christ and the church if they desire permanent reunion.

Augustine's next attempted ascent to God comes a bit further in *Confessions* 7. He opens again with the claim that God initiates the ascent: "I was astonished to find that already I loved you, not a phantom surrogate for you. But I was not stable in the enjoyment of my God. I was caught up to you by

---

25. *Confessions* 7.9.15. Eugene TeSelle notes that Augustine's use of Rom. 1:18–21 leads him into a twofold reading of idolatry: it may involve false fabrications (*phantasmata*) of God through the imagination, or it may begin with a true understanding of God that devolves into a false one because it is conducted in pride rather than humility (see TeSelle, *Augustine the Theologian*, 243–47). My point is not to dispute this but to underscore the anthropological ramifications of Augustine's claims on idolatry. That is, Augustine locates the effects of idolatry not only in the human upward relation to God (i.e., in false conceptions of God) but also within the soul itself (i.e., in distortions of the divine image), which in turn undermine attempts to move through the soul toward God.

26. *Confessions* 7.9.14; 7.10.16.

27. Meconi argues that Christ's humiliation is a—perhaps *the*—basic difference with Neoplatonism, which could never recommend humility as a fundamental virtue underlying humanity's inward participation in the divine. Meconi, "Incarnation and the Role of Participation," 69. Andrew Louth agrees with Meconi on this point; see Louth, *Origins of the Christian Mystical Tradition*, 140–41.

28. *Confessions* 10.29.40–10.40.65.

29. *Confessions* 13.11.12–13.12.13; 13.19.25–13.23.33.

your beauty and quickly torn away from you by my weight."[30] God's love has already caught hold of Augustine and, in conjunction with divine beauty, lifts him upward. He follows this with a reference to Romans 1:20 and the way the visible creation should raise humans to the invisible God. This leads into a second mystical ascent, which again has a basic Platonist structure, and now results in fleeting reunion with God. This reunion may indicate a successful ascent on Platonist grounds, as O'Donnell suggests, but Augustine leaves the experience profoundly dissatisfied. His failure to achieve permanent reunion with God again leads to an ensuing contrast between what the Platonists taught him (i.e., the immaterial, immutable nature of God) and what they did not teach him (i.e., the incarnation), with Romans 1 serving in the background as reminder and warning of the limits of human attempts to know God. At this point Augustine explicitly rereads the language of human upward *participatio* in God through God's downward *participatio* in Christ, identifying the incarnation as the precondition for humanity's reunion with God.[31] Significantly, Augustine draws on the language of Genesis 3:21—Christ participates in our "coat of skin"—to describe God's downward participation, and in this he connects that participation to the garden of Eden and humanity's original fall into sin and mortality.[32] The Platonist books may aid Augustine in moving toward a correct view of the spiritual nature of God, but they fail to understand the trinitarian God's downward participation in humanity and its connection to healing the undercurrents of human sin. They also then fail to understand the process necessary to overcome human unlikeness to God. In

---

30. *Confessions* 7.17.23.

31. *Confessions* 7.18.24.

32. According to Augustine, one of the consequences of the fall is that Adam and Eve take on mortal bodies. The best account of this comes in his *Literal Commentary on Genesis*, which is written several years after *Confessions*. Augustine argues that in the garden of Eden, Adam and Eve exist in a sinless condition that would eventually have resulted in the beatific vision. He maps this transition into blessedness in terms of their bodies: their "ensouled" bodies would eventually be transformed into spiritual bodies (*Literal Commentary on Genesis* 6.26.37). Augustine reads this transformation in relation to the tree of life, which he calls a sacrament of wisdom. The tree points to the spiritual feeding of the angels that allows them to be partakers (*particeps*) of eternity (11.32.42). Eventually God would have allowed the humans to eat of the fruit and exchange their "ensouled" bodies for spiritual bodies and permanent immortality. Humanity's sin of pride, however, turns them from the immortal, immutable God and into their own mutable, mortal origin. In this context, Augustine reads the serpent's words "and you will be like gods" as deceit that is turned back on itself and so as a warning for all future generations of humanity (11.39.53). Adam and Eve not only fail to become immortal like God but also find the divine image distorted. Augustine argues that the transition into mortality occurs between 3:7 and 3:21. Adam and Eve's realization of and shame at their nakedness signals that death and disease have now entered the human body (11.31.40–11.32.42). This culminates in Genesis 3:21 when God fashions coats of skin—mortal bodies—for Adam and Eve to replace the fig leaves in 3:7.

this, the ascent narratives, couched though they are in Platonist terminology, are a crucial part of Augustine's search to understand the christological and soteriological process necessary to overcome human unlikeness to God—the *regione dissimilitudinis*—and achieve stable unity with God.

Augustine's attempt to understand how humans overcome their dissimilarity with God finds profound and mature expression in his sermons on the Psalms.[33] In light of the above critiques of Augustine's trinitarianism, I would like to focus on the ecclesiological and sacramental context in which Augustine develops his account of deification. We can turn here to his sixteenth sermon on Psalm 118:

> This is the teaching of the Letter to the Hebrews: He who sanctifies and those who are sanctified are all of one stock; that is why he is not ashamed to call them his brothers; and, a little further on, Since "children" share in the same flesh and blood, he too just as truly shared in them (Heb. 2:11, 14). This plainly declares that Christ was made a participant [*particeps*] in our nature. We could not have become sharers [*participes*] in his godhead if he had not become a sharer [*particeps*] in our mortality. The gospel teaches that we have indeed become sharers [*participes*] in his divinity: He gave them power to become children of God; those, that is, who believe in his name, who are born not of blood, nor by the will of the flesh, nor by the will of man, but of God. But it goes on to show how this became possible through Christ's coming to share [*particeps*] in our mortality: The Word was made flesh, and dwelt among us (Jn. 1:12–14). Through his becoming one with us [*eius participationem nobis*], grace is dispensed to us, so that we may fear God with pure hearts and keep his commandments. Most surely Jesus himself is speaking in this prophecy. But he says certain things in the person of his members, in the unity of his body, as though in the voice of a single human being diffused throughout the whole world and continually growing as the ages roll on; and other things he says in his own voice, as our head.[34]

This passage highlights several key aspects of Augustine's now mature view of deification. Foremost, he locates the path to deification within the incarnation and God's downward participation in Christ. He states the matter succinctly in Sermon 192: "To make gods of those who were human, he was made a human who was God."[35] Elsewhere, Augustine expands on this notion, developing

33. Augustine comments on all the Psalms, mainly in the form of public sermons, beginning in 392 and finishing around 418.

34. *Expositions of the Psalms* 118.16.6. The English citation is taken from Augustine, *Expositions of the Psalms*, trans. Maria Boulding (New York: New City Press, 2003).

35. Sermon 192.1. "*Deos facturus qui homines erant, homo factus est qui Deus erat.*" We do not fully know the extent to which Augustine was familiar with the Greek tradition. In 394/95

the closely related claim that humans can participate in divine immutabil-
ity only because God first participates through Christ in human mutability.[36]
Augustine emphasizes also that the upward route established through Christ
is *ex gratia*, not *de substantia*—that is, through divine grace and not through
essential unity with God.[37] In other contexts, Augustine expands on this point
in various ways, including within the process of deification aspects of what
today we place within the categories of justification and sanctification: we can
participate in God only because God became a just man in Christ to forgive
our sins;[38] we can participate in God because Christ came to teach and become the way of humility to overcome human sin;[39] and we become adopted
children of God because our sins are forgiven when God joins us in the flesh
in Christ and dies for us.[40] Augustine concludes the above-quoted passage by
placing all of this within an ecclesiological and christological context. Drawing
on the Pauline head/body metaphor, he utilizes the prosopological method
common in his exegesis of the Psalms to connect the process of deification to
the mystical body of Christ.[41] As the quote indicates, he takes Christ to be the
subject (voice) of this psalm and to be, therefore, the one who brings about
human deification. But, noting that Christ speaks here as the head of the body,
Augustine reminds his readers that sharing in God's divinity occurs within the
wider context of one's incorporation into the body of Christ. Christ speaks

Augustine requests Latin translations of Greek biblical commentaries from Jerome, especially
Origen (Letter 28.2), but the request goes unfulfilled, as Jerome has begun his critique of Ori-
genism. Nevertheless, Augustine's summary statement on deification in Sermon 192 is close to
that of Irenaeus and Athanasius. Though differences would remain on issues such as original sin
and predestination, this is another area where we find cracks in the nineteenth- and twentieth-
century tendency to read the Greek East against the Latin West.

36. *Tractates on the Gospel of John* 2.15; 21.1; 22.1; *Expositions of the Psalms* 121.5; 146.11;
Letter 140.4.10.

37. *Expositions of the Psalms* 49.2.

38. *On the Trinity* 4.2.4.

39. *Expositions of the Psalms* 58.1.7; *On the Christian Struggle* 11.12.

40. *Tractates on the Gospel of John* 2.13.2; 2.15.2.

41. The concept of the *totus Christus* is a central theme that orients much of Augustine's
interpretation of the Psalms—Christ as the head and the church as the body of Christ. Augustine explicates the Psalms through a prosopological exegesis that delineates a shifting identity
of the voice (or speaker) of the Psalm based on the context and content of the passage. Among
the voices (identities) Augustine finds in the Psalms are the twofold voice of Christ when he
speaks in his divinity as the Word and in his humanity for sinful people (*pro nobis*), the voice
of individual Christians as part of Christ's body, and the voice of the church when it speaks as
the body of Christ. The diverse voices are united in the *totus Christus*. For recent studies on
Augustine's prosopological exegesis, see Michael Cameron, "The Christological Substructure of
Augustine's Figurative Exegesis," in *Augustine and the Bible*, ed. Pamela Bright (Notre Dame,
IN: University of Notre Dame Press, 1999), 74–103; Michael Fiedrowicz, *Psalmus vox totius
Christi: Studien zu Augustins "Enarrationes in Psalmos"* (Freiburg: Herder, 1997).

in the voice of the church as the head that unites the corporate body of the church into his risen body.[42] In other writings Augustine draws out the closely related sacramental context when he connects human participation in the body of Christ to baptism and the Eucharist. In Letter 98 Augustine argues that we share (communicatur) in grace through baptism and join all other Christians in the unity of the Spirit.[43] In Sermon 26 on John, Augustine argues that human participation in Christ is conditioned by partaking in the Eucharist. He again underscores that the initiative and power come directly from God, arguing that the efficacy of the sacrament is conditioned by divine predestination and justification of sinners.[44] Augustine goes on to interpret human participation in God through both a trinitarian context of the Son's eternal participation in the Father and a christological context of the Son's kenotic participation in Christ. Augustine uses the trinitarian context to establish the basic difference between humanity and the Son, which opens the way for the Son's kenotic mediation. The Son is God and so not made better by his participation in the Father, while humanity, who participates in the Son through the Eucharist, is bettered by this participation.[45] This contrast hinges in part on the creator/creation distinction and its attendant differences (e.g., eternal/temporal, immutable/mutable). This becomes apparent as Augustine continues with a discussion of the way humans are made better through their participation in Christ. Here he turns to a kenotic model to interpret human participation and the way this is opened through divine participation in humanity. The Son unites with humanity in Christ by emptying himself: by taking on that which he is not, namely mortality and death, the Son unites with humanity without giving up that which he is, namely God.[46] The Son's emptying—his incarnation in mortal flesh—opens the way for human participation in God, which Augustine connects directly to the human partaking of the body and blood of Christ in the Eucharist.[47] Through this, humans are able to become what they are not, namely eternal. In Sermon 123 on John, Augustine makes clear both the ecclesiological and eschatological dimensions of human participation in divine eternity that flow

---

42. Augustine draws on the corporate, ecclesiological context of participation in Christ's body in numerous contexts. For example, see City of God 10.6; 12.9; Tractates on the Gospel of John 123.2; Expositions of the Psalms 10.7; 26.2.13; 75.3; 125.13; 149.5.

43. Letter 98.2.

44. Tractates on the Gospel of John 26.15.

45. Tractates on the Gospel of John 26.19.

46. Here and elsewhere the kenotic language of emptying is part of Augustine's polemic against the Arian claim that the sending of the Son in the incarnation indicates that he is less than the Father. See also On the Trinity 2.1.3–2.2.4.

47. Tractates on the Gospel of John 26.19.

through the Eucharist.[48] Here he associates the participation in Christ that comes through the Eucharist with the unifying of the church in Christ and the church's movement toward eternal blessedness.[49] In this way, Augustine connects the human participation in God that results in eternal blessedness (i.e., deification that results in the *visio dei*) with the corporate dynamic of the church's unification in the body of Christ through the power of the Spirit.

The ecclesiological and sacramental themes that infuse the trinitarian structure of Augustine's account of deification should in turn lead scholars to revisit his place within contemporary trinitarian discussions. Critics of Augustine are right that he draws on Platonist concepts in his accounts of the Trinity and the human reunion with God. But this does not result in an intellectualistic monism that finds itself far afield from basic Christian soteriological concerns. The situation is far more complex. Augustine draws on a basic Platonist ascent model both to narrate his discontent with it and to reinterpret the human ascent to God within a trinitarian and incarnational model, a model the bishop of Hippo does not fail to connect with the life of the church. In so doing, Augustine's account opens the possibility of further dialogue with the Greek tradition and offers resources for contemporary theologians seeking to anchor Christian ecclesiology to the worship of the trinitarian God.

---

48. For a wider study of the connection between Augustine's account of deification and his ecclesiology and theory of signs, see David Meconi, "Becoming Gods by Becoming God's: Augustine's Mystagogy of Identification," *AugStud* 39, no. 1 (2008): 61–74.

49. Deification encompasses both the process and goal of the human return to God. In this, it has a basic eschatological dimension. Those redeemed through Christ are deified now in the hope that they will be resurrected and reunited with God (*Expositions of the Psalms* 49.2).

8

JUSTIFICATION AS DECLARATION
AND DEIFICATION

BRUCE D. MARSHALL

At least since the Reformation, theological controversy has repeatedly arisen over how two seemingly disparate elements in God's justification of sinful human beings fit together. On the one hand, justification has an irreducibly *forensic* aspect. God declares or reckons us righteous; he imputes saving righteousness to us, not on account of anything we are or do, but solely on account of what has been done for us by Christ, to whom the ungodly cling by faith. On the other hand, justification has an irreducibly *transformative* aspect. For those who are in Christ by faith, the old sinful self has passed away, and the new has come. It proves difficult, however, to do full justice to both of these claims at the same time. They appear to compete with one another: a vigorously forensic account of justification seems to threaten the transforming power of God's love for sinners, while introducing renewal of life into justification apparently endangers God's sure mercy toward the

This chapter first appeared as "Justification as Declaration and Deification," *International Journal of Systematic Theology* 4 (2002): 3–28. Reprinted with permission of Bruce D. Marshall. The author is grateful to Mark Edwards, Michael Root, and David Yeago for their comments on earlier versions of this essay.

undeserving. Centuries of interconfessional polemic about justification, while now largely muted, have made the apparent opposition between forensic and transformative accounts of justification seem set in stone.

At times this problem is thought of as a conflict between Lutheranism and the rest of the Christian world. The Lutheran view of justification, so the assumption regularly goes, is both thoroughly forensic and untethered to any insistence on transformation, holiness, and new life. Pretty much everyone else insists that justification involves or implies renewal of life, even if it also includes a wholly forensic element. To be sure, Lutherans sometimes give aid and comfort to this confessionalizing of the problem by insisting that any change God brings about in us belongs not to justification at all, but to "sanctification," and that a right understanding of the matter must always be vigilant to distinguish justification from sanctification—vigilant, in other words, to keep transformative elements out of justification. But the coherence of the forensic and the transformative is as much a problem for Lutherans as for anyone else. Luther himself is the clearest illustration of this. Under the rubric of justification he offers equally flamboyant accounts of God declaring sinners righteous in spite of their sin and of God transforming sinners into new selves.[1]

Luther can thus serve as an especially useful test case for pursuing the question of how justification as declaration and as transformation might fit together. While I will here analyze a number of Luther's texts, my concern is primarily systematic, not exegetical. A coherent account of justification presumably concerns Christian theology generally, of whatever confessional stripe. I do not take up Luther on the assumption, to which Lutherans sometimes seem prone, that Luther turned the trick on justification and that the rest of Christian theology can get justification right by learning to do Luther's trick. On the contrary: Luther looks like an exceptionally unpromising candidate to make the forensic and the transformatory cohere. If we can show how the two fit together in his case, then the results would seem promising

---

1. Recent discussion of justification has focused on the merits of the Lutheran/Roman Catholic *Joint Declaration on the Doctrine of Justification* (JD) of 1999 (Grand Rapids: Eerdmans, 2000). The JD was controversial primarily in Germany, and there chiefly among Protestant theologians. An assessment of that debate would be a topic for another paper. Here it may simply be observed that the coherence of forensic and transformative accounts of justification was central to the inner-Lutheran conflict over the JD. Indeed that conflict finds its way into the JD itself. Speaking for the Lutherans, §26 insists that "a distinction but not a separation is made between justification itself and the renewal of one's way of life that necessarily follows from justification." But the same paragraph immediately goes on to say that this renewal of life "comes forth from the love of God imparted to the person *in justification*" (emphasis added). Luther's view, as we will see, is the latter.

for Christian theology generally. A similar logic might be at work in, or be applicable to, accounts of justification quite different from his in both concept and emphasis.

I. Faith and Deification

Even when they hold aggressively transformationist views of justification, Western theologians often suppose that the characteristically Eastern Christian idea of deification goes too far. Yet, as is now well known, Luther makes some of his boldest statements about God's transformation of sinners by employing a concept of deification, along with various cognates.[2] He does this throughout his career, though I will look only at his writings after 1520 (which is to say, roughly, after the public beginnings of the Reformation).

Luther sometimes speaks of participation in the divine nature in order to characterize God's gift of righteousness and eternal life to us in Christ. Commenting, for example, on John 17:21, he invokes 2 Peter 1:4 in order to assert a real participation by Christians in the divine nature common to Christ and the Father.

---

2. Finnish Luther research in particular has extensively documented and developed this point. For a helpful overview of the Finnish research program and its accomplishments, see Olli-Pekka Vainio, ed., *Engaging Luther: A (New) Theological Assessment* (Eugene, OR: Cascade Books, 2010). Among the formative texts from this group of scholars, see Tuomo Mannermaa, *Der im Glauben gegenwärtige Christus: Rechtfertigung und Vergottung; Zum ökumenischen Dialog* (Hannover: Lutherisches Verlagshaus, 1989); Risto Saarinen, *Gottes Wirken auf Uns: Die transzendentale Deutung des Gegenwart-Christi-Motivs in der Lutherforschung* (Mainz: Verlag Philipp von Zabern, 1989); Simo Peura, *Mehr als ein Mensch? Die Vergöttlichung als Thema der Theologie Martin Luthers von 1513 bis 1519* (Mainz: Verlag Philipp von Zabern, 1994). See also Carl E. Braaten and Robert W. Jenson, eds., *Union with Christ: The New Finnish Interpretation of Luther* (Grand Rapids: Eerdmans, 1998).

Luther's talk of deification has naturally come to the attention of recent Lutheran/Orthodox ecumenical dialogue. See the detailed account in Risto Saarinen, *Faith and Holiness: Lutheran-Orthodox Dialogue 1959–1994* (Göttingen: Vandenhoeck & Ruprecht, 1997), esp. 29–78.

Gunther Wenz offers a critical but sympathetic assessment of the Finnish program, with references to further literature, in "Unio: Zur Differenzierung einer Leitkategorie finnisher Lutherforschung im Anschluß an CA I–VI," in *Unio: Gott und Mensch in der nachreformatorischen Theologie*, ed. Matti Reppo and Rainer Vinke (Helsinki: Luther-Agricola-Gesellschaft, 1996), 333–80. Mannermaa's response follows: "Über die Unmöglichkeit, gegen Texte Luthers zu systematisieren" (381–91). Reinhard Flogaus is less sympathetic, though the extent of his substantive differences with the Finns may not be as great as his negative tone suggests. Cf. Reinhard Flogaus, *Theosis bei Palamas und Luther: Ein Beitrag zum ökumenischen Gespräch* (Göttingen: Vandenhoeck & Ruprecht, 1997); see also Flogaus, "Palamas and Barlaam Revisited: A Reassessment of East and West in the Hesychast Controversy of 14th Century Byzantium," *SVTQ* 42 (1998): 1–32. For a preliminary assessment of Flogaus's position from the Finnish side, see Saarinen, *Faith and Holiness*, 244–48.

"I and you are one," [Jesus] wants to say, "in one divine being and majesty. Following this same example they should also be one and the same thing among themselves, in such a way that precisely the same unity may be [in them as is] in us, namely as is embodied in me and you. In sum: may they all be one and purely one in both of us, indeed may they be made of the same thing [as we are] to such an extent that they have everything which you and I are capable of having." Thus we too may become participants in the divine nature, as St. Peter says in II Pet. 1. For although the Father and Christ are one in another, higher, inconceivable way on account of their divine being, nonetheless we have all such things [as they have], so that they are truly ours, and we do enjoy them [*so haben wir doch solches alles, das es unser ist und sein geniessen*].[3]

By faith we have "everything" that the Father and the Son have; all these things "are truly ours, and we do enjoy them." Luther consistently interprets 2 Peter 1:4 in this sense and sometimes explicitly links the faith by which we receive righteousness and eternal life to participation in the divine nature. "This we have, [Peter] says, through the power of faith: that we are participants in, and have togetherness or communion with, the divine nature. This is an utterance without parallel in the New and Old Testament."[4] By faith (and so even now, in the present life) we have a real share in God's own nature. Luther here characterizes God's "nature" by specifying a series of attributes: eternal truth, righteousness, wisdom, life, peace, joy, and happiness. We receive, it seems, God's own attributes, not simply copies or effects of them. They belong to us as much as they belong to God, and by possessing them we are almighty conquerors of the devil, sin, and death, as only God can be.[5]

Luther's concept of human participation in God's own eternal righteousness and life is also eschatological, acknowledging a distinction between our present participation in the divine nature or essence (*wesen*), which makes us God's new creation, and its future completion. The Christian has only begun to be what he will one day be in full: "a divine creature" (*ein Göttliche Creatur*), indeed "a purely and completely divine being, as he himself is" (*ein lauter volkomen Göttlich wesen, wie er selbs ist*).[6] In God's final kingdom, "God

3. *D. Martin Luthers Werke, Kritische Gesamtausgabe* (Weimar, 1883ff.) (= WA) 28, pp. 183.28–184.16 (Das Siebenzehend Capitel Johannis, von den gebete Christi, 1530). All translations are my own.

4. WA 14, p. 19.3–6 (Die ander Epistel Sanct Petri . . . ausgelegt, 1523/24).

5. Cf. WA 14, p. 19.12–14: "As little as one can deprive God of being eternal life and eternal truth, so little can one also deprive us."

6. WA 41, p. 587.32, 37 (Ein ander predigt auff die Epistel Jacobi, 1536). Rörer's handwritten notes (hereafter = Hs.) on this sermon are not so strong as the printed version. In the end, the Christian will be a "perfect creature of God" (*volkomene Creatur Gottes*) (p. 587.11).

will be what everyone needs, and shall have."[7] Our eschatological possession of God's own attributes, already begun in this life by faith, is direct: God will not simply supply everything that we need; he will *be* everything that we need (*das wird Gott seyn*).

It seems that for Luther, believers have a real participation by faith in Christ's own divinity and so in his own divine attributes or characteristics. At the same time, a distinction remains between a divine and a creaturely way of possessing the divine attributes. As Luther observes on John 17:21, the divine unity belongs to the Father and Christ "in another, higher, inconceivable way" (*auff ein ander hoher unbegreifliche weise*) than it belongs to us, even though the church by faith truly enjoys a share in the divine unity itself. The eschatological completion of our participation in the divine nature will not obliterate this distinction. In the end God will be everything that we need, but we will have all that we need (namely God himself) from God and not from ourselves. The divine persons by contrast possess all these things without at all being in "need" of them, and so do not possess them by participation.[8] Luther thus strives to preserve a clear distinction between God and creatures while still asserting that we genuinely become participants in the divine nature.

Luther can also sometimes speak explicitly of our participation in God's own life as "deification" or "divinization" (*Vergottung*). He interprets Ephesians 3:19 by saying that "we are filled with [God's] Spirit," so that "everything that he is and can do is fully in us and powerfully at work, so that we become fully divinized (*wir gantz vergottet werden*). We do not have only a part or a few pieces of God, but all his fullness . . . in sum: your whole life is entirely divine."[9] Here it is specifically the person of the Spirit who divinizes

---

7. WA 14, p. 28.3–4.

8. Some trinitarian considerations come into view here. The Son and the Holy Spirit eternally receive the divine nature and attributes from the Father, the Son by generation and the Spirit by procession. In that sense one might say that the Son and the Spirit "need" the Father in order to possess the divine nature. But at no point can the Son or the Spirit be without divinity; they cannot fail to possess the divine nature and attributes as fully as the Father from whom they receive them. Therefore they do not *participate* in the divine nature, since to have a nature or characteristic by participation implies that one is subject to the possibility of existing without that nature or characteristic, or of possessing it more or less fully.

On the inner-trinitarian reception of divinity from the Father, Luther observes (here concentrating specifically on the divinity of the Son): "The one who generates pours his divine substance into the Son, yet the whole divinity nevertheless remains in him, in such a way that the Son is the perfect image of God" (WA 39/II, p. 23.31–3 [Disputation über Joh. 1:14, 1539]).

9. WA 17/I, p. 438.17, 20–22, 27–28 (Eyn Sermon von Stärke und Zunehmen des Glaubens und der Liebe, 1525).

us by imparting to us God's own life, blessedness, and love; Luther's concepts of participation in the divine nature and deification are thus genuinely trinitarian and not only christological. He stresses that human beings come to share the divine nature precisely by faith and not by works, but he conceives of faith as involving nothing less than the divinization of believers. "Faith, if I may speak in this way, is the creator of divinity—not in God's own substance, but in us."[10] Luther can thus conceive of the relationship to God in Christ that the Spirit brings about by faith in a way strikingly reminiscent of Athanasius: God "pours out Christ his dear Son upon us and pours himself into us and draws us into himself, so that he is entirely humanized and we are entirely divinized . . . and all with one another are one reality (*eyn ding*)—God, Christ, and you."[11]

We clearly have grounds in Luther for taking God's gift of righteousness and eternal life in Christ to involve participation in the divine nature and the deification of Christians. It is sometimes argued (in particular against the Finnish interpretation of Luther) that explicit appeals to "Vergottung" or "Durchgottung," while sometimes vivid, are relatively infrequent in his writings and cannot be regarded as one of his leading ways of talking about justification and salvation.[12] Whatever the merits of this textual claim, the decisive systematic question is not how often Luther talks about deification, but whether his assertions about it are consistent with the rest of what he says about justification. As it turns out, transformation is far more basic to Luther's account of justification than his periodic uses of deification language might, by themselves, suggest.

10. WA 40/I, p. 360.24–25 (In epistolam S. Pauli ad Galatas Commentarius, 1535). Cf. p. 390.22–23: "The believer is a wholly divine human being" (*divinus homo*).

11. WA 20, pp. 229.30–33; 230.10 (Ein Sermon aus dem 3. Kapitel Matthäi von der Taufe Christi, 1526; cited in Karl Christian Felmy, *Die Orthodoxe Theologie der Gegenwart: Eine Einführung* [Darmstadt: Wissenschaftliche Buchgesellschaft, 1990], 141). This passage echoes Athanasius, *De incarnatione* 54 (PG 25:192b): "He became man, that you might become God." This similarity should not, however, be taken to suggest that Luther had any direct acquaintance with Athanasius's treatise; the *De incarnatione*, it seems, became known in the West only in the seventeenth century. Cf. Bernhard Lohse, "Luther und Athanasius," in *Auctoritas Patrum: Contributions on the Reception of the Church Fathers in the 15th and 16th Century*, ed. Leif Grane, Alfred Schindler, and Markus Wriedt (Mainz: Verlag Philipp von Zabern, 1994), 97–115; Georg Kretschmar, "Kreuz und Auferstehung in der Sicht von Athanasius und Luther," in *Der Auferstandene Christus und Das Heil der Welt: Das Kirchberger Gespräch über die Bedeutung der Auferstehung für das Heil der Welt zwischen Vertretern der EKD und der Russischen Orthodoxen Kirche* (Witten: Luther-Verlag, 1972), 40–82.

12. Cf. Bernhard Lohse, *Martin Luther's Theology: Its Historical and Systematic Development*, trans. Roy A. Harrisville (Minneapolis: Fortress, 1999), 221; Lohse, "Luther und Athanasius," 98–99, 114–15.

II. Justification and Union with Christ

(A) Ways of Conceiving the Believer's Union with Christ

When he speaks of participation in the divine nature or deification, Luther regularly observes that these great gifts depend on and come about through the believer's union with Christ by faith. Here we do find an idea that is essential and central to Luther's understanding of justification. Commenting on Galatians 2:16, Luther reasons as follows: "We say that faith lays hold of Christ, who is the form which adorns and informs faith, as color does a wall. . . . If it is true faith, it is a certain trust of the heart and a firm assent by which Christ is grasped, so that Christ is the object of faith—indeed not the object but, if I may put it so, Christ is present in faith itself [*in ipsa fide Christus adest*]."[13]

By faith, Christ unites himself to the believer in a manner something like that in which a form is united to the substance in which it inheres: "Christ is my form."[14] As intimately as a color is one with the surface to which it gives a certain shade or hue, so Christ is one with those who believe in him. This can be taken in a strong sense. One might suppose that Luther here compares Christ to some particular color (green, white, or whatever), which can easily be replaced with a different color (the wall can readily be repainted). But Christ's union with us by faith goes deeper than this; he cannot so easily be replaced as the believer's "form." The comparison might better be taken to apply between Christ and color *simpliciter*. That a surface is colored at all, and not just that it has one color instead of another, seems to be the simile Luther wants to draw. Just as there are no surfaces without color, so there are no believers without Christ as their form; perhaps, indeed, just as a surface ceases to exist without a color united to it, so also believers as such cease to exist without Christ united to them.[15] Luther grants that this is a "crude" way of speaking, not, however, because it makes too much of the believer's union with Christ, but because it makes too little: "We are incapable of grasping spiritually how closely and intimately Christ inheres and dwells in us."[16]

Here (as generally for Luther) faith is at once a secure trust in Christ (*certa fiducia cordis*) and a confident assent (*firmus assensus*) to the church's proclamation of and teaching about him. Assent without trust would be empty; it would fail to grasp (*apprehendere*) Christ as the one he is—as the redeemer

13. WA 40/I, pp. 228.29–30, 33–229.15.
14. WA 40/I, p. 283.7 (Hs.).
15. Thus Luther's claim that "faith first makes [*facit*] the person, who then does good works" (WA 40/I, p. 402.15–16; cf. pp. 402.19–21; 407.30–32).
16. WA 40/I, p. 283.27–29.

of the world—and so would fail actually to have him present. A person who assented without *fiducia* "would truly be dead, because he would only have a historical faith about Christ, which the devil and all unbelievers also have" (cf. James 2:19).[17] Trust without assent would be blind; it would have nothing definite to grasp and so would equally fail to have Christ present. Where there is trusting assent to the gospel, however, Christ himself is immediately present: *in ipsa fide Christus adest.*[18]

For present purposes it is especially important to observe that Luther explicitly makes justification itself dependent upon this union with Christ. Faith justifies, and not works, because faith is the medium by which Christ makes himself intimately present to us, indeed gives himself to be possessed by us and united with us: "Faith justifies *because* it lays hold of and possesses this treasure, namely the present Christ."[19] It is precisely through faith's union with Christ that the believer receives God's gifts of righteousness and eternal life. These gifts, in fact, turn out to be nothing other than Christ's own person. He himself is our righteousness and life, in that we receive nothing less than his own divine qualities just because we are united with him and possess him dwelling within us by faith. The righteousness that justifies and saves is thus within us, closer to us than we are to ourselves. "We say that Christ forms or permeates faith, or is the form of faith. Therefore Christ grasped by faith *and dwelling in the heart* is Christian righteousness, *because of which God reckons us righteous* and gives us eternal life."[20]

While Luther willingly adapts the Aristotelian categories of form and substance in order to conceptualize our union with Christ by faith, he also thinks about the *unio cum Christo* in more personalistic terms. Following Bernard of Clairvaux, he often conceives of the believer's union with Christ as a nuptial relationship, but one more intimate than any human marriage. While the relationship of believers to Christ remains, like a marriage, genuinely interpersonal, in faith the believer becomes so closely bound to Christ that the two are "like one person" (*quasi una persona*). This comes out especially in Luther's commentary on Galatians 2:20: "Faith makes of you and Christ something like one person, so that you may not be separated from Christ; on the contrary, you inhere in him. It is as though you could say that you are

17. WA 40/I, p. 285.21–23.

18. For an interpretation of Luther (and especially of his 1535 *Galatians*) that takes the presence of Christ in faith to be the heart of his theology of justification, see Tuomo Mannermaa, "In ipsa fide Christus adest. Der Schnittpunkt zwischen lutherischer und orthodoxer Theologie," in *Der im Glauben gegenwärtige Christus*, 11–93.

19. WA 40/I, p. 229.22–23 (emphasis added).

20. WA 40/I, p. 229.27–30 (emphasis added). To the troublesome term "reckons" (*reputat*) and its cognates we will return in the third section of this chapter.

Christ, and [he] conversely: I am that sinner who inheres in me, and conversely. [We are] joined by faith in one 'flesh and bone,' by a bond much closer than that of husband and wife."[21]

Here Luther clearly thinks of the believer's union with Christ by faith as a relationship of interpersonal reciprocity. Pure inertia or passivity obtains on neither side of the relationship; it is acting subjects distinct from one another—individual persons—who here come to be "like one person." This union involves the total reality of the person on each side, both that of the believer who clings to Christ in faith and that of Christ who gives himself totally to the believer in love. "Thus faith brings it about that Christ is ours, and his love brings it about that we are his. He loves, we believe, and thus we become one with him" (*da wirt eyn kuch auß*).[22]

The personal character of the *unio cum Christo* does not, however, diminish for Luther the ontological realism of the union. To be sure, Luther insists that the presence of Christ in faith is not quite the most intimate possible form of unity among persons. The highest form of unity (in "one natural essence") belongs to the persons of the Trinity themselves, but our union with Christ exceeds any we can attain with a person who is not true God.[23]

(B) Justifying Union with Christ as Transforming

In light of the passages like these, Luther's concept of a *unio personalis* between the believer and Christ seems to lie at the heart of his teaching about justification by faith.

> When it comes to *justification*, Christ and I must be joined as closely as possible, so that he lives in me, and I in him (what a wonderful way of speaking this is!). Because he lives in me, whatever grace, righteousness, life, peace, and salvation is in me belongs to Christ. But nevertheless it is all mine, because of the sticking together and adhesion which happens by faith, since by faith we are made to be like one body in the Spirit.[24]

21. WA 40/I, pp. 285.5–286.1 (Hs.).

22. WA 10/I/1, p. 74.16–18 (Kirchenpostille on Luke 2:14, 1522), cited in Werner Elert, *Morphologie des Luthertums* (Munich: C. H. Beck, 1931; repr., 1952), 1:151. Elert's chapter on "unio mystica" (135–54) contains an abundance of citations from Lutheran sources bearing on the union of believers with the Trinity and their divinization. On this see also Albrecht Peters, *Rechtfertigung* (Gütersloh: Gerd Mohn, 1984), 38–46. As Elert observes (*Morphologie des Luthertums*, 151), Luther "clearly says . . . that here there is relationship of love, which includes the moment of reciprocity. 'The Lord loves me, and I love him back'" (WA 45, p. 178.35–36 [Predigt über Matth. 22, 1537]).

23. WA 33, p. 232b.2–3; cf. p. 232b.33–39 (Wochenpredigt über Joh. 6, 1531).

24. WA 40/I, p. 284.20–26 (emphasis added).

This personal union with Christ by faith seems to be the crucial conceptual link for Luther between justification and salvation, on the one hand, and deification, on the other. Without the *unio personalis*, there is no justification and no salvation. "Who is that 'I' about whom [Paul] says, 'It is no longer I'? This I is the one who has the law, must do good works, and is a person separated from Christ. This I Paul rejects, because I as a person distinct from Christ belong to death and hell."[25] But with the *unio personalis*—which is to say, with the faith that lays hold of Christ—there can only be justification and salvation, since Christ by uniting us to himself gives us all that he is and has, his own divine righteousness and life. In short, he deifies us. "Therefore Christ, [Paul] says, adhering to me, cemented to me, and dwelling in me, lives in me this life that I live; indeed the life by which I live is Christ himself."[26]

Thus, to be justified is to be united with Christ by faith, and to be united with Christ is to be deified. Since faith does nothing less than deify the believer on account of his union with Christ, Luther evidently teaches a transformatory or (in the language of traditional Lutheran dogmatics) "effective" notion of justification. He does not think of the believer's new life, the life of increasing holiness in conformity to Christ, as an event or process different from faith and justification, or in some sense subsequent to justification. Rather, the believer's new life belongs to justification itself. To become a new self is just to cling to Christ for salvation and thereby be united with him. It could hardly be otherwise, since in faith we are righteous by Christ's own righteousness and we live his own eternal life. By faith we are one with Christ, and where Christ is there can be no sin and death; "at his presence these things can only vanish."[27]

We can see that when Luther conceives of Christ himself as the "form" of the believer, he at the same time thinks of the believer as taking on Christ's own shape, of being conformed to Christ. Christ as form and the Christian as conformed are two sides of one and the same state of affairs—namely, the believer's union with Christ.[28] Christ and the believer are related, as it were, like the inside and the outside of a curve. Made one with Christ by faith, believers can no more fail to take on his qualities than a curve's outside can fail to conform to its inside. It belongs to justifying faith itself, therefore, to make us those who think and act like Christ himself. Thus Paul urges the Galatians "to have the form or likeness of Christ . . . the image of Christ and of God,

25. WA 40/I, p. 283.22–25.
26. WA 40/I, p. 283.30–31.
27. WA 40/I, p. 283.34–35.
28. WA 40/I, p. 649.23: "The heart endowed with such faith has the true form of Christ."

which is to feel, be affected, will, understand, and think just like Christ. . . . This is 'the new man, who is generated.'"[29]

Luther's characterization of the new life in Christ often has a decidedly pneumatological flavor. Upon Christ rests the Holy Spirit in all his fullness. Joined to Christ by faith, we share in all that he is and has, and so by faith we receive the fullness of the Spirit. "We live," Luther argues, "by faith in Christ and are made new creatures, that is, truly righteous and holy by the Holy Spirit; this is not sham or fakery."[30] The Spirit brings about in us a genuine and radical change (*mutatio*) and renewal (*renovatio*) not only of the heart and mind but also of will, the flesh, and even the senses. "The new creature . . . [is] the renewal of the mind by the Holy Spirit, after which comes an external change of the flesh, the members, and the senses. . . . These changes, I should say, are not verbal but real; they introduce a new mind and will, new senses and actions, even of the flesh."[31]

There is no suggestion here that justification is the work of Christ, while new life or sanctification is the work of the Spirit. Rather, the Spirit is given through faith in the gospel of Christ—the very faith by which we are justified and saved—and the reception of the Spirit changes the whole self.

III. Imputation and Transformation

(A) The Forensic Dimension of Justification

So far Luther appears committed to an understanding of the believer's transformation in Christ as bold as any on the Christian theological spectrum, including Orthodox *theosis*. Another central element in Luther's teaching about justification, however, seems to compete with these transformationist commitments. This is the legal or forensic aspect of justification, in which the concept of imputation plays a central role.

The idea that God "reckons" or "imputes" saving righteousness to us stems, of course, from Scripture, and in particular from Romans 4. Using Abraham and David as examples, Paul there argues that we are "reckoned righteous" or "credited with righteousness" on account of our faith in Christ and without the works of the law. Luther dwells especially on Paul's citation of Genesis 15:6: "Abraham believed God, and it was reckoned [*elogisthē*; Vulg.: *reputatum*]

---

29. WA 40/I, p. 650.6, 8–9 (Hs.), cited in Mannermaa, "In ipsa fide Christus adest," 89.

30. WA 40/II, p. 180.23–24. On Christ as the bearer of the Spirit, and on the dependence of the new life in Christ upon baptism, cf. below, n. 56.

31. WA 40/II, pp. 178.31–33; 179.11–13; cf. 40/I, p. 572.21–23: "The Holy Spirit, who comes with the preached word, purifies hearts by faith and begets spiritual impulses [*motus*] in us."

to him as righteousness" (Rom. 4:3 RSV; cf. Gal. 3.6). Spurred on by these passages, Luther reasons as follows (here commenting on Galatians 2:16).

> God accepts or counts you as righteous, solely for the sake of Christ in whom you believe. And this acceptance or reckoning is most necessary. First, because we are not yet entirely righteous, but in this life sin still dwells in the flesh. God cleanses this remnant of sin in the flesh. Nevertheless we always have to go back to this article, that our sins are covered and that God does not want to impute them to us, as Rom. 4 teaches. It is not that sin is no longer present. . . . Rather sin is truly present and the faithful feel it, but it is ignored and hidden before God because Christ the mediator stands in between.[32]

Characteristically Luther here regards two notions as mutually implicative: the imputation of righteousness and the nonimputation of sin. The believer's sins are forgiven in that they are covered (*tecta*) or hidden (*abscondita*) from God by the perfect righteousness of Christ and so are not held against the sinner. God does not want to reckon (*imputare*) our sins to our account, but instead regards as our own the righteousness of another, in whom we have faith: "God . . . counts you as righteous, solely for the sake of Christ in whom you believe."

In Romans 4 Paul surely does claim that God reckons us righteous on account of Christ and that the people whom God reckons or counts righteous—the justified—are those who have faith in Christ, regardless of Torah observance. It is some distance, though, from these Pauline ideas to Luther's apparent claim that God forgives our sins by covering them up, indeed hiding them from himself by interposing Christ the righteous between the believer and himself. Neither does it follow directly from Romans 4 that God counts us as righteous or just simply by imputing or ascribing to us the perfect righteousness of another, even while our own continuing sin and unworthiness teach us not to regard this righteousness as our own. Why does Luther think it necessary to extend Paul's ideas so as to conceive of justification in this boldly forensic way?

His chief motives are two: to console terrified consciences and to give Jesus Christ his due. One motive is more pastoral, the other more doctrinal, though of course they are interrelated.

In the first place, Luther wants a teaching about justification that ensures that the gospel of Christ comes across as genuinely good news, a word of grace and peace to those who recognize that they have sinned against God's law and have no claim upon his favor. The need for assurance of salvation was a particularly

---

32. WA 40/I, pp. 233.23–234.14.

pressing problem in the context of the sometimes highly rigorous penitential practices of the late medieval West. These practices had helped to heighten the awareness of continuing sin in the lives of believers. According to the prophet Isaiah, "all our righteous deeds are like a polluted garment" (64:6 RSV). "And he," as Luther likes to observe, "was a holy prophet. So if our righteousness is impure and stinks before God, what will our unrighteousness do?"[33]

In this context the central question about salvation was one of trust or assurance. Upon what can I rely for salvation? Luther responds: upon God in Christ alone and not at all upon yourself. In spite of your continuing sin, which indeed warrants eternal death and the loss of God, you may be confident of salvation on account of Christ. Because Christ has destroyed sin and death by his own death and resurrection, God will not hold your sins against you and will regard you as righteous for Christ's sake. For salvation you may therefore rely with complete confidence upon Jesus Christ, who died for sinners—for the ungodly (*asebēs*), as Paul says (Rom. 4:5; cf. 5:6, 8).

To cling to Christ for salvation is of course the Spirit's free gift, given by way of the public practices of the church; no human capacity can produce this act except by the Spirit's power, and no individual can cling to Christ without the church.[34] In Luther's view, to rely by the Spirit's power on Jesus Christ alone for salvation just is to have faith, and God justifies, or reckons as righteous, the ungodly on account of this faith. Because God in Christ promises salvation precisely to sinners, Luther regards the imputed righteousness of Christ, rather than any righteousness that believers may be able to detect in themselves, as essential to justification and the key to the consolation of consciences terrified by the recognition of their own sin. "We define a Christian in this way: not a person who neither has nor feels sin, but one to whom God does not impute that sin on account of faith in Christ. This teaching offers solid consolation to genuinely terrified consciences."[35]

The second motivation for the claim that God justifies by imputed righteousness is christological and trinitarian. Our salvation depends upon the conquest of sin, death, and the devil, which hold us in their grip. But neither we nor any creature can overcome these forces opposed to salvation; only God

---

33. WA 7, p. 433.25–27 (Grund und Ursach aller Artickel D. Martin Luthers, 1521).

34. The place outside ourselves where we may look to find the Word incarnate crucified, risen, and exalted for us, and so have legitimate confidence about our salvation, is the church, where the gospel of Christ is proclaimed and baptism and the eucharist celebrated. "In the place where . . . I have called you to the gospel you have baptism, the sacrament, and the fellowship of the church. There you have the greatest certainty, so that you may be entirely sure that he is favorable to us" (WA 40/I, p. 591.2–4 [Hs.]). I am grateful to David Yeago for pointing this passage out to me.

35. WA 40/I, p. 235.15–19.

can.[36] God conquers sin, death, the devil, and hell by the cross and resurrection of Jesus Christ. Since the human being Jesus destroys death and sin by his own death and resurrection, this human being must himself be God. The church's ancient faith in the divinity of Christ follows from its conviction that he is the savior of the world.

> Here you see how necessary it is to believe and confess the article concerning the divinity of Christ. When Arius denied it, it was necessary that he also deny the article on redemption. For to conquer the sin of the world, death, and the curse and wrath of God in himself is not the work of any creature, but of divine power. Therefore it is necessary that he who conquers them in himself be God truly and by nature.[37]

Conversely, to rely for salvation on our own works or capacities is to deny that Jesus Christ is true God and to attribute his divinity to ourselves.[38] Thus for Luther the ultimate basis of the claim that justification is by faith alone, without works, is the ancient Christian doctrine of the incarnation of the Logos. Of those who seek confidence about salvation in themselves and their works, he asks: "If they by their own righteousness and austerity of life can abolish sins and merit the forgiveness of sins and eternal life, of what use is it to them that Christ was born, suffered, poured out his blood, rose, and conquered sin, death, and the devil—since they can overcome these monsters by their own powers?"[39]

In this connection Luther often claims that the righteousness that justifies and saves us is "alien" to us—that is, another's rightful possession rather than our own. Together with this he insists that the righteousness that justifies us is to be found outside of ourselves—*extra nos*—rather than within us. Especially when it comes time to stand before the judgment seat of God, even the most righteous prophet or apostle knows that he cannot rely on his own resources, but must place his ultimate trust in the works of the Word incarnate. Indeed in the day of judgment we cannot rely even upon those good works that God brings about in us by his grace. For all God's gifts of grace we surely owe him boundless gratitude, and we glorify him for them. But before the throne of God, would even St. Peter or St. Paul be able—or indeed want—to say to the righteous judge, "'O Lord God, behold this good work which I have done with the help of your grace. There is in it no defect

---

36. See WA 40/I, p. 404.30–33.
37. WA 40/I, p. 441.14–19; cf. pp. 436.24–437.17.
38. Cf. WA 40/I, p. 405.15–16.
39. WA 40/II, pp. 10.30–11.12.

or sin, and it has no need of your forgiving mercy. . . .' Does this not fill you with horror and trembling?"[40]

At least in his later theology, Luther's well-known teaching that the believer is *simul iustus et peccator*—at the same time righteous and a sinner—finds its chief motive in his conviction that we may ultimately rely for salvation wholly on Christ outside of ourselves. His pastoral and doctrinal insistence on this point creates the conceptual space into which this much-disputed teaching naturally fits.

If, Luther argues, the right to be confident about the favor of God and our salvation depended on finding a certain level of righteousness or purity within ourselves, we would be driven to despair. At best we would be unsure whether sufficient purity was really present, and if we were honest we would likely find that no part of ourselves, no inner recess, is exempt from resistance to God. "Even though a Christian does not fall into coarse sins like murder, adultery, or theft," Luther maintains, nonetheless "in the *holy* man (*sancto viro*) impatience, grumbling, hate, and blasphemy against God are powerful."[41] Faced with this problem of introspective uncertainty, it will not suffice to point out, as the Augustinian tradition had always done, that any good capacity or achievement of our own is a gift of God's free grace. While surely correct as far as it goes, this Augustinian observation may well lead the saintly man who scrutinizes his life to doubt God's grace and favor in his own case, rather than to rejoice in the unmistakable abundance of God's gracious gifts.

Luther's solution to this problem is to argue that it does not matter what we find within ourselves. We can acknowledge the continuing reality of sin when we look within ourselves and yet be confident of our salvation when we look outside ourselves at Jesus Christ crucified and risen. He has won for us the favor of God and defeated the "monsters" that assail us within. "How can these two contradictory claims be true at the same time: I have sin and am most worthy of divine wrath and hate, and yet the Father loves me? Here nothing can intervene but Christ the mediator."[42]

Indeed it seems, on Luther's view, that the christological and trinitarian motive for talk of justification by an alien righteousness would hold good even for a conscience that had never known the terrors of sin. Even a human being who had entirely kept God's commands—someone who was not implicated in the fall of Adam—would not be able to rely on her or his obedience for salvation before the judgment of God. The terrified conscience can say with

40. WA 8, p. 79.21–23, 28–29 (*Rationis Latomianae confutatio*, 1521).
41. WA 40/I, p. 524.21–22, 27–28 (emphasis added).
42. WA 40/I, p. 372.14–17.

confidence, "I do not seek an active righteousness. Of course I ought to have and do it. But even granted that I did have and do it, I could not trust in it, or take my stand on it before the judgment of God."[43]

This kind of remark suggests that for Luther we human beings are not only redeemed, but created, in such a way that we can attain secure knowledge of our destiny with God, and ultimately of our union with God, only "extrospectively" (if the neologism may be allowed) and not introspectively. Even Adam and Eve in paradise, so to speak, would have been justified by faith alone. In this way "alien righteousness" appears to have a certain conceptual priority over "imputed righteousness" in Luther's view. Because sin infects the lives even of the redeemed until the day of judgment, we need the forgiveness of sins and the imputation of righteousness in order to reach God and so attain salvation, but the righteousness that brings us to God would be "alien" to us even if we had no need of forgiveness.

Luther thus has biblically resonant, pastorally compelling, and doctrinally coherent reasons for making forensic elements central in his theology of justification. Nonetheless his forensic approach to justification poses an obvious problem, which has drawn critical attention since the sixteenth century and remains troubling to non-Lutherans. Indeed it has sometimes proven troubling to Lutherans.

Despite its salutary pastoral and doctrinal motives, it seems as though Luther's forensic view of justification denies, or at best is indifferent to, the creative and renewing power of God's love in Christ. Before we dismiss this conclusion as a mere misunderstanding, a reading of Luther *in malem partem*, let us recall the following passage. The forgiveness of sins, Luther argues,

> prevents God from seeing the sins which still dwell in my flesh [*obstat, ne Deus videat peccata*]. The flesh distrusts God, is angry at him, does not rejoice in him, and so forth. God actually plays make believe with these sins [*Verum haec peccata dissimulat Deus*], and for him it is as though they were not sins. What does this is imputation, for the sake of the faith by which I begin to lay hold of Christ. For his sake God counts imperfect righteousness as perfect righteousness, and sin as though it were not sin, even though it really is sin.[44]

Here, in a fashion that can hardly be regarded as uncharacteristic, Luther apparently makes explicit the disturbing implications of his forensic view of justification. To be justified is to be the beneficiary of a legal verdict on God's

43. WA 40/I, pp. 42.29–43.12.
44. WA 40/I, p. 367.15–21. The Hs. (p. 367.5–7) has "sum apud eum": "for him *I* am as though they were not sins."

part. As Luther happily concedes, however, this verdict flies in the face of the known facts. Our sins, it seems, are covered (*tecta*), not removed.[45] Rather than making us new creatures, as Paul insists (cf. 2 Cor. 5:17), for Luther Christ's obedient passion and death seem to prompt a deliberate act of self-deception on God's part, in which he *regards* believers as righteous even though *in reality* they remain sinners.

This way of thinking, so the long-standing objection goes, apparently offers the faithful a spurious assurance of salvation. By resting content with this radically forensic view of justification, Luther apparently teaches believers to rely on a supposed divine favor that leaves them unchanged. But the love of the triune God for sinners is no such legal fiction. The favor of this God does not leave sinners unchanged, but imparts to them that holiness without which, as the New Testament warns, "no one will see the Lord" (Heb. 12:14).

(B) Justification as at Once Forensic and Transforming

To return to the question with which we began: how, if at all, can Luther have it both ways? He insists that unless Christ dwells within us and thereby really renews our whole life, there is no justification and no salvation. Yet at the same time he insists that we always remain sinners in God's eyes who may and must ultimately rely for salvation only on God's free declaration of forgiveness in Jesus Christ and not at all on ourselves.

Lutheran theology has regularly tried to cope with this problem by assigning all of Luther's forensic language to "justification," and all of his transformative language to "sanctification." Luther, however, explicitly blocks this recourse. He includes the transforming presence of Christ in his idea of justification and apparently has no trouble making justification—the favor of God announced in his declaration of forgiveness—*depend* upon the new life wrought by our union with Christ through faith.[46] Luther's refusal to distill all transformative elements out of justification is evidently bound up with the very reasons that drive him to think of justification in a radically forensic way. Did justifying

45. Cf. the passage cited above, n. 32.
46. See the texts cited above, notes 19, 20, 24, 30, 31. Cf. WA 8, p. 107.34–35: "A person is not pleasing to God and does not have grace, except on account of the gift of God laboring to drive out sin" ("grace" = "the favor of God . . . not a quality of the soul" [p. 106.10–11]; "the gift" = "righteousness . . . that is, faith in Christ" [p. 106.1–2]); also p. 112.12–13: "Behold, this faith is the gift of God, which obtains the favor of God for us." But cf. p. 114.19–21: "They are safe under the grace of [Christ], not because they believe and have faith, or the gift, but because they dwell in the grace of Christ. For no one's faith could stand fast, unless he relied on Christ's own righteousness and was kept under his protection." Here again Luther apparently wants to have it both ways.

faith in Christ not already include new life, the faithful would have to look for it elsewhere, since without holiness there is no salvation—no one will see the Lord. In so doing they would fail to give Christ his due and so fall once again into the terrors of conscience that await sinners who seek confidence about salvation outside of Christ.

At one level, Luther responds to the apparent incoherence of imputation and transformation by suggesting that we have to think about union with Christ in a new way. We become one with Christ, Luther apparently wants to say, precisely by relying upon him outside ourselves. The tradition had of course always said that Christ lives at once *extra nos* and *in nobis* (for example, when the scholastics spoke of both a visible mission of the Son of God in incarnation and an invisible mission of the incarnate Son in grace).[47] Luther's innovation, to the extent that he makes one, is to say that the faith that lays hold of Christ *extra nos* for salvation is itself enough to unite us to him.

Writing as an Anglican, John Henry Newman puts this point quite nicely. Indeed Newman here credits Luther, despite his generally critical attitude toward the Reformer.[48] "True faith," Newman says, "is what may be called colourless, like air or water; it is but the medium through which the soul sees Christ; and the soul as little really rests upon it and contemplates it, as the eye can see the air."[49] The genuinely believing mind is wholly possessed, not by its own faith, but by its object—Jesus Christ.[50]

United by faith with Christ outside ourselves, we genuinely take on his qualities and attributes. In *this* way, Christ himself becomes our "form," "coloring" us with his victorious righteousness and life as truly as whiteness colors a surface to which the color white adheres. Or, in Luther's more personalistic idiom, the crucified and risen Christ genuinely gives his destitute spouse, who clings to him by faith, all that he is and has. By faith's union with him *extra nos* we become new selves, who share in his conquest of sin and death once for all, and he subdues within us the sinful remnants of the old self. Our sin, as Luther has it, becomes "reigned over" by Christ (*peccatum regnatum*), instead of reigning over us as it once did (*peccatum regnans*).[51] In this way

---

47. See, e.g., Thomas Aquinas, *Summa theologiae* I, 43, 5, especially ad 3; 43, 7, ob 2 and ad 1.

48. See John Henry Newman, *Lectures on the Doctrine of Justification*, 8th ed. (London: Longmans, Green, and Co., 1900; first published 1838), 331–33 (the long passage from Luther that Newman cites on p. 332 is in WA 40/I, pp. 282.16–283.14). As these lectures indicate, Newman did not gain his impression of Luther simply from the British evangelicals of the day, but had clearly read Luther's 1535 Galatians commentary with considerable care.

49. Newman, *Lectures on the Doctrine of Justification*, 336.

50. Cf. ibid., 337.

51. See WA 8, p. 96.18–21; cf. p. 94.3–5 (with reference to Rom. 6:12); p. 89.6–8, 34–35.

"sin is different outside of grace than it is in grace"—precisely the grace of baptism, which joins us to Christ.[52] "Outside of grace [the flesh] prevails," but "in grace it can do nothing"; it cannot get the upper hand over Christ, and so it cannot "damn or harm."[53]

It will be evident that Luther thinks of faith primarily as a relation in which human beings stand rather than as an action they undertake or a disposition that belongs to them. In this sense faith is not chiefly a *qualitas* of human beings, to put the point in scholastic terminology; it belongs in a different (Aristotelian) logical category. As a relation faith has the character of ultimate trust or reliance; its subject is the sinful human being and its term is Jesus Christ, who embodies and promises the favor or grace of God toward us. Luther is sometimes explicit about the primarily relational character of faith, though some of his interpreters have probably made rather more of this than his scattered remarks warrant, seeking in Luther's occasional suggestions a full-blown "relational ontology," sometimes depicted as a decisive insight that the rest of the tradition has lacked.[54]

In any case Luther's notion of faith goes some distance toward explaining how he can freely mix forensic and transformative ideas when he talks about justification. As Luther sees it, the two are not opposites; rather each implies and requires the other. Understood as reliance upon God's free and unmerited favor in Christ—upon God's promise to forgive our sins and regard us as righteous on account of Christ outside ourselves—faith "snatches us away from ourselves and places us outside ourselves"; it "takes us out of our own skin."[55] In just this way faith joins us to Christ and makes us new creatures. Through this very faith we come to have a new heart; we are transformed in the depths of ourselves precisely by relying upon that which is outside ourselves, namely the righteousness of Christ that God imputes to us. Luther is explicit about this. He interprets the forensic and apparently extrinsicist language of being "clothed in" or "putting on" Christ and his righteousness precisely in terms of transformation and new creation: "According to the gospel to put on Christ is not a matter of imitation, but of new birth and new creation. . . . This does not happen by a change of clothes, or by any laws or works, but by the rebirth

---

52. WA 8, p. 126.29. On the way baptism changes sin, see, e.g., pp. 91.24–92.11.

53. WA 8, pp. 91.39–40; 102.7.

54. Suggestions like "Paul is one human being, who confesses [in Rom. 7] that he exists in two different relations [*alio et alio respectu*]: under grace he is spiritual, and under the law he is carnal, yet it is the same Paul in both cases" (WA 8, p. 119.14–16); cf. p. 96.3–4: "in this life there is no separating these two relations" (*conspectus*). For a standard attempt to work up remarks like this into a distinctive ontology, see Wilfried Joest, *Ontologie der Person bei Luther* (Göttingen: Vandenhoeck & Ruprecht, 1967), esp. 233–50.

55. WA 40/I, p. 589.25–26; 284.17.

and renewal which takes place in baptism."[56] What makes us new creatures is apparently nothing other than the *iustitia Christi* outside ourselves, the same righteousness that God imputes to us and by which our sins are "covered" (*tecta*) so that God does not reckon them to our account.

By conceiving of faith as the medium of a *unio personalis* with Christ *extra nos*, Luther thinks it possible both to honor the pastoral and doctrinal imperatives that prompt us to think in forensic terms of grace as the favor of God who reckons us righteous in spite of our sin, *and* to uphold the transforming and renewing power of God's same favor and love. Sinners though we are, we may rely entirely upon God's promise of mercy in Christ and have no need to look within ourselves for signs of new life. God's favor makes such introspection unnecessary, not because his favor fails to transform us, but because it makes us new creatures *by* leading us to look away from ourselves to Christ outside ourselves. When we set our hearts on him, all that we need for salvation is ours, including that holiness without which no one will see him in the end.

From the foregoing, Luther appears to follow certain specific rules for thought and speech about justification. By way of summary, we can identify four such rules as at least implicitly present in Luther's account of justification.

1. Forensic and transformatory affirmations must not be regarded as inconsistent or mutually opposed, nor may their consistency be preserved only by excluding transformation from justification, as though talk of transformation changes the subject from justification to something else (for example, sanctification).

2. Forensic and transformatory affirmations must not only be treated as consistent with one another but must both be regarded as necessary in thinking and speaking about justification.

3. Whatever is affirmed to have forensic value in justification must also have transformatory value. That is: if any x that justifies (for example, the *iustitia Christi*) is imputed to us, then x transforms us. There is no converse rule: an x that justifies (examples: the Holy Spirit, the faith that clings to Christ) may transform us even though it would be senseless to say that this x is "imputed" to us.

56. WA 40/I, p. 540.17–18, 26–28. Cf. Schmalkaldische Artikel III [13]: "'By faith,' as St. Peter says (Acts 15:9), we get a different, new, and pure heart, and for the sake of Christ our mediator, God will and does regard us as entirely righteous and holy. . . . The whole human being, with regard both to his person and his works, *shall be called and shall be* righteous and holy, out of pure grace and mercy poured out on us in Christ." *Die Bekenntnisschriften der evangelisch-lutherischen Kirche*, 8th ed. (Göttingen: Vandenhoeck & Ruprecht, 1979), p. 460.8–11, 16–19 (= WA 50, pp. 250.15–22; 251.1–5) (emphasis added).

4. For any disposition or action *x* that is affirmed to justify, whether divine or human (examples: God's imputation of righteousness, our faith in the righteousness of Christ), *x* transforms. As long as "transforms" means "gives us new life in Christ, and thereby an eschatologically perfectible share in the divine nature" (as it must when the issue is justification before God), this rule appears fully convertible: if *x* transforms in this sense, then *x* justifies.[57]

Stating these claims as rules for speech helps to highlight the fact that significant agreement or disagreement about justification does not depend upon how the forensic and transformatory aspects of justification are conceived, but on whether certain basic types of affirmation (those identified by the rules) can be made in common. These rules might therefore be followed by theologies of justification whose content was quite different from Luther's own.

It will be observed that these rules join the forensic and transformatory aspects of justification to each other with increasing stringency. The point of distinguishing between (3) and (4) might not be immediately apparent. Consider, though, the following text, a comment on John 16:10.

> [Christ says,] "This is righteousness: that I go to the Father." . . . But such righteousness is completely concealed and hidden, not only for the world and reason, but also for the saints. For it is not a thought, word, or work in us. . . . Rather it is entirely outside us and above us; it is Christ's going to the Father (that is, his passion and resurrection, or ascension). . . . This is a marvelous righteousness: that we should be called righteous or have a righteousness which really is no work or thought, indeed nothing at all in us, but is entirely outside us in Christ, while nevertheless it truly becomes ours through his grace and gift. So much our own, in fact, that it is as though we had achieved and acquired it ourselves.[58]

Here the righteousness that justifies us is utterly "alien" to us, lodged outside us in the act of another, in "Christ's going to the Father." At the same time, this very act outside us genuinely transforms us and makes us righteous; when Jesus Christ goes to the Father, his own righteousness "truly becomes ours." Rule (4) seems necessary to cover such cases. While requiring that whatever is reckoned to sinners also transforms them, (3) permits the reckoning and the transformation to be two different acts. Prompted by texts like these comments

---

57. If "transforms" simply means "changes in some morally significant respect," then the rule is not convertible; our dispositions and actions can transform us without justifying us before God (for example, moral renewal that takes place without faith in the gospel of Christ).

58. WA 46, p. 44.1, 23–25, 27–28, 34–38 (Das 16. Capitel S. Johannis gepredigt und ausgelegt, 1539).

on John 16, (4) blocks this permission, so that if God reckons us righteous on account of Christ, the divine reckoning itself entitles us to believe that we are new creatures in Christ, however much we continue to struggle with the remnants of sin. Rule (4) thus maximizes the consolation offered by the gospel of Christ.

IV. The Trinitarian Unity of Imputation and Transformation

Of course it is one thing to state a rule, another to follow it. Lutheran theology from its earliest days has looked for ways of integrating the forensic and transformatory aspects of justification. At least in this century, Luther's followers have most often sought the coherence of justification in anthropology—for example, by concentrating, as I have so far done, on how to conceive of faith. But in order to observe the rules we have just found in Luther, one need not share Luther's particular conception of faith; still less need one submit to the speculative claims of this or that school of Lutheran theology (for example, by seeing Luther as the revolutionary proponent of a "relational," as opposed to a "substantialist," view of the human person). On the contrary, the unity of the forensic and transformatory aspects of justification lies chiefly in the doctrine of God: in trinitarian convictions common to all of the historic Christian confessions. Indeed on Luther's view the doctrine of justification by faith cannot even be stated in an adequate way unless the God who does the justifying has been identified as the Trinity. That is: each element in the total divine work of justification belongs chiefly to one of the persons of the Trinity and can be understood properly only if it is grasped in its distinctive connection to the action of that particular divine person.[59]

For Luther the divine person who initiates and sustains the justification of sinners is the Father. Luther is sometimes quite explicit about the Father's distinctive role in the divine act of justification, as when he characterizes the *iustitia* that justifies and saves as that "of Christ and the Holy Spirit which we do not accomplish, but undergo, which we do not have, but receive, when God the Father gives it to us through Jesus Christ."[60] In particular the imputation of righteousness, and likewise the nonimputation or forgiveness of sins, follows this trinitarian pattern. The one who imputes (or not) is the Father;

59. At least since the late nineteenth century, accounts of justification that stem from Luther have often paid little or no attention to the trinitarian shape of God's justifying work, even when they belong to theologies that are energetically trinitarian in other ways. For one exception to this generalization, see Robert W. Jenson, "Justification as a Triune Event," *Modern Theology* 11 (1995): 421–27.

60. WA 40/I, p. 43.15–17.

he takes this action "for the sake of Christ," and brings us to believe that he has taken it by the persuasion of the Spirit. Even when Luther ascribes this role in justification simply to "God" (as he often does, following the linguistic patterns of the New Testament), the imputer is clearly the Father.[61]

The Father forgives our sins and reckons us righteous, passes his saving verdict upon us, not on account of what we have done, but on account of what his only begotten Son has done: taken our flesh and died for our sins. The Father, that is, sends the eternal Son to the cross out of love for sinners, and the Son accepts the cross out of love for the Father and for us. "Christ not only was found among sinners, but by his own decision, together with the Father's will, he wanted to be the friend of sinners, having assumed the flesh and blood of those who are sinners, who are thieves and immersed in every kind of sin."[62] In so doing the Son willingly became, as Paul says, "a curse for us" (Gal. 3:13). For Luther, this transaction between the Father and the Son at the heart of their saving work in time, in which the Father commands and the Son obeys, "is the most joyous of all doctrines and the one most full of consolation. . . . When the merciful Father saw that we were crushed by the law and held under a curse, and could not be liberated from it by anything, he sent his own Son into the world, upon whom he heaped the sins of all, and said to him . . . , 'Plan to pay the debt for them and make satisfaction for them.'"[63]

At the Father's bidding there comes to pass on the cross an "astounding battle" (*mirabile duellum*), in which the Son of God, "a person . . . of un-conquered and eternal righteousness," puts the devil, sin, and death to rout.[64] "Of this astounding battle the church beautifully sings, 'Death and life came to blows in an astounding conflict. The slain lord of life lives and reigns.' Therefore death is conquered and abolished by Christ in the whole world, so that now only a shadow of its former self remains."[65] As in this conflict "all sin is conquered, killed, and buried," so also "Christ . . . has become the death of death, as Hosea sings: 'I will be your death, O death.'"[66]

61. See, inter alia, WA 40/I, pp. 365.29–366.12.

62. WA 40/I, p. 434.16–19.

63. WA 40/I, p. 437.18, 20–23, 26–27.

64. WA 40/I, p. 439.24.

65. WA 40/I, p. 439.31–34. Luther here quotes the Easter Sequence *Victimae paschali laudes*, which originated in the eleventh century and was in widespread use by the twelfth: "Mors et vita duello / conflixere mirando: / dux vitae mortuus, / regnat vivus." Thus the quotation ends with "reigns," and not, as the Weimar editor mistakenly supposes (WA 40/I, p. 439.32), with "conflict."

66. WA 40/I, pp. 439.26; 440.13–14. Christ wins this *duellum* by his own means and in his own way, "without weapons and combat, in his own body and in himself" (p. 440.22–23), but the martial language of strife and victory remains for Luther especially suitable for extolling what happens on the cross (perhaps most famously in his hymn "Ein feste Burg ist unser Gott," 1529). Of course Luther here relies on the common coin of Christian faith in the paschal

But the Son's absolute victory over all the powers of hell is not the only outcome of his cross and resurrection. Luther notices that for Paul, Christ "became a curse for us" (Gal. 3:13) "in order that . . . we might receive the promise of the Spirit through faith" (Gal. 3:14 RSV). By accepting the cross and conquering its curse Christ wins for us the promised Holy Spirit. The Spirit is freedom from the law, sin, death, curse, hell, and the wrath and judgment of God.[67] The Spirit himself justifies, when he comes "on account of Christ," a point Luther generally links to the gospel proclamation of Christ's death and resurrection. "To hear the voice of the bridegroom, to hear the proclamation of faith—this justifies, when the proclamation is heard. Why? Because it brings the Holy Spirit, who justifies."[68]

To the Father, then, ultimately belongs the right to decide both whether to extend salvation to sinful human beings and, if he does, how this salvation will come to pass. In fact the Father has decided to save sinners by sending his Son to the cross in our flesh, by raising him from the dead in the power of the Spirit, and by pouring out that Spirit on all flesh. Equally, it is the Father's prerogative to decide whether his saving will has been adequately carried out by the Son and the Spirit to whom it has been entrusted. This means that the Father's decision about our salvation, his final judgment on the destiny of sinners, takes the form of a verdict on the work of his Son and thereby also on the work of his Spirit (since it is the Father's saving will that the Son win the outpouring of the Spirit for the world). The resurrection and exaltation of Jesus leave no doubt as to the Father's verdict on the work of his Son in our flesh and, above all, on the cross: he has done all things well. There is no sin of which the Father will say to the Son: for *this* one your death is not enough. At the Father's command the Son has borne and conquered our human sin and death in their totality: by his obedience unto death "all sins have been expiated and purged from the world. Therefore the world has been freed from death and from all evils."[69] For this reason the Father's attitude toward us is wholly determined by and included in his attitude toward his crucified Son. The Father will never tell the Son that what he has done for the salvation of sinners is not enough, that there is any sin or evil that his death fails to "purge and expiate" from the world.

---

mystery. Besides *Victimae paschali laudes*, upon which he depends directly, see, e.g., the second antiphon of the Divine Liturgy of St. John Chrysostom: "O Christ our God, trampling down death by death."

67. WA 40/I, p. 455.32–34. Christ does not, to be sure, acquire the Spirit for us only by his cross. Luther stresses, for example, the role of Christ's prayer; cf. WA 45, pp. 563.32–564.1 (Das 14. und 15. Kapitel S. Johannis gepredigt und ausgelegt, 1538).

68. WA 40/I, p. 336.30–31; cf. p. 401.16–18.

69. WA 40/I, p. 438.14–15.

Luther clearly maintains that the *simul iustus et peccator* needs to be understood in this trinitarian context. He puts one of his sharpest statements of the *simul* in the form of a rhetorical question about the trinitarian Father: "How can these two contradictory claims be true at the same time: I have sin and am most worthy of divine wrath and hate, and the Father loves me? Here nothing can intervene but Christ the mediator."[70] Christ "intervenes," Luther goes on to say in this passage, by being the one who fixes the Father's attitude toward us. "The Father, [Christ] says, does not love you because you are worthy of love, but because you love me and you believe that I have come from the Father."[71] The Father loves us, that is, precisely by loving his crucified Son, who obediently accepted the cross in order that he might deliver the lost and undeserving from sin, death, and hell. The believer "turns to Christ and through Christ strengthens himself against the feeling of divine wrath and judgment, and believes that he is loved by the Father—not for his own sake, but for the sake of Christ the beloved."[72]

Because the Father's attitude toward the Son fixes his attitude toward us, the Father never sees and knows us except in connection with his Son and what his Son has accomplished and therefore as those whose sin and death are vanquished. That even the justified continue to sin, that our faith is feeble and tenuous, changes this not at all. The Father's attitude toward us remains determined by what his Son has done for us rather than by what we have done for ourselves. In just this sense the Father "imputes" the righteousness of Christ to us, "covers" our remaining sins with Christ's sinless perfection: not because the Father fails to recognize the reality of our sin, but because he recognizes that his Son has now and forever "purged and expiated" it, destined it to pass away. "Because sin and death are taken away by that one man, God no longer sees anything else in the whole world, especially if it believes, than complete cleansing and righteousness. And if any remnants of sin remain nonetheless God does not notice them, on account of Christ, the shining Sun."[73] Any self-deception here lies not with the Father, who sees us as we are in his Son and therefore in truth, but with us, who continue to think and act as though we were other than what God's Son become our flesh has made of us—who in our meager faith decline to take ourselves at the estimate the Father of Jesus Christ places upon us. "The victory of Christ is entirely certain. There is no defect in the reality, since it is entirely true, but in our unbelief. For reason finds it difficult to believe in these inestimable goods."[74]

70. Cf. n. 42 above.
71. WA 40/I, p. 372.17–18.
72. WA 40/I, p. 372.22–23.
73. WA 40/I, p. 438.15–18.
74. WA 40/I, p. 444.22–24. Cf. WA 41, p. 556.2–7 (Hs.) (Predigt . . . bei der Hochzeit Caspar Crucigers in Eilenburg, 1536).

This perhaps makes it easier to see the sense in which the righteousness that saves us is "outside" us and "alien" to us. Our salvation depends entirely upon the Father's judgment that the Son has fulfilled all righteousness, and thus upon a divine verdict wholly ordered to the deeds of another from whom we will always be distinct (none of us, after all, has been or will be born of the virgin Mary, or crucified under Pontius Pilate). The destiny of the eternal Son in our flesh entitles us to confidence, indeed certainty, about our salvation precisely because he alone, and not any feature of our own person or history, is the adequate basis of the Father's decision to save us; his incarnation, cross, and resurrection display with complete clarity and finality the Father's attitude toward us.

But the Father's verdict does not simply determine that the Son's work is enough to save us, come what may. The same verdict determines that the Son's saving work, accomplished at the Father's bidding, transforms the world. Christ comes in order that through his destruction of sin and death "all creation might be changed."[75] This transformation of the world takes hold in us by the Spirit's gift of faith, which unites us with Christ *quasi una persona* and so begins to deify us. The Son's conquest of sin and death reaches its completion, the perfection that the Father's omnipotent verdict guarantees, when each believer "becomes a perfect and indeed a divine creature."[76]

We may be tempted to see here not, as I have just suggested, a single divine verdict, but rather two different acts and attitudes of the Father pertaining to salvation. On the one hand there appears to be a judgment after the fact, as it were, on the work Christ and the Spirit have accomplished in us, a discernment by the Father of the change that has actually taken place in us. On the other hand there seems to be a judgment in spite of the fact that we are not changed, a verdict based not on discernment of what has actually happened but on forbearance in the face of what has not happened. Distributing transformation and forgiveness into two different judgments by the Father threatens, however, to reintroduce in trinitarian terms the fruitless conflict between renewal and imputation. Justification has to involve both, but treating each as the content of a separate divine verdict encourages the thought that the knowledge of the two must also come separately, so that, for example, we know that the Father renews us by looking at ourselves and know that he forgives us by looking at Christ. This naturally leaves us wondering how to be sure that both verdicts apply to us—that we in fact have salvation.

Because the Father never sees us or passes judgment on us except in his Son, there is no need to take new life and forgiveness as belonging to two different

75. WA 40/I, p. 440.29–30.
76. WA 41, p. 587.31–32 (cf. n. 6 above).

verdicts. The Father's decision to forgive us and his decision to deify us can be seen as one and the same act and as belonging to one and the same attitude: the Father's love for his Son. The content of the act that forgives and of the act that transforms is determined in the same way, by the Father's attitude toward the Son, who, above all on the cross, does all things well for us.

As Luther is aware, the use of temporal categories in describing justification, necessary though it is, can mislead us. It seems natural to speak of transformation as involving the Father's recognition of what has already taken place, while imputation involves his favor despite what has not yet taken place. From God's point of view, however, these distinctions apparently reduce to the Father's unalterable perception of us in his Son.[77] From "before the foundation of the world" (Eph. 1:4) the Father sees us for what he has made us to be in the end: his deified creation, those who by the death and resurrection of his Son and the outpouring of his Spirit share his life as fully as creatures are able. It makes no difference in the Father's estimate of us whether we are in the process of being transformed, have been transformed fully, or still await even the beginnings of transformation; his attitude toward us is equally, and fully, determined by his attitude toward his Son in any case. The Father does not see us in his Son and so love us only when we have been united to the Son by faith and baptism and thus have the beginnings of deification. He sees us in just the same way not only before we have begun to be deified but before we have begun to be at all—from "before the foundation of the world."

As the Father sees us only in his Son and loves us even when we have yet to exist at all—despite the absolute disparity there between what he sees and what presently is—so, a fortiori, he continues to see us only in his Son and love us when we have fallen into sin. From and to all eternity, the Father sees us—reckons us—as righteous on account of Christ. This loving regard of the Father on account of his Son transforms and deifies us, since the incarnation of the Son and the sending of the Spirit to make us partakers of the divine nature are simply the enactment of the Father's eternal vision of us. But this is to say that the Father's declaration of forgiveness for Christ's sake transforms us. The forgiveness of sins and the imputation of righteousness are, one can say, simply the Father's faithful persistence about seeing us only in his Son,

---

77. Though prompted by a different problem, the following remark is pertinent: "It ought to be said that the Son is always born, not that he is born in the present, nor that he is always to be born in the future. Grammar has to do with the future and the present. But these speculations have no place when it comes to divine things. Christ cannot be said to be born in the past, the future, or the present. . . . Therefore whether you take it [grammatically] as future, present, or past, it is always true: he always is born, was born, and will be born. . . . For here there is no time" (WA 39/II, p. 293.18–24, 26 [Die Promotionsdisputation von Georg Major und Johannes Faber, 1544]).

even when what we are fails to conform to what he sees there. It is just this persistence that guarantees our transformation.

Luther, to be sure, insists that the Father presently sees us in the Son only when we have faith. In faith the believer's attitude toward Christ coincides, however weakly and inadequately, with the Father's own. Faith, as Luther likes to say, "justifies because it gives God his due; the person who does this is righteous."[78] As Luther sees it, unbelief is a deliberate refusal to accept God's verdict on us in Christ, such that "where Christ and faith are truly absent, there is no remission of sins, no hiding of them, but pure imputation and condemnation of sins."[79] Since faith is the Spirit's gift, entirely dependent upon the Spirit's presence and action, remarks of this kind might seem to separate once again the Father's saving will toward us from his verdict on the work of his Son: for salvation we need the Father to see us in Christ, and he sees us in Christ only when he gives us faith by the Spirit. Here too, though, the Father's verdict on the cross of his Son works for us rather than against us. As the Father sees it, the Son does all things well, including—or rather, chiefly—gaining for us the Spirit who unites us to him *quasi una persona* and so makes us sharers in the divine nature. Here too the Father will never say that the Son has not done enough; on account of Christ we can be sure that the Father supplies all things needful for salvation, most of all the Spirit himself.

So one might develop on the basis of Luther's theology a trinitarian account of his insistence that the same divine attitude and act that declares us righteous *propter Christum* also transforms us into new creatures—his insistence, in other words, on the four rules for thinking about salvation that we have proposed.

To conclude. Even the boldest forensic claims about justification need not compete with equally bold transformationist claims. As Luther's theology shows, we have at least two ways to display the logical coherence of imputation and transformation. A distinctive concept of union with Christ *extra nos* by faith can join the two. Attention to the Father's eternal verdict on the work of his incarnate Son joins them in a different way. If the first strategy for dealing with the problem relies on ideas that are to some extent distinctively Lutheran, the second does not. It turns on trinitarian convictions shared by Christians who have traditionally conceived of justification in quite different ways. This suggests that any Christian theology that takes the justification of the sinner to be the work of the triune God should be able to verify that in this saving work, declaration and deification cohere.

78. WA 40/I, p. 361.12–13.
79. WA 40/I, p. 234.15–17.

Postscript (2014)

Rarely is anything to be gained by trying to improve upon what one said when stirred by motives, once powerful, that no longer guide one's life and work. This essay was originally published in 2002, and much of it was written several years earlier than that, for the international Lutheran-Orthodox dialogue. I have lightly updated the notes and made a few other changes, but this is essentially the essay I wrote more than ten years ago.

At the time I wrote as a Lutheran, one greatly concerned to make a case for the catholic character of Luther's theology of justification. Substantively, this meant more than showing that Luther's mature theology of justification is not purely forensic (a common enough claim). I needed to show that Luther's sometimes astonishingly strong teaching on transformation and holiness fully coheres with, and is indeed implied by, the sharply forensic statements for which he is best known, rather than being adventitious or even contradictory to those statements.

Thus the argument of this essay. It was of a piece with the efforts of a number of others, some of whom it cites for support, to offer a catholic—or, as we regularly put it, an "evangelical catholic"—interpretation of Lutheranism, over against the more common view that Lutheranism is irreconcilably opposed to essential features of Roman Catholicism and, *mutatis mutandis*, of Eastern Orthodoxy. It was also the work of a Christian who wanted to be Catholic, more deeply, no doubt, than I myself was aware of at the time. Three years after this essay was published, I was received into the Catholic Church. With that, the urgency about finding a catholic reading of Luther began to fade, though this, I can clearly say, was a result rather than a cause of my conversion to Catholicism. I have in fact returned to the subject of "imputation" in the theology of justification as a Catholic, but my interlocutor was Thomas Aquinas, not Luther, and the results not only were more satisfying substantively but also rested rather more comfortably on the texts I was trying to interpret than is the case here.[80]

Were I to write this essay today, I would be more candid—or more relaxed—about Luther's apparent determination to keep the sinner's transformation out of justification. That is, of course, the subject of sections III and IV of this essay, and I remain convinced that arguments of the sort developed there

---

80. See "*Beatus vir*: Thomas d'Aquin, Romains 4, et le rôle de l'imputation dans la justification," *RThom* 111, no. 1 (2011): 3–34; a shorter English version, "*Beatus vir*: Aquinas, Romans 4, and the Role of 'Reckoning' in Justification," in *Reading Romans with St. Thomas Aquinas: Ecumenical Explorations*, ed. Michael Dauphinais and Matthew Levering (Washington, DC: Catholic University of America Press, 2012), 216–36.

are the best way to pursue a coherent account of Luther's thinking about this vexed matter. The starkly forensic elements in Luther's theology of justification serve important pastoral and doctrinal purposes, but they can and should be integrated with the transformationist elements in his theology. This approach is, in particular, far more convincing than the more usual interpretation of Luther, which more or less ignores, or dismisses, the many texts in which he asserts that justification itself is profoundly transformative. Still, the textual resistance in Luther to the interpretation I give here is, I now see, even stronger and more pervasive than this essay suggests.

To take one example, from the beginning of the Reformation 1 Corinthians 13:2 was used, understandably, against Luther's theology of justification: "if I have all faith . . . but have not love, I am nothing" (RSV). In his Galatians commentary of 1535, frequently cited here, Luther emphatically dismisses the relevance of this text to the theology of justification, concluding that "faith justifies without love and before love"—that is, without the charity of which 1 Corinthians 13 speaks.[81] Here Luther evidently goes out of his way, in the face of potent scriptural evidence, to insist that the sinner's transformation is no part of justification. In fact he appears to play off "the heart's possession of Christ the Savior himself" by faith against the transforming charity of 1 Corinthians 13. Faith's possession of Christ, deliberately contrasted with the charity that forms faith, is "the power that justifies" (*vis iustificandi*).[82] How a text like this squares with Luther's description of faith in vividly nuptial terms, where the believer embraces Christ in love as a bride embraces her bridegroom, is a bit difficult to say.[83]

To be sure, one could argue that Luther is here objecting to certain late medieval views of infused charity (as he understood them) and not to the Bible's deeper insistence on the unity of faith and love. This only serves to underline, though, a seemingly intractable problem facing any attempt, "catholic" or otherwise, to interpret Luther on imputation, holiness, and justification. You can read Luther the way I do here—if you want to be a Catholic, you certainly will—and I think this is the most persuasive way, on the whole, to make Luther's texts on justification hang together. But Luther can also be read in a different and much less Catholic fashion. There are a lot of pages in the

---

81. "Haec fides sine et ante charitatem iustificat" (WA 40/I, pp. 239.26–27, 240.16).

82. "Sola fide, non fide formata charitate, nos iustificari. Quare non isti formae gratificanti tribuenda est vis iustificandi, sed fidei quae apprehendit et possidet in corde ipsum Christum Salvatorem" (WA 40/I, pp. 239.31–240.16).

83. See above, pp. 120–21. Michael Waldstein helpfully lays out the difficulty in interpreting Luther on this point. See his "The Trinitarian, Spousal, and Ecclesial Logic of Justification," in Dauphinais and Levering, *Reading Romans with St. Thomas Aquinas*, 274–87.

Weimar Ausgabe, and those whose main motives in interpreting Luther on justification are other than Catholic will always be able to find another text that speaks for their reading rather than a Catholic one, requiring another counterargument from the other side. It may be possible to resolve the conflict between "Catholic" and "Protestant" readings of Luther by meticulous textual interpretation, but after centuries of effort on all sides this seems more like an eschatological hope than a sober estimate of what theological exertion can actually achieve.

PART 3

THE
TRINITY
AND ECCLESIAL
BEING

9

PERSONHOOD, COMMUNION, AND THE TRINITY IN SOME PATRISTIC TEXTS

KHALED ANATOLIOS

The conception of the Divine Trinity as a communion of persons is a privileged motif in modern Eastern Christian theology. This characterization typically presents the interpersonal communion of the Holy Trinity as an exemplar for the communion of the church and, more universally, as the "structure of supreme love," to use the words of the great Romanian Orthodox theologian, Dumitru Stăniloae.[1] While Eastern theologians often freely employ motifs from modern personalist philosophy, they follow the standard Eastern strategy of rooting their theological speculation in the tradition of the fathers. A model of this approach is the popular and highly influential work of the Greek Orthodox theologian, now Metropolitan of Pergamon, John Zizioulas. Zizioulas borrows motifs from modern personalist philosophy, such as the priority of personal freedom over nature, but it is to patristic theology that he defers as the normative guide for a genuine theology of the

1. See Dumitru Stăniloae, "The Holy Trinity: Structure of Supreme Love," in *The Experience of God*, trans. and ed. Ioan Ioniță (Brookline, MA: Holy Cross Orthodox Press, 1994), 245–80.

Trinity. Zizioulas characterizes this theology, particularly in the doctrine of the Cappadocian fathers, as indicating a vision of "being as communion": all being, beginning with the absolutely archetypal being of God himself, has its source in personal freedom that enacts itself as communion of love.[2] In the divine Trinity, the Father is that personal source who enacts his loving freedom in eternally generating the Son and causing the Spirit to proceed. Zizioulas's work not only contributed considerable momentum to the modern personalist stream of Eastern trinitarian thought but also struck a powerful chord that resonated in much of Western theology.[3]

At the same time, Zizioulas's work also typifies the vulnerabilities of the claims of modern Eastern theology to derive a personalist reading of trinitarian theology more or less directly from the patristic tradition. Bishop Zizioulas sought a foundation for his personalist trinitarian theology in what he considered to be "the Cappadocian revolution" of Greek ontology. According to Zizioulas's reading, this revolution was unleashed when the Cappadocians, especially St. Basil of Caesarea, identified the category of *hypostasis* with *prosōpon*. Up until that time, so goes Zizioulas's account, *hypostasis* signified an existent being, while *prosōpon* carried relational connotations associated with its use in Greek drama to denote a "mask," or dramatic "role," the face that a being presents to others. By advocating for the understanding of *hypostasis* as *prosōpon* and asserting the co-incidence of these two categories, the Cappadocians were affirming that each of the divine subsistents is to be identified with his relational role within the divine communion.[4] More generally, for Zizioulas, this understanding of divine persons could be legitimately broadened to indicate a vision of being as radically relational: "*to be* and *to be in relation* becomes identical."[5] Despite the initial enthusiasm that Zizioulas's work generated and that still endures in many quarters, his speculative edifice suffered considerable structural damage with the publication of the French patristic scholar André de Halleux's critical response in his article "Personnalisme ou Essentialisme Trinitaire chez les Pères Cappadociens?"[6] There, de Halleux countered the characterization

2. John Zizioulas, *Being as Communion: Studies in Personhood and the Church* (Crestwood, NY: St. Vladimir's Seminary Press, 1985).

3. Catherine LaCugna's *God for Us: The Trinity and Christian Life* (San Francisco: Harper-SanFrancisco, 1991), which has been highly influential in some strands of modern Western trinitarian theology, is strongly influenced by Zizioulas (see esp. 260–66). However, her conflation of God's being with God's relation to the world is not to be attributed to Zizioulas.

4. Zizioulas, *Being as Communion*, 33–41.

5. Ibid., 88.

6. André de Halleux, "Personnalisme ou Essentialisme Trinitaire chez les Pères Cappadociens?" *RTL* 17 (1986): 129–55, 265–92.

of Cappadocian trinitarian theology as "personalist" rather than essentialist and as placing primary emphasis on the personal monarchy of the Father rather than on the shared divine nature. In another article, de Halleux pointed out, quite rightly, that in fact Basil was suspicious of the application of the category of *prosōpon* to the divine *hypostaseis*, considering the former term as masking over a reluctance to affirm the ontological subsistence of each of the Three.[7] It was not so much that Basil affirmed the co-incidence of the ontological category of *hypostasis* and the relational notion of *prosōpon* but that he insisted that *hypostasis* was the more helpful term and that *prosōpon* was vulnerable to modalist understandings, as if the distinctions between the divine persons were merely the effect of different roles undertaken by one and the same entity.[8]

The interchange between Zizioulas and de Halleux is typical of a discernible pattern in modern discussions of the Trinity. Eastern theologians, at least Eastern systematic theologians, are generally favorably disposed to a personalist vision of the Trinity that endorses the application of the categories of person and communion to the divine Trinity and that presumes continuity between the signification of these concepts in patristic trinitarian doctrine and in modern accounts of personhood, freedom, and relationality. Such a personalist vision of the Trinity tends to be well received by mainstream currents in Western theology and to strike a responsive chord among modern Christians generally. Thereupon, patristic scholars arrive on the scene and spoil the party, pointing out the invalidity of personalist trinitarian arguments that claim patristic endorsement and suggesting that the last call for talk of trinitarian personhood and communion has already come and gone. In a recent review of Lucian Turcescu's book on the concept of divine persons in Gregory of Nyssa, Michel Barnes provocatively stipulates: "If the word [person] disappeared entirely from English and other modern languages our reading of patristic trinitarian writings would be greatly improved."[9]

7. "'Hypostase' et 'Personne' dans la formation du dogme trinitaire (*ca* 375–381)," *RHE* 79 (1984): 313–69, 625–70, esp. 318–30.

8. Cf. Basil, *Ep.* 210, 214.

9. Michel Barnes, review of *Gregory of Nyssa and the Concept of Divine Persons*, by Lucian Turcescu, *Modern Theology* 23 (2007): 642. Insofar as Barnes's statement is suspicious of the imposition of later connotations attached to this term on patristic texts, it has an undeniable wisdom. But it also evokes the important question of whether there are any elements of continuity between patristic trinitarian theology and modern notions of personhood. It should be noted that Barnes's concern with the hermeneutical contamination of patristic trinitarian texts by modern notions of personhood is not an exclusively Western phenomenon. See, for example, the cautions of the Orthodox theologian John Behr on reading notions of "personhood" or "personal communion" into Gregory of Nyssa's *Epistle to Peter (Ep. 38)*, in Behr's *The Nicene Faith* (Crestwood, NY: St. Vladimir's Seminary Press, 2004), 2:420–27.

For my own part, I would like to suggest in this essay that the lessons to be derived from recent unsuccessful attempts to anchor a personalist trinitarian theology in the patristic tradition are not quite so drastic. There needs to be a middle way between simply presuming continuity between patristic and modern understandings of "person" and "communion" and presupposing absolute discontinuity.[10] Moreover, in negotiating this middle path, I suggest that we should observe at least three basic rules. First, we need to guard against a methodological flaw that afflicts historical scholarship on the Trinity in general, and that is the tendency to reduce the focus of inquiry to a word study of the very narrow repertoire of conciliar trinitarian vocabulary, such as *hypostasis*, *ousia*, *prosōpon*, and *koinōnia*. What is needed instead is a more comprehensive analysis of the complex reception of the biblical narrative as a whole by the patristic tradition.

Second, it is high time to impose a moratorium on the rather glib proposition that patristic notions of personhood cannot be retrieved simply because modern post-Enlightenment notions of personhood are quite different. That patristic characterizations of the hypostases of the Trinity are indeed quite different from modern notions of human personhood is a truism. That the differences are such that there are absolutely no lines of continuity between the two sets of meanings has by no means been sufficiently demonstrated or, to my estimation, even closely argued. Thus, both Barth and Rahner point out that an essential difference between modern and patristic notions of "person" is that the former includes the notion of self-consciousness, but neither in fact has a closely argued theology of divine consciousness that encompasses both trinitarian unity and distinction.[11]

Third, in this case as with all theological language, the dialectics of analogical predication must govern our understanding and discussion. Whenever the same language is applied to God and creation, its signification is realized only through a dialectic of likeness and difference. Difference does not negate likeness, and likeness does not cancel out difference. So we can simply take it as a foregone conclusion that if we understand trinitarian persons and trinitarian communion as simply equivalent to the human realities of these predications, we will end up with tritheism. But the question is not whether the relations

10. The origin of the blanket assertion of such a discontinuity is not attributable so much to patristic scholarship as it is to the influence of Barth and Rahner, both of whom advised against continuing the language of "person" to apply to Father, Son, and Spirit. See Karl Barth, *Church Dogmatics*, vol. I.1, *The Doctrine of the Word of God*, trans. G. W. Bromiley (New York: T&T Clark, 2004), 353–60; Karl Rahner, *The Trinity*, trans. Joseph Donceel (New York: Crossroad, 2004), 42–45.

11. See Barth, *Church Dogmatics* I/1, 355–60; Rahner, *The Trinity*, 43.

and distinctions and self-subsistence of the trinitarian hypostases are equivalent to the human counterparts of these realities, but rather whether there is a continuity within difference that is revelatory of who God is and how God is related to the world and how we are meant to be related to each other in God. In this case, the analogy happens to be recommended by, among other things, the dominical prayer in the Gospel of the evangelist John, "that they may be one, even as we are one" (John 17:11 RSV).

I propose that there are at least three ways in which we can find analogical continuities between the biblical narrative, patristic trinitarian reflection, and modern conceptions of personhood and communion:

1. Father, Son, and Spirit are *persons* inasmuch as the scriptural narrative presents them in conversation with one another that cannot be reduced to a mere monologue without destroying the intelligibility of that narrative;

2. Father, Son, and Spirit are *persons* inasmuch as the biblical narrative presents each of them as a distinct agent, a possessor of active intentionality, even though together they constitute a single unified agency in relation to creation;

3. Father, Son, and Holy Spirit are *persons in communion* not only in the minimally ontological sense that they all equally share in the divine nature but also inasmuch as the biblical narrative indicates that the mutual relations by which they equally share in the divine substance may be appropriately characterized according to the interpersonal categories of delight and mutual glorification.

I will now take up each of these theses in turn.

1. Father, Son, and Spirit as Speaking Persons

The Roman Catholic philosopher and practitioner of phenomenology, Robert Sokolowski, defines a person as "a responsible speaker."[12] This is to say that a person is the kind of being who can say "I" in a declarative manner. The utterance of this "I" declares the speaker as "a rational agent" who is "actually exercising his rationality at the moment he uses the word. This use of the term *I* reveals the person of the speaker in its actual exercise, in its being-at-work as a person."[13] Sokolowski's definition of person has the merit of appealing

---

12. Robert Sokolowski, "The Revelation of the Holy Trinity: A Study in Personal Pronouns," in *Christian Faith and Human Understanding: Studies on the Eucharist, Trinity, and the Human Person* (Washington, DC: Catholic University of America Press, 2006), 133.
13. Ibid., 136.

to our common spontaneous understanding of what a person is. A person is a being who can declare his or her rationality by acting as an agent of intelligible utterance, by saying "I." In short, a person is a being who can speak and be spoken to. Using this understanding of person, Sokolowski proceeds to analyze the biblical disclosure of the trinitarian being of God through Jesus's speaking to the Father, a dialogue that reveals both Father and Son as persons. Sokolowski observes that the Spirit is not typically presented in the New Testament as one who speaks and is spoken to. Rather, the distinctive character of the Spirit's personhood, as the bond of unity between Father and Son, resides in his facilitating the dialogical exchange between Father and Son and in drawing humanity into that exchange.[14]

Sokolowski's project of tracing the scriptural disclosure of the trinitarian persons through their dialogical interchange can be much enhanced by recalling Tertullian's response to modalism in the third century. The latter theological position, associated with a certain Praxeas about whom we know very little directly, apparently proposed that the Son was a mere mode of appearance of the Father. Father and Son were radically and ultimately the very same reality without real distinction. Histories of doctrine typically focus on Tertullian's efforts to create two sets of vocabulary in order to express the co-incidence of unity and diversity in trinitarian being: Father, Son, and Spirit are one in "substance," "condition," and "power" (*substantia*, *status*, *potestas*) while three in "degree," "form," and "aspect" (*gradus*, *forma*, *species*).[15] But heeding our own warning about reducing trinitarian theology to a word study within a narrow range of terms for unity and diversity, we need to look further at Tertullian's objections to the doctrine of Praxeas. For our purposes, his most pertinent objection is that Praxeas's teaching nullifies the dramatic space in which Father and Son can interact as distinct speaking persons. The effect of nullifying this dramatic conversational space is that the biblical narrative is collapsed into a cryptic and altogether unintelligible monologue. Recalling Sokolowski's definition of the person as the being who can say "I" helps us to appreciate the aptness of Tertullian's demonstration of how his opponent's doctrine distorts the biblical narrative. In what may appear to be merely a rhetorical polemical ploy but is actually a profound theological argument whose logic is essentially continuous with Sokolowski's, Tertullian chooses the most dramatic instances in Scripture where the Son's "I" is posited in dialogical relation to the Father and collapses these dialogical situations into the "I" of the Father

14. Ibid., 144–46.
15. Tertullian, *Against Praxeas* 2.

in order to reveal the absurd consequences of applying Praxeas's teaching to the biblical narrative.

Thus, the verse of the psalm that in the New Testament is applied to Christ, "You are my Son, today I have begotten you" (Ps. 2:7 NRSV; cf. Heb. 5:5), becomes "The Lord said to himself, I am my son, today I have begotten myself."[16] The Johannine introduction to the foot washing, where Jesus is presented as "knowing that the Father had given all things into his hands, and that he had come from God and was going to God" (John 13:3 NRSV), filtered through a Praxean doctrine, would have to finally equate to: "The Father himself came forth from himself and went away to himself."[17] To cite one final example, Tertullian refers to the mutual glorification of Father and Son manifested in Jesus's prayer, "Father, glorify your name," and the Father's response, "I have glorified it, and I will glorify it again" (John 12:28 NRSV). Tertullian comments:

> The Son makes request from earth, the Father makes a promise from heaven. Why do you make both Father and Son a liar? If it is the case that either the Father was speaking to the Son from heaven while being himself the Son on earth, or that the Son was praying to the Father while being himself the Father in heaven, how is it that the Son is actually making a request to himself when he is making a request to the Father or again that the Father, by making a promise to the Son, would actually be making a promise to himself if he were himself the Father?[18]

Tertullian sums up the positive point of the personal distinctions of Father and Son in language that could be seamlessly inserted into Sokolowski's thesis: "All the Scriptures display both the demonstration and the distinctness of the Trinity and from them is derived also our standing rule, that the speaker and the one of whom he speaks and the one spoken to cannot all be regarded as one and the same."[19]

The overlapping arguments of Tertullian in the third century and Sokolowski in the twentieth should help us recognize a fairly simple point that is in danger of being obfuscated in the contemporary backlash against trinitarian personalism. This point is that despite the undeniable differences between modern psychological conceptions of personhood and ancient Christian conceptions of the distinct being of each of the Trinity, there is a basic common denominator in the characterization of each of the Trinity as a distinct agent

---

16. Ibid., 11.

17. Ibid., 23; ET: Ernest T. Evans, *Tertulliani Adversus Praxean Liber: Tertullian's "Against Praxeas"* (London: SPCK, 1948), 166.

18. Ibid.

19. Ibid., 11; ET: Evans, 100.

in acts of speech that animate the biblical narrative. As Tertullian amply demonstrates, we have to do nothing less than jettison the intelligibility of the biblical narrative if we are not willing to accept that Father, Son, and Spirit are such agents. If we are going to let the trinitarian economy lead us into God's very being, we have to conceive of the trinitarian persons as agents of speech and conceive of trinitarian communion as a *conversation* between Father and Son through the Holy Spirit.

2. Father, Son, and Spirit as Willing and Acting Agents

The biblical narrative presents Father, Son, and Spirit not only as agents of speech but also as agents of willing and acting. Indeed, the distinction between speaking and doing is not finally pertinent in the case of the scriptural identification of the God of Israel, who acts through his word. Characterizing Father, Son, and Spirit as willing and acting agents represents another strand of continuity between biblical and patristic characterizations of the trinitarian persons, on the one hand, and modern conceptions of personhood, on the other. The central content of this continuity is the affirmation that Father, Son, and Spirit each distinctly have a personal will. Now, such a statement may immediately raise the alarm of tritheism for some; for Rahner, it is tritheism to think of the divine persons as "centers of activity."[20] Many perhaps would consider it a settled dogmatic point that there is only one will in the Trinity, inasmuch as will pertains to essence, and there is only one essence. But that statement is only a half-truth and presupposes a dogmatic fallacy. This fallacy is the understanding of the difference between *language* of unity and *language* of distinction as delineating different *areas of the divine being*. But, in fact, the co-incidence of unity and distinction in the Trinity is such that there is nothing of the divine *being* that is singular without also and at the same time being diversified and there is nothing that is diversified without also and at the same time being unified. This principle pertains first and foremost to the correspondence between the divine essence and the three divine persons. There is only one essence, of course, but this one essence is not a separate *thing* from the three distinct persons. Rather, as Orthodox theologians tirelessly insist, the one essence exists only as tripersonal. It strictly follows, therefore, precisely on the premise of the co-incidence of will and essence, that the one will also exists only as tripersonal. Just as the essence is distributed distinctly among the persons, so is the divine will appropriated distinctly by Father, Son, and

20. *The Trinity*, 43.

Spirit such that each of them enjoys a personal will within the unity of divine being and action.

Once again, what is at stake, immediately and ultimately, is the plain and obvious sense of the biblical narrative. To restrict ourselves for the moment to the New Testament, it is clear that the Father, the incarnate Son, and the Spirit are each presented as intentional agents; each acts toward the others and toward and upon the world. None is simply the action or effect of the agency of the other, but each is an agent in his own right. The Father speaks to the Son and sends the Son and raises Jesus from the dead; the Son speaks to the Father and hands over his life to the Father and sends the Spirit; the Spirit descends on the Son and leads Jesus into the wilderness and blows where he wills.

In the patristic tradition, the insistence on the distinct hypostases of Father, Son, and Spirit as self-standing and active agents comes into prominence especially with Origen in the third century. Origen's caution about misunderstanding the title of "Wisdom" is typical of this emphasis: "Let no one think, however, that when we give him the name 'wisdom of God' we mean anything without hypostatic existence, that is, to take an illustration, that we understand him not to be as it were some living subsistent but a certain thing which makes people wise."[21] The contrast that Origen seeks to draw is between understanding Wisdom as merely an impersonal power or a power exercised by the agency of another and identifying this Wisdom as a power rooted in a self-standing being, who is thus an intentional agent. In his treatment of both Son and Spirit, Origen focuses on the activity, the *energeia*, of each and even seems to suggest that each has a distinct sphere of operation.[22] Yet that does not mean that each acts autonomously. Each acts in concert with the other so as to compose one harmonious movement: "And when wisdom is called the unspotted mirror of the Father's power and working, she would have us understand her nature to be like the image reflected in a mirror, which moves and acts in correspondence with the movements and actions of the one looking into the mirror, not deviating from them in any way whatsoever."[23]

Origen's emphasis on the tri-hypostatic coactivity of Father, Son, and Spirit achieves much more precise and coherent expression in certain formulations of Cappadocian theology, where we find a double insistence on both the personal agency of each of the divine hypostases and the unity of activity among them. This double insistence is modeled in Basil's *On the Holy Spirit*, written in the mid-370s. A central argument in this classic work is that the Spirit is an agent in

21. Origen, *On First Principles* 1.2.1; ET: G. W. Butterworth, *Origen: On First Principles* (Gloucester, MA: Peter Smith, 1973), 14.
22. Cf. Origen, *On First Principles* 1.3.5–7.
23. Ibid., 1.2.12; ET: Butterworth, 26.

the divine work of creation and salvation, even unto deification, and therefore must be honored with divine titles equivalently to the Father and the Son.[24] But Basil describes the trinitarian unity of operations as not an undifferentiated unity but a unity that is structured by and composed of the tripersonal distinctions. The bishop of Caesarea typically presents the common work of the Trinity in ways that highlight the distinct appropriation of that unified agency by the hypostases, each of whom remains a distinct agent within the common agency of the Trinity. For example, in the act of creation, "the source of being is one, which makes through the Son, and which perfects through the Spirit," and the angelic beings "exist by the will of the Father, . . . are brought into being by the energy of the Son, and they are perfected by the presence of the Spirit."[25] The basic linguistic structure of such statements consists of three distinct verbs, each delineating a single action. The immediate caveat to this pattern of distributing the common agency of the Trinity according to the personal distinctions is that this distribution cannot be understood as indicating that any of the three performs an action that is not performed by the other. In Basil's own words, none of them *completes* the separate work of the other that would otherwise be incomplete.[26] Rather, just as each of the persons possesses the common essence according to a particular modality, so each of the persons enacts the common action of the three according to his personal modality.

For Rahner, part of the problem of speaking of trinitarian "persons" is that it carries the danger of conceiving of the divine persons as distinct "centers of activity."[27] Rahner gives no precise definition of what exactly he means by "centers of activity." Basil, on the other hand, is clear that the unity of activity among the persons does not at all preclude that each is in himself an intentional agent. Indeed, it is precisely the fact that each of the persons is an intentional agent that is the basis for the unity of operation among the three. Basil's integration of unity of operations and distinct personal agency is on display in

24. See especially Basil, *On the Holy Spirit* 15.36–17.41.

25. Basil, *On the Holy Spirit* 16.38; ET: Stephen Hildebrand, trans., *On the Holy Spirit: St. Basil the Great*, Popular Patristics Series 42 (Crestwood, NY: St. Vladimir's Seminary Press, 2011), 71.

26. "And let no one think that I am saying that there are three persons as sources or that I am asserting the activity of the Son to be imperfect. For the source of beings is one, who makes through the Son and perfects through the Spirit. And neither is the Father, 'who works all in all,' imperfect in activity; neither is it the case that the Son is defective in creative power, unless it be perfected by the Spirit" (ibid. [ET modified]).

27. "There can be no doubt about it: speaking of three persons in God entails almost inevitably the danger (as a rule we try much too late to overcome it through explicit corrections) of believing that there exist in God three distinct consciousnesses, spiritual vitalities, centers of activity, and so on" (Rahner, *The Trinity*, 43).

his treatment of 1 Corinthians 12:4–6: "Now there are a variety of gifts, but the same Spirit, and there are a variety of ministries, but the same Lord; and there are a variety of operations, but it is the same God who inspires them all in every one" (translation mine). In Paul's sentence, "gifts," "ministries," and "operations," each qualified as comprising a "variety" (*diaireseis*), clearly refer to human activities; the ultimate source of these activities, however, is the one God, Lord, and Spirit. A modern reader is not likely to see Paul's use of these three divine titles in this context as referring to the Trinity. But Basil does, and he attributes the operations, ministries, and gifts distinctly to Father, Son, and Holy Spirit, within a common "unity and indivisibility of operation," emphasizing that the Holy Spirit participates in this united agency with its own intentionality (*autexousiōs*): "And so you should have learned the unity and indivisibility in every activity of the Holy Spirit, which is from the Father and the Son. God works the variety of operations, and the Lord the variety of ministries, and the Holy Spirit is also present, of his own will [*autexousiōs*] dispensing the distribution of gifts according to each one's worth."[28] In order to further substantiate his emphasis on the integral agency of the Spirit, Basil goes on to quote a later verse from the same chapter of 1 Corinthians, which he understands as ascribing willing to the Spirit: "One and the same Spirit works [*energei*] all these, distributing to each one individually as he wills [*kathōs bouletai*]" (1 Cor. 12:11, translation mine).

In Basil's *On the Holy Spirit*, we see the Spirit presented as a divine agent, who exercises a distinct modality of agency within the unified activity of the Trinity and who can be said to possess his own intentionality. In Gregory of Nyssa's *Catechetical Orations*, written in the early or perhaps mid-380s, we have a more systematic elaboration of the doctrine that each of the trinitarian hypostases must be conceived as an agent possessing a personal will.[29] Gregory begins his presentation of the contents of Christian faith by identifying Christian trinitarian doctrine as the mean between Greek polytheism and Jewish unitarianism. While Christians fundamentally share the Jewish adherence to monotheism, Christian monotheism involves confession of the "distinction of hypostases."[30] Gregory then proceeds to give an account of the distinct hypostases of Son and Spirit that applies scripturally derived trinitarian doctrine to the human analogues of the spoken word and the emitted breath that carries this word and makes it audible. The fundamental principle of Gregory's mode

---

28. Basil, *On the Holy Spirit* 16.37 (ET: Hildebrand, 70, modified).

29. For a fuller exposition of this text, see Khaled Anatolios, *Retrieving Nicaea: The Development and Meaning of Trinitarian Doctrine* (Grand Rapids: Baker Academic, 2011), 194–204; on Gregory's conception of divine personhood and intentionality, see esp. 215–20.

30. Gregory of Nyssa, *Catechetical Orations* 1.

of reasoning is that whatever is constitutive of the perfection of human nature must be applied to God supereminently, with a signification elevated according to the proportion that obtains between the creature and the transcendent God.[31] With reference to the analogical correspondence between the human word and the divine Logos, the key difference is that the former is a transient effect of the agency of the speaker, while the divine Word is in itself a center of vitality and subsistence. It is notable that, for Gregory, the hypostatic existence of the Word is considered to be integral to divine dignity and honor; he considers it impious and irreverent to suppose that the Word is unhypostatic. And it is equally clear that being a possessor of intentionality and agency is a central feature of Gregory's conception of hypostatic existence. He arrives at this conclusion by arguing from the divine simplicity of the Word and its innate vitality to its intrinsic power of intentionality. It is irreverent to suppose that the divine Word is lifeless. But if it is endowed with life, then divine simplicity demands that it not participate in life as something other than its own subsistence, or else it would be composite. Therefore, he concludes, "If the Word is alive because it is life then it certainly has the power of willing [*proairetikēn*]; for no living thing is without it. It is pious too to conclude that this faculty of will is filled with power [*dynatēn*]. . . . Whatever is good, it wills [*touto kai boulesthai*] and having willed it, is altogether able to do it. Being powerful [*dynamenēn*], it is not inactive [*mē anenergēton*] but brings to actualization every good purpose [*alla pasan agathou prothesin eis energeian agein*]."[32] Creation, he continues, "is the work of the Logos which, living and subsisting because it is God's Word, has will because it lives. It is capable of doing whatever it purposes and it chooses what is absolutely good and wise and everything else indicative of excellence."[33] In the above quotations from Gregory, we see a strict line of association between the Word's hypostatic existence, his goodness and power, and his intrinsic possession of intentionality. Gregory has no trouble applying the language of human willing (*boulēma*; *proairetikos*) to characterize the distinct personal existence of the Logos.

With regard to the Spirit, Gregory again applies the analogical reasoning of beginning with the likeness between the human and divine and then elevating this signification in keeping with our conception of the transcendent perfections of the divine being. While the Spirit may be likened to the emission of

31. "In reference, however, to the transcendent nature, everything said of it must be super-elevated because of the greatness of the object we contemplate" (*Catechetical Orations* 1; ET: Cyril Richardson in *Christology of the Later Fathers*, ed. Edward R. Hardy [Philadelphia: Westminster, 1954], 270).

32. Ibid.; ET: Richardson, 271 (modified).

33. Ibid.; ET: Richardson, 271–72 (modified).

breath that sustains human speaking, its divine perfection is bound up with the dignity of hypostatic existence, which includes being a possessor of intentionality and active agency:

> In the same way, when we learn that God has a Spirit, which accompanies his Word and manifests his activity, we do not think of it as an emission of breath. For we should degrade the majesty of God's power if we were to conceive of his Spirit in the same way as ours. Rather, we think of it as a power [*dynamin*] really existing by itself and in its own particular subsistence. . . . Like God's Word, it exists hypostatically, is capable of willing [*proairetikēn*], self-moved [*autokinēton*] and active [*energon*]. It always chooses the good [*to agathon hairoumenēn*] and it has the power that corresponds to its will [*syndromon echousan tē boulēsei tēn dynamin*] in fulfilling every good purpose.[34]

Here again, we see Gregory applying the vocabulary of intentionality, willing, self-movement, and active agency in order to characterize the distinct hypostatic existence of the Spirit. We can gather at least three points from Gregory's brief comments on the hypostatic existences of the Word and Spirit. First, hypostatic existence is intrinsic to divine perfection. To ascribe proper honor to Son and Spirit we must acknowledge their self-subsistences. Indeed, the perfection of God in comparison with the human being is precisely that the unhypostatic differentiations that constitute the human being as a rational and communicating being are hypostatic in God. Or, we can say that God's rationality and communicability are intrinsically interpersonal. Second, for Gregory, to say that Word and Spirit are hypostatic is to say that each is possessed of the power of willing; each is an agent. Third, for Gregory, to speak of divine personhood in terms of agency is not at all to reduce divine agency to a level equivalent to human agency. He is careful to point out crucial differences; for example, the Word and the Spirit will only the good, and their will is always perfectly potent and efficacious. But, conversely, these differences do not render the attribution of the power of willing altogether unsuitable to the Word and Spirit. According to Gregory, we must conceive the personal existences of the Word and Spirit by sublimating anagogically our conceptions of the perfections of human personhood. We do this by interpreting the biblical characterization of God dialectically with a view to both the likeness and difference between human and divine agency. The likeness cannot be reduced to equivalence, and the difference cannot be exaggerated into blank otherness. Gregory thus presents us with a model of analogical reasoning with respect to conceiving the trinitarian persons.

34. Ibid., 2; ET: Richardson, 273 (modified).

Even more explicitly than Basil, he considers agency and intentionality to be integral to divine hypostatic existence.

3. Father, Son, and Holy Spirit as "Persons in Communion"

There has been some recent discussion as to whether the language of "communion of essence," which can be found in Gregory of Nyssa and Basil, indicates a genuinely personal communion, a communion *between* persons, or merely denotes that each of the persons shares the properties of the nature.[35] Once again, however, we need to transcend an atomistic focus on the mere terminology of person, substance, and communion. The question of the kind of communion that can be appropriately attributed to Father, Son, and Holy Spirit has to be asked of the biblical narrative as a whole and with respect to the categories that arise organically from within that narrative. The canonical Gospels present Jesus as enjoying a communion of love, joy, trust, and intimacy with the God he called "Father," by the power of the Spirit. No one would deny that the relation between the man Jesus and the God he called Father can be appropriately characterized in terms of interpersonal communion. If one also believes that the humanity of Jesus has its ultimate ontological foundation in his preexistent divinity, then it seems consistent, moving from the economic to the immanent Trinity, to also conceive the relation between the divine Son and the Father in terms of interpersonal communion. So it should not surprise us that Athanasius, for example, had no trouble applying the declaration of Wisdom in Proverbs 8:30, "I was daily his delight, rejoicing before him always" (NRSV), to the preexistent Christ. Indeed, Athanasius argues that it is most appropriate to divine glory and transcendence that the delight that God has in creation is preceded and superseded and altogether enfolded by the intradivine delight between Father and Son:

> Therefore all the earth is filled with his knowledge. For one is the knowledge of the Father, through the Son, and of the Son, from the Father, and the Father rejoices in the Son and in this same joy, the Son delights in the Father, saying, "I was beside him, his delight. Day by day, I rejoiced in his presence" (Prov 8:30). . . . When was it then that the Father did not rejoice? But if he has always rejoiced, then there was always the one in whom he rejoiced. In whom, then, does the Father rejoice (cf. Prov 8:30), except by seeing himself in his own image, which is his Word? Even though, as it is written in these same Proverbs,

35. For a fuller discussion of this point, with reference to Nyssen's Ep. 38 and *To Ablabius: On Not Three Gods*, see Anatolios, *Retrieving Nicaea*, 220–35.

he also "delighted in the sons of people, having consummated the world" (Prov 8:31), yet this also has the same meaning. For he did not delight in this way by acquiring delight as an addition to himself, but it was upon seeing the works that were made according to his own image, so that the basis of this delight also is God's own Image. And how does the Son too rejoice, except by seeing himself in the Father? For to say this is the same as to say: "The one who has seen me has seen the Father" (John 14:9), and "I am in the Father and the Father is in me" (John 14:10).[36]

Athanasius here makes a critical point about the necessary connection and order between intratrinitarian communion and God's personal communion with creation. If we deny the attribution of interpersonal communion to the Trinity and yet are constrained by the biblical narrative to say that God rejoices in his communion with creation, then creation would be adding to the divine glory instead of simply participating in it. If communion with creation can be a delight for God, then surely we have to conceive of that delight as merely an extension outward of the intradivine interpersonal delight of the Holy Trinity.

A similar point is made by Basil and then taken up by his brother, Gregory, in reference to the Spirit. In his *On the Holy Spirit*, Basil takes as his point of departure Jesus's announcement to his disciples of the advent of the Paraclete: "When the Spirit of truth comes, he will guide you into all the truth. . . . He will glorify me, because he will take what is mine and declare it to you" (John 16:13–14 NRSV). In a fascinating exposition of this passage, Basil differentiates between two kinds of glory; there is a natural glory, such as the light, which can be called the glory of the sun, and there is a glory that is bestowed on another as an act of volition and judgment. We should note that up to that point, there had been a venerable tradition of speaking of the substantial union between the Father and the Son precisely in terms of the imagery of light and radiance. Such imagery is pervasive throughout Athanasius's work, for example. Yet here we find Basil rejecting this kind of emanationist conception in favor of something that we would characterize as more personal, inasmuch as it involves volition and judgment. He goes on to make a further distinction in reference to this kind of intentional glory, based on a quotation from Malachi 1:6, "A son honors his father, and servants their master" (NRSV). The glory of a servant is rendered to God by a creature, he explains, whereas the glory of intimate kinship is fulfilled by the Spirit.[37] Basil concludes this line of argument by insisting that divine glory is fulfilled not by the glory

36. Athanasius, *Oration* 2.82; ET: Anatolios, *Athanasius*, Early Church Fathers (London: Routledge, 2004), 174–75.
37. Basil, *On the Holy Spirit* 46.

and honor rendered by creatures to God but by the mutual glorification of Father, Son, and Holy Spirit. He finds warrant for this conception especially in the Johannine language of Jesus's Last Supper discourse: "And just as the Son will be glorified by the Father who says, 'I have glorified you, I will glorify you again' (Jn 12.28), thus also the Spirit is glorified through the communion that he has with the Father and the Son as well as through the witness of the Only-begotten."[38]

In his own treatise on the Holy Spirit, directed against the so-called Macedonians, and composed around the time of the Council of Constantinople in 381, Gregory of Nyssa takes up his older brother's conception of divine glory as fulfilled within the intratrinitarian communion. On the basis of the Johannine Jesus's saying that the Holy Spirit will glorify him, Gregory argues that in order for the Spirit to render adequate glory to the Son—presumably the "glory of intimates" of which Basil spoke—the Spirit must be in possession of an equally superabundant glory. Following this line of reasoning, Gregory conceives of the divine Trinity as "a circle of glory":

> Obviously, the one who gives glory to another must himself be in the possession of superabundant glory, for how could one who is bereft of glory glorify another? . . . So the power to glorify could never be displayed by one who was not in himself glory and honor and majesty and greatness. Now the Spirit does glorify the Father and the Son. And he is not a liar who said, "I glorify those that glorify me." "I have glorified you," says the Lord to the Father; and again he says, "Glorify me with the glory which I had with you before the world was." The divine voice responds, "I have both glorified and will glorify again." You see the circle of glory revolving among those who share a likeness. The Son is glorified by the Spirit; the Father is glorified by the Son; again the Son has his glory from the Father; and the only-begotten thus becomes the glory of the Spirit.[39]

It seems to me that this characterization of trinitarian life as a circle of mutual glorification is a scripturally appropriate way to conceive of the Trinity in terms of interpersonal communion, one that is far more fruitful than fixating on the mere phrase "communion of nature." Once again, it is by attending to the patristic appropriation of biblical categories, such as delight and mutual glorification in this case, that we can find a basis for conceiving of the Trinity as a communion of persons.

---

38. Ibid.; ET: Hildebrand, 82.
39. Gregory of Nyssa, *Against the Macedonians: On the Holy Spirit* (NPNF[2] 5:324–25 [modified]).

Conclusion

The premise of this essay has been that the tendency of modern Eastern Orthodox theology to invoke categories of personhood and personal communion in trinitarian theology is fundamentally sound but requires more solid ground in claiming to base itself on the legacy of patristic theology. Methodologically, the focus on the bare terminology of personhood and communion will always be vulnerable to the objection that the signification of these terms has become equivocal because of the intervention of the Enlightenment and modern psychology and philosophy. What is required, therefore, is a more integrated approach that seeks to uncover continuities between the trinitarian structure of the biblical narrative, patristic doctrinal formulations, and modern characterizations of personhood and communion. In this essay, I have proposed three such continuities that enable us to speak meaningfully of the divine Trinity as a communion of persons: (1) as disclosed by the biblical narrative, Father, Son, and Spirit are each agents of mutually referring speech-acts such that we can characterize their ontological relationship as radically *conversational*; (2) Father, Son, and Spirit are each distinctly possessors of intentionality and agency within the unified agency of trinitarian coactivity; (3) Father, Son, and Spirit enjoy a personal communion that can be appropriately characterized as a perichoretic circle of delight and mutual glorification. As I have stressed at various points throughout this essay, in no way does the application of these categories to the divine Trinity reduce the scope of their signification so as to make them univocal with their reference to human and creaturely realities. Rather, it is through the way of analogy, by applying creaturely perfections to the divine in a preeminent degree and by subtracting creaturely deficiencies in crossing over from human to divine predication, that we can glimpse the glory of the living God of whom we are trying to speak. We can say finally that such maneuvers of anagogical signification are not merely conceptual but existential and ethical. When Gregory of Nazianzus speaks of the unity of the Trinity, he explains that "each of these Persons possesses unity, not less with that which is united to it than with itself, by reason of the identity of essence and power."[40] Gregory explicitly contrasts this trinitarian unity with the unity of human nature in which individuals are necessarily separated from one another in many ways; indeed, the mutability of human nature is such that each human person is even at variance with him- or herself. Yet, notwithstanding this great difference between divine and human communion of persons, Nazianzus's description of trinitarian unity should remind us of

---

40. Gregory of Nazianzus, *Theological Orations* 5.16; ET: Richardson, 203.

the exhortation of St. Paul to the Philippians that precedes the great hymn of christological *kenōsis*: "Let each of you look not to your own interests, but to the interests of others" (Phil. 2:4 NRSV). To the extent that human persons heed that exhortation, we will indeed be traveling on the path of being not less united with our fellow humans than we are with ourselves, and thus also the path of assimilating ourselves to the trinitarian mode of being. We can joyfully tread that path even while recognizing that its destination cannot be reached until the time "when that within us which is godlike and divine . . . shall have mingled with its like, and the image shall have ascended to the archetype, of which it now has the desire."[41]

41. Ibid., 2.17; ET: Richardson, 147.

10

THE TRINITARIAN BEING
OF THE CHURCH

JOHN BEHR

The relationship between trinitarian theology and ecclesiology has been
much discussed in recent decades. It is an intriguing subject and perhaps
an odd juxtaposition. It has often been noted that although a confession of
faith in "one church" is included in most ancient creeds along with "one
baptism," the church herself is seldom directly reflected upon; the person of
Jesus Christ, his relation to the Father and the Spirit, was endlessly discussed
and was the subject of a great many conciliar statements, but not the church
or ecclesiology more generally. The question of ecclesiology, it is often said,
is our modern problem, one (at least for the Orthodox) provoked by the ecumenical encounter of the twentieth century. One fruit of this encounter is that
we have realized the trinitarian dimensions of the church herself, so providing
continuity with the theological reflection of earlier ages and grounding the
church in the Trinity.

This chapter is the revised version of a paper presented to the North American Lutheran-
Orthodox Dialogue, May 2003. It was originally published as "The Trinitarian Being of the
Church," *SVTQ* 48, no. 1 (2004): 67–88. Reprinted with permission.

Following in the wake of the Second Vatican Council, ecumenical dialogue in recent decades has emphasized the connection between the Trinity and the church largely through the exploration of what is commonly referred to as "communion ecclesiology." *Koinōnia*, "communion," was the theme of the Canberra Assembly of the World Council of Churches in 1991 and also of the Fifth World Conference on Faith and Order in Santiago de Compostela in 1993. In this approach, the *koinōnia* of the three persons of the Holy Trinity, the very being of God, is taken as the paradigm of the *koinōnia* that constitutes the being of the ecclesial body, the church. As Metropolitan John (Zizioulas) put it in his address to the meeting at Santiago de Compostela: "The Church as a communion reflects God's being as communion in the way this communion will be revealed fully in the Kingdom."[1] Such communion ecclesiology readily dovetails with the "eucharistic" ecclesiology espoused by many Orthodox during the twentieth century: it is in the sacrament of the Eucharist, the event of communion par excellence, that the church realizes her true being, manifesting already, here and now, the kingdom that is yet to come. Although, as Metropolitan John continues, "*Koinonia* is an eschatological gift,"[2] the fullness of this eschatological gift is nevertheless already given, received, or tasted in the celebration of the Eucharist.

Painted in these admittedly rather broad strokes, the oddity of juxtaposing the Trinity *and* the church can be seen. What is said of the church is certainly based upon what is said of the Trinity, but the effect of speaking in this manner, paradoxically, is that the church is separated from God, as a distinct entity reflecting the divine being. Another way of putting this, using terms that are themselves problematic, would be to say that communion ecclesiology sees the church as parallel to the "immanent Trinity": it is the three persons in communion, the one God as a relational being, that the church is said to "reflect." This results in a horizontal notion of communion, or, perhaps better, parallel "communions," without being clear about how the two intersect.

Metropolitan John is very careful to specify that the *koinōnia* in question "derives not from sociological experience, nor from ethics, but from *faith*."[3] We do not, that is, start from our notions of what "communion" might mean in our human experience of relating to others and then project this upon the Trinity. Rather, we must begin from faith, for "we believe in a God who is in his very being *koinonia*. . . . God is trinitarian; he is a relational being by definition;

---

1. Metropolitan John (Zizioulas) of Pergamon, "The Church as Communion," *SVTQ* 38, no. 1 (1994): 8.
2. Ibid.
3. Ibid., 5.

a non-trinitarian God is not *koinonia* in his very being. Ecclesiology must be based on Trinitarian theology if it is to be an ecclesiology of communion."[4] However, only after stating the principles of trinitarian *koinōnia* does Metropolitan John affirm, as a second point, that "*koinonia* is decisive also in our understanding of the person of Christ. Here the right synthesis between Christology and Pneumatology becomes extremely important."[5] He rightly emphasizes (correcting V. Lossky) that the "economy of the Son" cannot be separated from "the economy of the Spirit"—that is, both that the work of (or the "relation to") the Spirit is constitutive for the person of Christ and that there is no work of the Spirit distinct from that of Christ.[6]

Nevertheless, besides the very serious question concerning the appropriateness of characterizing the Trinity as a communion of three persons,[7] this approach does not adequately take into account the "economic" reality in which all trinitarian theology is grounded and in terms of which the Scriptures describe the church. Christology and pneumatology may have been synthesized, but trinitarian theology is still considered as a realm apart. Although Metropolitan John emphasizes that "the Church is not a sort of Platonic 'image' of the Trinity; she is communion in the sense of being the people of God, Israel, and the 'Body of Christ,'" this is followed, in the next sentence but one, with the affirmation that "the Church as communion *reflects* God's being as communion."[8] Despite the tantalizing mention of the church as the "Body of Christ," we are left with a communion of three divine persons and the image of this in the communion that is the church, whose structure, authority, mission, tradition, and sacraments (especially, of course, the Eucharist,[9] a point to which I will return) are correspondingly "relational." We have the Trinity *and* the church.

4. Ibid., 6.
5. Ibid.
6. Cf. J. Zizioulas, *Being as Communion* (Crestwood, NY: St. Vladimir's Seminary Press, 1985), 124–25.
7. A point already noted by Lossky, who observes that "in speaking of three hypostases we are already making an improper abstraction: if we wanted to generalize and make a concept of the 'divine hypostasis,' we would have to say that the only common definition possible would be the impossibility of any common definition of the three hypostases" (*In the Image and Likeness of God* [Crestwood, NY: St. Vladimir's Seminary Press, 1975], 113). See also L. Ayres, "On Not Three People: The Fundamental Themes of Gregory of Nyssa's Trinitarian Theology as Seen in *To Ablabius: On Not Three Gods*," and L. Turcescu, "'Person' versus 'Individual,' and Other Modern Misreadings of Gregory of Nyssa," both in *Rethinking Gregory of Nyssa*, ed. S. Coakley (Oxford: Blackwell, 2003).
8. Metropolitan John, "Church as Communion," 8 (emphasis added).
9. Cf. ibid., 15: "Baptism, Chrismation or Confirmation, and the rest of the sacramental life, are all given in view of the Eucharist. Communion in these sacraments may be described as 'partial' or anticipatory communion, calling for its fulfillment in the Eucharist."

The three primary scriptural images for the church—that is, the church as the people of God, the body of Christ, and the temple of the Holy Spirit— offer us, as suggested by Bruce Marshall, a way of looking at the trinitarian being of the church that integrates the church directly and intimately to the relationship between the Father, Son, and Holy Spirit.[10] Moreover, each of these images links the church in a particular way to one member of the Holy Trinity without undermining the basic Cappadocian point, that the actions of God are differentiated but not divided: it is the one God, the Father, who calls the church into being as the body of Christ indwelt by the Holy Spirit; and, in return, the church is conceived in terms of communion, but communion with God, as the body of his Son, anointed with his Spirit, and so calling upon God as Abba, Father.

I would like to begin with the basic content of these images and then continue by suggesting how trinitarian theology, as expounded in the fourth century and beyond, directs us to combine these various images, as different aspects of the single mystery that is the church. Following this I will offer some further considerations concerning the calling of the church and her eschatological perfection; concerning baptism (with which the church is invariably connected in creedal formulations) as the foundational sacrament of the church and the implications this has for the question of the boundaries of the church; and lastly concerning how, as the place where the human being is born again through baptism, the church can also be considered as our mother, in which each Christian puts on the identity of Christ.

The People of God, the Body of Christ, and the Temple of the Holy Spirit

Most fundamentally, the word "church," *ekklēsia*, means a "calling-out," the election of a particular people from the midst of the world by God, who forms them as his own people, "a chosen race, a royal priesthood, a holy nation, God's own people" (1 Pet. 2:9 RSV). For Christians this calling is, of course, that of the gospel of Christ, proclaiming with the power of the Spirit the divine work wrought in and by Christ, destroying death by his death and by his blood breaking down the dividing wall so that those "separated from Christ, alienated from the citizenship of Israel" (Eph. 2:12 RSV) may enter into the covenant, in the one body of Christ, having access in the one

10. Bruce D. Marshall, "The Holy Trinity and the Mystery of the Church: Toward a Lutheran/ Orthodox Common Statement" (paper presented to the North American Lutheran-Orthodox Dialogue, May 2002).

Spirit to the Father (Eph. 2:11–18). The "citizenship of Israel" is defined by relation to Christ. Though a specific, "once for all" event, the passion of Jesus Christ—his death, resurrection, and bestowal of the Spirit, as another advocate leading us into the fullness of the truth of Christ[11]—as preached by the apostles, "according to Scripture," is of eternal significance and scope. It is this gospel that was preached in advance to Abraham, so that all who respond in faith to the Word of God, as did Abraham, receive the blessings that were bestowed upon him (Gal. 3:3–14). Going further back, many of the fathers affirmed that the creation of Adam already looks toward, and is modeled upon, the image of God, Christ Jesus (and that the world itself is impregnated with the sign of his cross), and also that the breath that Adam received, making him a "living being," prefigures the Spirit bestowed by Christ, which renders Christians "spiritual beings." The Word, by which God calls forth and fashions a people for himself, is unchanging. The revelation of this mystery hidden from all eternity both enables us to look back into the Scriptures, and creation itself, to see there an anticipatory testimony to Christ and also introduces the gentiles into the covenant, for its basis is now clearly seen to be Christ himself, not race or fleshly circumcision: the church, the new creation called into being by the cross of Christ, is the Israel of God (Gal. 6:16).

Called into being by God through his Word, Jesus Christ, and by the power of the Spirit, the church is the body of Christ. God "has put all things under [Christ's] feet and has made him the head over all things for the church, which is his body, the fulness of him who fills all in all" (Eph. 1:22–23 RSV). As "firstborn of the dead," in whom "the whole fullness of divinity dwells bodily," Christ is "the head of the body, the church" (Col. 1:18–19; 2:9). It is by holding fast to the head that "the whole body, nourished and knit together through its joints and ligaments, grows with a growth that is from God" (Col. 2:19 RSV). The identity is complete; it is not a loose analogy or metaphor: "You are the body of Christ and individually members of it"—all, that is, who "by one Spirit . . . were baptized into one body" (1 Cor. 12:27, 13 RSV). Christians are called to be the "one body," by living in subjection to the head, Christ, allowing his peace to rule in their hearts (Col. 3:15). As members of his body, they depend for their life and being upon their head and also upon one another: "We, though many, are one body in Christ, and individually members of one another" (Rom. 12:5 RSV). The grace given to each is for the benefit

11. Cf. John 14:25–26; 16:13–15. The pentecostal bestowal of the Spirit is intimately connected with the passion of Christ, for it was at his death, when the work of God was "fulfilled" and Christ rested on the Sabbath, that Christ "gave up the ghost" or, more literally, "handed down [traditioned] the Spirit" (John 19:30).

of the one body, so that everything is to be done in love for the building up of the one body (1 Cor. 12–13).

The subsequent reflection devoted to identity of the one body, the body of Christ assumed by the Word who now dwells in those who have "put on Christ," is so vast and profound that it is impossible to treat it here. But as it is also not satisfactory to pass it by in silence, one example must suffice. The identity of the body is the central nexus in the classic work *On the Incarnation* by Athanasius, integrating trinitarian theology, Christology, ecclesiology, and soteriology. As he puts it:

> For being over all, the Word of God, by offering his own temple and his bodily instrument as a substitute for all, naturally fulfilled the debt by his death; and, as being united to all by the like [body], the incorruptible Son of God naturally clothed all with incorruption by the promise concerning the resurrection; and now no longer does the actual corruption in death hold ground against humans, because of the Word dwelling in them through the one body. (*Inc.* 9)

The Word clothed himself with our body so that he might conquer death by offering his body to death and so that we might now be clothed with his incorruption through the identity of the one body. It is very striking that when treating the resurrection of Christ, Athanasius makes no mention of the postresurrection appearances of Christ to the disciples as described in the Gospels: that Christ is alive and his own, proper body raised is shown by the fact that those who have "put on the faith of the Cross," as he put on our body, "so despise death that they willingly encounter it and become witness for the Resurrection the Savior accomplished against it" (*Inc.* 27–28). The presentation of Christian theology, characteristic of many textbooks, as a collection of discrete realms—Trinity, incarnation, passion, soteriology, ecclesiology—only serves to obscure the vitality of such a vision.

As a body, the church also has a structure, a variety of members with a variety of gifts and ministries. From the earliest times, the congregation gathered around the bishop, together with his presbyters and deacons; so intrinsic were these to the structure of the body that Ignatius asserts that without these three orders, the community cannot be called a "church" (*Letter to the Trallians* 3.1). That there is only one Christ means that there can be only one Eucharist, one altar, and one bishop (*Letter to the Philadelphians* 4). However, for all the importance given to the clergy, and especially the bishop, their roles are historically and geographically specific; as it is often pointed out, the church of God is also always the church of a particular place, gathering together all Christians (*epi to auto*, 1 Cor. 11:20). On the other hand, the significance of the apostles, upon whose proclamation the church is based, is universal and eternal, and so, in the typologies that Ignatius proposes, they always appear on the divine side.[12] The changing understanding of the ordained ministry through history need not detain us here; what is important for the present purposes is the essential role that they have in the constitution of the church. Yet their essential role should not be overstated; it is not by virtue of being gathered around the bishop that a community is the church, but by virtue of Christ himself. As Ignatius puts it, in words that are often misquoted: "Whenever the bishop appears, let the congregation be present, just as wherever Christ is, there is the catholic Church" (*Letter to the Smyrnaeans* 8). It is Christ who makes the congregation to be his body, the church, and so when Ignatius writes his letters, he does so to the whole community, not to the bishop, warning them to "be deaf when anyone speaks to you apart from Jesus Christ" (*Letter to the Trallians* 9).

Finally, it is "by the one Spirit that we are baptized into the one body" (1 Cor. 12:13), and so it is as "a holy temple in the Lord" that we are fashioned into a "dwelling place of God in the Spirit" (Eph. 2:21–22 RSV). Those in whom the Spirit of God dwells are the temple of God (1 Cor. 3:16). The Spirit is bestowed through Christ, so that we receive the Spirit of the Father as the Spirit of Christ (cf. Rom. 8:9–11). But it is also the Spirit who enables us to recognize Christ, to call him Lord—that is, the one spoken of in the Scriptures (1 Cor. 12:3)—and who unites us to Christ, making us to be one body with him, as a bride to her spouse (as in the imagery of Eph. 5), so that "the Spirit and the Bride say, 'Come'" (Rev. 22:17 RSV), and who enables those united in one body with Christ to call on God as Abba, Father (Gal. 4:6; Rom. 8:15–16). It is in "the communion of the Holy Spirit" (2 Cor. 13:14) that Christians have their unity as the one body of Christ; they are to "maintain the unity of the Spirit in the bond of peace," so that "there is one body and one Spirit, just as you were called to the one hope that belongs to your call, one Lord, one faith, one baptism, one God and Father of us all, who is above all and through all and in all" (Eph. 4:3–6 RSV).

All of these images describe the activity of the Trinity, the Father, the Son, and the Holy Spirit, in the divine economy of salvation. Yet they are not merely "economic" activities different from the "immanent" relations of the Father, Son, and Spirit, "missions" as distinct from "processions." As debate

---

12. Cf. John Behr, *The Way to Nicaea* (Crestwood, NY: St. Vladimir's Seminary Press, 2001), 82. For Ignatius, the bishop, deacon, and presbyters image the Father, Christ, and the apostles, respectively (*Letter to the Trallians* 3.1; *Letter to the Magnesians* 6.1). Only with Cyprian are the apostles considered to be the first bishops and the bishops considered, in turn, the successors of the apostles.

concerning trinitarian theology intensified during the fourth century and beyond, discussion inevitably became more abstract, but its content remained constant. As the Cappadocians in the fourth century were keen to emphasize, we know God only from his activities, as he reveals himself, and what he reveals of himself is what he is. The crucified Jesus Christ, "designated Son of God in power according to the Spirit of holiness by his resurrection from the dead" (Rom. 1:4 RSV), of whom it is said, "You are my Son; today I have begotten you" (Acts 13:33; Ps. 2:7 RSV), is the same one about whom, when the Spirit rested upon him at his baptism, the Father declared, "You are my Son, the Beloved; with you I am well pleased" (Mark 1:11; cf. Matt. 3:17; in Luke 3:22, ancient variants have the "begotten you" of Ps. 2:7), and who was conceived in the womb of the Virgin by the Holy Spirit, the power of the Most High (Matt. 1:20; Luke 1:35)—this is the one who is eternally, or better, timelessly, begotten from the Father, not, as Arius would have it, begotten as a discrete event in a quasi-temporality before the aeons, before which God was not Father. Likewise, the Holy Spirit, who proceeds from the Father, is bestowed upon Christians by Christ, as the Spirit of Christ, and so it is affirmed that while the Son is begotten directly from the Father, the Spirit derives from the Father "by that which is directly from the first cause, so that the attribute of being Only-begotten abides unambiguously in the Son, while the Spirit is without doubt derived from the Father, the intermediacy of the Son safeguarding his character of being the Only-begotten and not excluding the Spirit from his natural relation to the Father."[13]

Later Byzantine theology, especially that of Gregory of Cyprus and Gregory Palamas in the thirteenth and fourteenth centuries, develops these points by differentiating between the "procession" of the Holy Spirit from the Father, by which the Spirit derives his subsistence and existence, and the "manifestation" or "shining forth" of the Spirit through the Son, a relation that is not only temporal but eternal.[14] The Spirit, who proceeds from the Father, rests upon the Son; the activity that is depicted at every key moment in the apostolic presentation of Christ manifests, and provides the basis for our understanding of, the eternal relation between Father, Son, and Spirit. But the Spirit does not simply rest upon the Son as a termination, for, as we have seen, it is always through the Spirit that Christ is shown to be the Son of God, through the Spirit that he is begotten, raised, and revealed, and through the Spirit that Christians are led to Christ, incorporated into his body, and so have access to the Father.

13. Gregory of Nyssa, *To Ablabius* (GNO 3.1, p. 56).
14. Cf. D. Stăniloae, "Trinitarian Relations and the Life of the Church," in *Theology and the Church* (Crestwood, NY: St. Vladimir's Seminary Press, 1980), 11–44.

The trinitarian order, from the Father through the Son in the Spirit, finds its reciprocating movement in the Spirit through the Son to the Father. In a very striking passage, Gregory Palamas relates these two movements by speaking of the Spirit as "an ineffable love of the Begetter towards the ineffably begotten Word," a love that is "also possessed by the Word towards the Begetter," for the Spirit also belongs to the Son, who "rejoices together with the Father who rejoices in him," so that "the pre-eternal joy of the Father and the Son is the Holy Spirit," as common to both of them, but whose existence depends upon the Father alone, from whom alone he proceeds.[15]

That the Spirit is "manifested" through the Son, not only in the temporal realm but eternally, means that the distinction between "procession" and "manifestation" does not correspond to a distinction, often made, between intratrinitarian "processions" and extratrinitarian "missions." One fork of the argument against the term *filioque* developed by Photius, in the ninth century, confines the procession of the Spirit through the Son solely to the temporal realm (where the Son, as human, is anointed with the Spirit, and so the Spirit can be said to be "of Christ"), so introducing a distinction between the "immanent" and the "economic" Trinity.[16] The consequence of this is that the intratrinitarian communion becomes a realm apart, and the work of the Spirit becomes almost independent from that of Christ.[17] Following the Byzantine fathers mentioned, we must say that Christ's relationship to the Holy Spirit not only is constitutive for his being on an "economic" level (the inseparability of Christology and pneumatology, noted by Metropolitan John), but also

15. Gregory Palamas, *The One Hundred and Fifty Chapters*, chap. 36; on this aspect of Palamas's theology and its connection to Augustine, cf. R. Flogaus, "Palamas and Barlaam Revisited: A Reassessment of East and West in the Hesychast Controversy of 14th Century Byzantium," *SVTQ* 42, no. 1 (1998): 1–32.

16. Photius, *On the Mystagogy of the Holy Spirit*, esp. 93. Cf. M. A. Orphanos, "The Procession of the Holy Spirit according to Certain Later Greek Fathers," in *Spirit of God, Spirit of Christ: Ecumenical Reflections on the Filioque Controversy*, Faith and Order Paper no. 10 (London: SPCK; Geneva: WCC, 1981), 21–45; J. Meyendorff, *Byzantine Theology: Historical Themes and Doctrinal Themes*, 2nd ed. with revisions (New York: Fordham University Press, 1987), 60–61.

17. Cf. Vladimir Lossky, who states categorically that "theologians have always insisted on the radical difference between the eternal procession of the Persons . . . and the temporal mission of the Son and the Holy Spirit in the world," and then continues on the next page: "Intimately linked as they are in the common work upon earth, the Son and the Holy Spirit remain nevertheless in this same work two persons independent the one of the other as to their hypostatic being. It is for this reason that the personal advent of the Holy Spirit does not have the character of a work which is subordinate, and in some sort functional, in relation to that of the Son. Pentecost is not a 'continuation' of the Incarnation. It is its sequel, its result" (*The Mystical Theology of the Eastern Church* [Crestwood, NY: St. Vladimir's Seminary Press, 1976], 158–59).

determines how we speak, more abstractly, of the relation between Father, Son, and Spirit. As the Cappadocians already realized, the relation between Father, Son, and Holy Spirit is identical, and it must be so, with the pattern of divine life revealed in the Scriptures: the Spirit, who proceeds from the Father, rests upon the Son, as a bond of love returned to the Father. It is in this specific pattern of communion (and not as imaging a communion of three divine persons) that the church, as the body of Christ and the temple of the Spirit, has her being: the "institutional" dimension and the "pneumatic" dimension cannot be separated, but together form the one body of Christ giving thanks to God in the Spirit. The church is not just a communion of persons in relation, but the body of Christ giving thanks to the Father in the Spirit.

The Calling of the Church and Her Eschatological Perfection

This very high theology of the church as the body of Christ and the temple of the Spirit must not blind us to the other trinitarian aspect of the church, that she is the one called by God. As called, the church is a response, a dynamic response growing to the fullness to which she is called. We who were "separated from Christ, alienated from the commonwealth of Israel," have been introduced into the promised covenant of Christ (Eph. 2:12 RSV), but nevertheless "our commonwealth is in heaven, and from it we await a Savior, the Lord Jesus Christ, who will change our lowly body to be like his glorious body" (Phil. 3:20–21 RSV). Our prayer is that "when he appears we shall be like him" (1 John 3:2 RSV). But he is still "the Coming One," to whom "the Spirit and the Bride say, 'Come'" (Rev. 22:17 RSV). Therefore, the church, though scattered throughout the world, is not located on earth but in the Spirit: "Where the church is, there is the Spirit of God, and where the Spirit of God is, there is the church."[18]

It is within this dynamic that we can best explain such issues as "the visibility of the church," whether "the church" is to be fully identified with the gathering of the baptized around the sacraments of word and Eucharist, and the all too visible failings both of the individual believers, ordained and lay, who belong to the church and of the particular church of any given place. We are called by God to be his holy church, and by conversion and repentance we enter into that reality, becoming the body of Christ by the grace of the Spirit; the church is holy not by the virtues of the individual believers but by receiving the holy mysteries, through the hands of sinful believers.

18. Irenaeus of Lyons, *Against the Heresies* 3.24.1.

More to the purposes of an ecumenical dialogue, it is perhaps by virtue of this dynamic that we can also best understand the claim of the Orthodox Church to be the true church. Georges Florovsky stated this in unequivocal terms, asserting that the conviction of the Orthodox Church is that she "is in very truth the Church, i.e., *the true* Church and the *only* true Church."[19] With this conviction, he admits, he is "compelled to regard all other Christian churches as deficient," and so "Christian reunion is simply conversion to Orthodoxy." But, he continues, this is not meant to be an arrogant or triumphalistic claim, for it goes hand in hand with the acknowledgment that "this does not mean that everything in the past or present state of the Orthodox Church is to be equated with the truth of God. Many things are obviously changeable; indeed, many things need improvement. The *true* Church is not yet the *perfect* Church." Or, as he puts it elsewhere: "The Orthodox Church claims to be *the Church*. There is no pride and no arrogance in this claim. Indeed, it implies a heavy responsibility. Nor does it mean 'perfection.' The Church is still in pilgrimage, in travail, *in via*. She has her historic failures and losses, she has her own unfinished tasks and problems."[20] Although stressing the orientation toward the eschatological perfection to which the church is called, Florovsky himself, in his "return to the Fathers," sought for the Christian unity in the past, the common mind that existed in the diversity of early Christianity and that has been preserved intact by the Orthodox Church:

> The Orthodox Church is conscious and aware of her identity through the ages, in spite of all historic perplexities and changes. She has kept intact and immaculate the sacred heritage of the Early Church. . . . She is aware of the identity of her teaching with the apostolic message and the tradition of the Ancient Church, even though she might have failed occasionally to convey this message to particular generations in its full splendor and in a way that carries conviction. In a sense, the Orthodox Church is a continuation, a "survival" of Ancient Christianity.[21]

Florovsky's insistence that ecumenical dialogue be not only an "ecumenism in space, concerned with the adjustments of the existing denominations as

19. G. Florovsky, "The True Church," in *Ecumenism I: A Doctrinal Approach*, Collected Works of Georges Florovsky (Belmont, MA: Notable & Academic Books, 1989), 13:134; this text is an extract from "Confessional Loyalty in the Ecumenical Movement," *The Student World* 43 (1950): 57–70. This paragraph is indebted to an unpublished paper of John Erickson, "The One True Church: Thoughts Concerning an Ecumenical Conundrum" (August 2001).

20. G. Florovsky, "The Quest for Christian Unity and the Orthodox Church," in *Ecumenism I: A Doctrinal Approach*, Collected Works of Georges Florovsky (Belmont, MA: Notable & Academic Books, 1989), 13:139–40 (an article originally published in *Theology and Life* 4 [August 1961]: 197–208).

21. Ibid., 140.

they are at present," but also an "ecumenism in time,"[22] thus turns out to be a return to the past: "The way out of the present confusion and into a better future is, unexpectedly, through the past. Divisions can be overcome only by a return to the common mind of the early Church. There was no uniformity, but there was a common mind."[23]

In what sense there was a "common mind" in Christian antiquity has become an extremely thorny question, especially since the work of Walter Bauer, *Orthodoxy and Heresy in Earliest Christianity* (or at least since its translation into English). However, what was recognized as normative Christianity by the end of the second century was based (through the interplay of the "canon of truth," a common body of Scripture, apostolic tradition, and apostolic succession) on nothing other than the proclamation of the gospel "according to Scripture" as delivered by the apostles (cf. 1 Cor. 15:3).[24] It was the one Christ, proclaimed in this manner, who was then, and will always be, the uniting force for those who gather together in expectation of him as his body. The full, perfect, identity of the church, therefore, is not something located in the ecclesial bodies and structures of the past, to be recovered by archaeology, but, as Florovsky intimates, in the future, in the eschaton, when Christ will be all in all, an orientation maintained by remaining in faithful continuity with the "faith which was once for all delivered to the saints" (Jude 3 RSV) regarding Christ, the coming Lord. The implications that this has for the recognition by the Orthodox Church of the ecclesial reality beyond its own bounds are best seen from the point of view of the abiding significance of baptism as our entry into the church and the historical practice of the Orthodox Church regarding reception of converts.

Baptism, Eucharist, and the Boundaries of the Church

Entry into the body of Christ is through baptism in the name of the Father, the Son, and the Holy Spirit. "One baptism for the remission of sins" is ubiquitously included in creedal confession along with "one church." As the body of Christ that we are speaking of is his crucified and risen body, baptism itself is understood as sharing in his death: "Do you not know that all of us who have been baptized into Christ Jesus were baptized into his death? We were

---

22. Ibid., 139.

23. G. Florovsky, "Theological Tensions among Christians," in *Ecumenism I: A Doctrinal Approach*, Collected Works of Georges Florovsky (Belmont, MA: Notable & Academic Books, 1989), 13:13 (originally published in *The Christian Leader* 5 [1950]).

24. Cf. Behr, *Way to Nicaea*, 11–48.

buried therefore with him by baptism into death, so that as Christ was raised from the dead by the glory of the Father, we too might walk in newness of life. For if we have been united with him in a death like his, we shall certainly be united with him in a resurrection like his" (Rom. 6:3–5 RSV). It is very important to observe the tenses used by Paul: if we *have died* with Christ in baptism, we *shall rise* with him. Although baptism is a specific, sacramental event, until our actual death, in witness to Christ, we must preserve our state of being baptized: "If we have died with Christ, we believe that we shall also live with him. . . . So you must consider yourselves dead to sin and alive to God in Christ Jesus" (Rom. 6:8, 11 RSV). In other words, the "one baptism for the remission of sins" is not simply a gateway to be passed through as we enter into the "one church," and then left behind. Rather, the paschal dimension of baptism characterizes the totality of the Christian life, shaping and informing every aspect of it, until we are finally raised in Christ.[25] As Aidan Kavanagh puts it, "The whole economy of *becoming* a Christian, from conversion and catechesis through the eucharist, is thus the fundamental paradigm for *remaining* a Christian. . . . The paschal mystery of Jesus Christ dying and rising still among his faithful ones at Easter in baptism is what gives the Church its radical cohesion and mission, putting it at the center of a world made new."[26] The "one true Church" must maintain her baptismal character until, in the eschaton, she is, as Florovsky puts it, the "perfect Church."

It is in the Eucharist, the "banquet of the kingdom," the event of "communion" par excellence, that Christians are given a foretaste of the kingdom, invoking the Spirit "upon us and upon the gifts now offered," and praying to God to "unite all of us to one another who become partakers of the one Bread and Cup in the communion of the Holy Spirit" (Liturgy of St. Basil). But we must not forget that this is given to us in anticipation, as a foretaste of the kingdom to come, not as its final realization; no eschatology can be exclusively "realized"; Christian eschatology is always already *but not yet*. The church is still *in via*, seeking, and receiving proleptically as a gift, her perfection that is yet to be fully manifest.

Whether the sacrament of the kingdom, already celebrated in anticipation by the church *in via*, can be used to define the boundaries of the one true church is a very serious question. This is, of course, how the "eucharistic ecclesiology" espoused by many Orthodox theologians during the twentieth

25. See especially J. Erickson, "Baptism and the Church's Faith," in *Marks of the Body of Christ*, ed. C. E. Braaten and R. W. Jenson (Grand Rapids: Eerdmans, 1999), 44–58, to which the following paragraphs are indebted.

26. A. Kavanagh, *The Shape of Baptism: The Rite of Christian Initiation* (New York: Pueblo Publishing Company, 1978), 162–63.

century views the matter. This has undoubtedly contributed to an increased ecclesial awareness, but it has also been deleterious in two respects. First, the "eucharistic revival" that has accompanied such ecclesiology has emphasized participation in the Eucharist to such a point that it often overshadows, if not obscures, the perpetual baptismal dimensions of Christian life; baptism is regarded as the necessary preliminary step into the body that celebrates the Eucharist.[27]

Taken to its extreme, this results in a community of, in John Erickson's phrase, "eucharisticized pagans"—members of the church who participate in the Eucharist but do not otherwise have any consciousness of the life in death that is the Christian life in this world.[28] Second, it results in a view that sees life outside the Orthodox Church, defined as coextensive with participation in her celebration of the Eucharist, in uniformly negative terms: "The boundaries of the body of Christ depend entirely on the eucharistic life. Outside that life, humanity is ruled by alien powers. Separation and destruction can only be averted by those who unite in Christ and prepare themselves for the joint assembly of the eucharist."[29] In this perspective, not only do the Orthodox regard themselves, rightly, as belonging to "the one true Church," but they deny the designation "church" to any other body gathering together in the name of Christ: outside the Orthodox Church, "humanity is ruled by alien powers."

This approach began with Cyprian in the third century. When faced with various schisms resulting from different responses to persecution, Cyprian defined the boundaries of the church in terms of adherence to the bishop, but with the bishop being understood not, as with Ignatius and Irenaeus, as the bearer of the true teaching (for the schismatic groups with whom Cyprian was dealing were perfectly orthodox in their beliefs) but rather as the bearer of apostolic authority, especially the ability to forgive sins (which is connected with the only mentions of the word "church" in the Gospels: Matt. 16:18; 18:17). Cyprian ultimately ends up identifying the bishop with the church herself: "You should understand that the bishop is in the church and the church in the bishop, and whoever is not with the bishop is not in the church" (Cyprian, *Ep.* 66.8). The images for the church preferred by Cyprian all emphasize the sharp boundaries of the church and her exclusivism: "You cannot have God

27. Recall the remarks of Metropolitan John mentioned earlier, at n. 9 above.
28. As Erickson ("Baptism," 57) puts it: "We forget that the eucharist is but a foretaste of the kingdom, not its final realization. And then, this tendency towards a realized eschatology begins to creep from the eucharist into other aspects of church life, so that the church qua church comes to be seen as perfect in every respect. Its dependence on Christ, and him crucified, is forgotten. We want the glory and forget the cross."
29. G. Limouris, "The Eucharist as the Sacrament of Sharing: An Orthodox Point of View," in *Orthodox Visions of Ecumenism*, ed. G. Limouris (Geneva: WCC, 1994), 254.

for your Father if you no longer have the church for your mother. If there was any escape for one who was outside the ark of Noah, there will be as much for one who is found to be outside the church."[30] Most famously, "Outside the church there is no salvation" (Cyprian, *Ep*. 73.21). Finally, when faced with the issue of receiving into communion those who had been baptized in a schismatic group, Cyprian insisted that they were to be baptized (i.e., "re-baptized," though Cyprian, naturally, does not use this term). Because of the connection between baptism and remission of sins, there can be no baptism outside of the catholic church, defined as adherence to the bishop, who alone bears this apostolic gift: as baptism is entry into the church, one cannot be outside the church and yet baptized into it.

Cyprian's position concerning (re)baptism has been repeatedly advocated through the centuries and, especially since Nikodemus the Hagiorite (1748–1809), is promoted by many in the Orthodox Church today.[31] But, as Florovsky points out, while Cyprian was right, theologically, to state unequivocally that the sacraments are performed only *in* the church, "he defined this *in* hastily and too narrowly."[32] Moreover, as Florovsky also points out, "the *practical* conclusions of Cyprian have not been accepted and supported by the consciousness of the Church."[33] Cyprian's position was an innovation,[34] and one that has not been uniformly followed by the church. Indeed, there are several important witnesses against it. The First Ecumenical Council, at Nicaea in 325, speaks of receiving "the pure ones"—that is, those of the Novatianist schism—by the laying on of hands (Canon 8). Addressing the same issue several decades later, Basil, in a letter (*Ep*. 188) that was subsequently included in the canoni-

30. Cyprian, *On the Unity of the Church* 6. Cf. Erickson, "Baptism," 55–56, for Cyprian's static, exclusivist imagery of the church, in contrast to the variety of images to be found in Scripture and the fathers: the temple, vine, paradise, body; not only Eve and Mary, but also Tamar, Rahab, Mary Magdalen, the Canaanite woman, Zacchaeus: "not just images of achieved perfection, which might incline us to hold a triumphalist and exclusive view of the church, but also images of repentance, conversion and striving."

31. For a critical analysis of the issue, see J. Erickson, "The Reception of Non-Orthodox into the Orthodox Church: Contemporary Practice," *SVTQ* 41, no. 1 (1997): 1–17; and Erickson, "On the Cusp of Modernity: The Canonical Hermeneutic of Nikodemus the Haghiorite (1748–1809)," *SVTQ* 42, no. 1 (1998): 45–66.

32. G. Florovsky, "The Boundaries of the Church," in *Ecumenism I: A Doctrinal Approach*, Collected Works of Georges Florovsky (Belmont, MA: Notable & Academic Books, 1989), 13:37; this essay is stated to be "combined from a Russian original and an English translation which appeared in" *Church Quarterly Review* 117 (October 1933): 117–31.

33. Ibid., 37.

34. It is noteworthy that Cyprian does not challenge the claim made at Rome that Pope Stephen's policy was in accord with the traditional practice of that church, nor does Cyprian appeal to "tradition" to support his case: "One must not prescribe by custom, but overcome by reason" (*Ep*. 71.3).

cal corpus of the Orthodox Church, differentiated between "heretics" (who are completely broken off and alien as regards their faith, shown in the form of their "baptism," for instance "in the Father and the Son and Montanus or Priscilla"), "schisms" (which have resulted "from some ecclesiastical reasons and questions capable of mutual remedy," in this case regarding penance), and "paraecclesial gatherings" ("assemblies brought into being by insubordinate presbyters or bishops or by uninformed laity"). Basil mentions Cyprian's practice, but sides with "the ancients [who] decided to accept that baptism which in no way deviates from the faith," so that "the ancients decided to reject completely the baptism of heretics, but to accept that of schismatics, as still being of the Church." In other words, those baptized in the right faith, even if not in eucharistic communion with the main body of the church, still belong to the church. This is not to succumb to some kind of "branch theory" of the church, nor to advocate immediate eucharistic communion with, in the paradoxical phrase, the "separated brethren." Rather it is to place the issue in terms of the eschatological tension in which the church exists in this world. But this does present a challenge, perhaps especially to the Orthodox, to reconsider how they view those outside their own eucharistic community. The celebration of the Eucharist is the sacrament of the kingdom, giving a foretaste of what is already but not yet; it seems, as suggested earlier, that we should perhaps not take the character of the "perfect Church," to use Florovsky's expression once again, as the definition of the boundaries of the "one true Church."

As we are to live baptismally, "considering ourselves dead to sin and alive to God in Christ Jesus," until we actually die in good faith and are raised with Christ, so also the Eucharist in which we already partake is also, in a sense, "not yet," but is fulfilled in our own death and resurrection. As Irenaeus put it:

> Just as the wood of the vine, planted in the earth, bore fruit in its own time, and the grain of wheat, falling into the earth and being decomposed, was raised up by the Spirit of God who sustains all, then, by wisdom, they come to the use of humans, and receiving the Word of God, become eucharist, which is the Body and Blood of Christ; in the same way, our bodies, nourished by it, having been placed in the earth and decomposing in it, shall rise in their time, when the Word of God bestows on them the resurrection to the glory of God the Father, who secures immortality for the mortal and bountifully bestows incorruptibility on the corruptible. (*Against the Heresies* 5.2.3)

By receiving the Eucharist, as the wheat and the vine receive the fecundity of the Spirit, we are prepared, as we also make the fruits into the bread and wine,

for the resurrection effected by the Word, at which point, just as the bread
and wine receive the Word and so become the body and blood of Christ, the
Eucharist, so also our bodies will receive immortality and incorruptibility
from the Father. The paschal mystery that each baptized Christian enters by
baptism is completed in that believer's resurrection, celebrated as the Eucharist
of the Father.

The Mother Church and Christian Identity

Finally, just as Paul says, "I am . . . in travail until Christ be formed in you"
(Gal. 4:19 RSV)—in those, that is, whom he (though this time as a father)
has "begotten . . . through the Gospel" (1 Cor. 4:15 KJV)—so also, until the
day when we die in the witness (*martyria*) of a good confession, the church
is our mother, in travail, giving birth to sons of God. The motherhood of the
church is an ancient theme, one that has its roots in Isaiah, who, after foretell-
ing the passion of Christ, proclaims: "Sing, O barren one, who did not bear;
break forth into singing and cry aloud, you who have not been in travail! For
the children of the desolate one will be more than the children of her that
is married, says the Lord" (Isa. 54:1 RSV). Of the many ways in which this
imagery has been explored, one of the most stimulating brings it directly into
conjunction with the incarnation of the Word. According to Hippolytus, "The
Word of God, being fleshless, put on the holy flesh from the holy virgin, as
a bridegroom a garment, having woven it for himself in the sufferings of the
cross, so that having mixed our mortal body with his own power, and having
mingled the corruptible into the incorruptible, and the weak with the strong,
he might save perishing man."[35]

He continues with an extended image of a loom, of which the web beam is
"the passion of the Lord upon the cross," the warp is the power of the Holy
Spirit, the woof is the holy flesh woven by the Spirit, the rods are the Word,
and the workers are the patriarchs and prophets, "who weave the fair, long,
perfect tunic for Christ."[36] The flesh of the Word, received from the Virgin and
"woven in the sufferings of the cross," is woven by the patriarchs and prophets,
whose actions and words proclaim the manner in which the Word became
present and manifest. It is in the preaching of Jesus Christ, the proclamation
of the one who died on the cross, interpreted and understood in the matrix,

---

35. Hippolytus, *On Christ and the Antichrist* 4; see also the extended metaphor in *Antichrist* 59.

36. For further use of the imagery of weaving as applied to the incarnation, see N. Constas
and M. W. Morgenstern, *Proclus of Constantinople and the Cult of the Virgin in Late Antiquity:
Homilies 1–5, Texts and Translations*, VCSup 66 (Leiden: Brill, 2003).

the womb, of Scripture, that the Word receives flesh from the virgin. The virgin in this case, Hippolytus later affirms following Revelation 12, is the church, who will never cease "bearing from her heart the Word that is persecuted by the unbelieving in the world," while the male child she bears is Christ, God and man, announced by the prophets, "whom the Church continually bears as she teaches all nations."[37]

In and through the images of the church that we have explored—the church as the people of God, the body of Christ, and the temple of the Holy Spirit—together with testimony to the life of the church expressed in the sacraments of baptism and Eucharist, we can perhaps now glimpse more fully what is meant by speaking of the trinitarian dimensions of the church and why it is that the church herself was never a direct subject of theological reflection in the early centuries. The church, as the body of Christ and the temple of the Spirit, incarnates the presence of God in this world, and does so also as the mother of the baptized, in travail with them until their death in confession of Christ, to be raised with him, as the fulfillment of their baptism and the celebration of the Eucharist.

---

37. Hippolytus, *Antichrist* 61.

11

THE RELEVANCE OF GREGORY OF NYSSA'S *AD ABLABIUM* FOR CATHOLIC-ORTHODOX ECUMENICAL DIALOGUE ON THE TRINITY AND THE CHURCH

THOMAS CATTOI

The trinitarian theology of Gregory of Nyssa (335–95) provides useful background for contemporary Catholic-Orthodox conversations about the nature of the church and the exercise of church authority.[1] Gregory's construal of the unity of operations of the three divine persons and his understand-

1. The literature on Gregory of Nyssa is vast; the latest significant addition is Morwenna Ludlow, *Gregory of Nyssa: Ancient and [Post]modern* (Oxford: Oxford University Press, 2012). Other important volumes published in recent years are Michel René Barnes, *The Power of God: Dynamis in Gregory of Nyssa's Trinitarian Theology* (Washington, DC: Catholic University of America Press, 1999); Sarah Coakley, ed., *Rethinking Gregory of Nyssa* (Oxford and Malden, MA: Blackwell, 2003); Martin Laird, *Gregory of Nyssa and the Grasp of Faith: Union, Knowledge, and Divine Presence* (Oxford: Oxford University Press, 2004); Lucian Turcescu, *Gregory of Nyssa and the Concept of Divine Persons* (Oxford: Oxford University Press, 2005); and again by Morwenna Ludlow, *Universal Salvation: Eschatology in the Thought of Gregory of Nyssa and Karl Rahner* (Oxford: Oxford University Press, 2009).

ing of intratrinitarian causality, as seen through one of his shorter works, the letter *Ad Ablabium* (also known as *Quod Non Sint Tres Dei*),[2] may translate into a new paradigm of ecclesial unity and ecclesial primacy-in-communion. As "oppositional" readings of "Eastern" and "Western" approaches have fallen out of favor, it has become more possible to bridge the gap between Catholic-Orthodox dialogue and current scholarship on Gregory of Nyssa. Perhaps, as trinitarian theology lets go of its old conceptual paradigms and moves into uncharted territory, one can hope that new life shall also be breathed into Catholic-Orthodox dialogue on church unity, conciliarity, and authority.

With its challenge to the "traditional" scholarly reading of Western and Eastern trinitarian theology, Michel Barnes's 1995 article on Augustine and the Trinity marked an important turning point in the *Rezeptionsgeschichte* of early Christian thought.[3] For most of the twentieth century, a partial reading of Théodore de Régnon's massive *Études de théologie positive de la Sainte Trinité* had popularized a methodological division between Augustine's preoccupation with God's essence and unity, on one hand, and the Cappadocian fascination with the distinction of the trinitarian persons, on the other.[4] While the actual purpose of de Régnon's study was to highlight a methodological shift between the patristic and the Scholastic era,[5] this reductive interpretation of his work gained enormous popularity: generations of theologians came to accept an oppositional narrative in which Latin theology viewed the persons of the Trinity as a manifestation of God's general nature and used the latter as its starting point, whereas Greek thinkers viewed God's nature as the shared possession of the three hypostases and tended to emphasize the plurality of the divine persons. Barnes's contention in 1995—echoed a few years later by Orthodox theologian David Bentley Hart—was that this kind of dialectical hermeneutics had really succeeded only in obscuring the shared heritage of East and West and perhaps even in fomenting an old-fashioned and sterile opposition between the two traditions.[6] Rather than asking what is the "starting point"—the essence or the person—in the trinitarian theology of particular

2. References to the works of Gregory are from the multivolume Greek edition *Gregorii Nysseni Opera* (*GNO*), ed. Werner Jaeger (Leiden: Brill, 1960–92). The standard English translation by W. Moore and H. A. Wilson is in *NPNF*[2], vol. 5.

3. Michel René Barnes, "Augustine in Contemporary Trinitarian Theology," *TS* 56 (1995): 237–50.

4. Théodore de Régnon, *Études de théologie positive de la Sainte Trinité* (Paris: Victor Retaux, 1892/98).

5. See Lewis Ayres, *Nicaea and Its Legacy: An Approach to Fourth-Century Trinitarian Theology* (Oxford: Oxford University Press, 2004), 302–4.

6. David Bentley Hart, *The Beauty of the Infinite: The Aesthetics of Christian Truth* (Grand Rapids: Eerdmans, 2004), 169–70.

thinkers, what is needed is a retrieval of their overall speculative vision, giving attention to the broader theological context as well as the intended audience of their writings.

In the past few decades, another branch of theology—ecclesiology—has also been marked by an analogous form of oppositional thinking. In the wake of the Second Vatican Council, the Orthodox tradition of relational ecclesiology furnished Catholic theology with a useful conceptual bridge between two distinct paradigms: on the one hand, the older, centripetal approach stressing the universal jurisdiction of the Roman see, and on the other hand, the renewed appreciation of the role of the local churches, which eventually led to the establishment of national episcopal conferences.[7] The schematic version of de Régnon's vision actually provided an apposite prop for this approach: assuming that ecclesiology reflects trinitarian theology, Catholic thinkers saw the purported Augustinian emphasis on the unity of the divine essence as dovetailing with the Roman teaching on universal jurisdiction, whereas some Orthodox apologists saw the well-advertised personalism of the Cappadocians as mirroring the more "democratic" approach of Orthodox ecclesial governance.[8] And indeed, while recent scholarship in the field of trinitarian theology has abandoned the dichotomy between Western essentialism and Eastern pluralism, this oppositional reading appears to survive in ecclesiological conversations: in the same way as the much-praised "social trinitarianism" of the Cappadocians was an antidote to the essentialism of Augustine, the Orthodox tradition of autocephaly becomes the all-healing balm for the poisons of Roman centralism.

This approach continues to echo at the highest levels of ecumenical dialogue between representatives of Eastern and Western Christianity, as is clear from the proceedings of the tenth plenary session of the Joint International Commission for the Theological Dialogue between the Roman Catholic and the Orthodox Churches, which was held in the northern Italian city of Ravenna in 2007.[9] Reflecting the desire of both parts for dialogue and greater mutual

7. See Michael Buckley, *Papal Primacy and the Episcopate: Towards a Relational Understanding* (New York: Crossroad, 1998), 68–74; Archbishop John Quinn, *The Reform of the Papacy: The Costly Call to Christian Unity* (New York: Crossroad, 1999).

8. A balanced presentation of Orthodox ecclesiology can be found in Timothy (Kallistos) Ware, *The Orthodox Church* (Oxford and New York: Penguin, 1997), 239–63. See also Emilianos Timiadis, *Lectures on Orthodox Ecclesiology* (Joensuu, Finland: Joensuu University Publications, 1992).

9. The Joint International Commission for the Theological Dialogue between the Roman Catholic Church and the Orthodox Church was established in 1979 by the Holy See and by fourteen Orthodox churches. The first meeting was held in Patmos and Rhodes in 1980. Following the 2007 meeting in Ravenna, the commission met in Cyprus in 2009 and in Vienna in

understanding, the final declaration that was signed on October 13, 2007, by all conference delegates—save for the representatives of the Russian Patriarchate—chose to present the relationship between different ecclesial communities as an expression of the loving bond between Father, Son, and Holy Spirit, whose unity in difference the followers of Christ are called to imitate.[10] Despite this avowedly irenic character, however, the document appeared reluctant to address questions such as the ecclesiological foundation of church primacy or the ontological relationship of the "first see" with the other churches. In paragraphs 5–6, we are told that the perichoretic exchange of wisdom and love within the Trinity is the ground for the church's dialectic of conciliarity and primacy, and also that the ordering (*taxis*) without inequality that binds the three trinitarian hypostases ought to model the ordering of the local churches within the universal *ekklēsia*. While numerous appreciative references to the "Orthodox" emphasis on plurality in unity show the extent to which this concept is now part of a broader "Catholic" ecclesiology, we are left without clear markers as to the way in which the ecclesial *taxis* is supposed to mirror its trinitarian counterpart. Clearly, ecclesiological reflection is not a self-enclosed branch of theology. Can the much-vaunted "social trinitarianism" of the Cappadocians offer a way out from this ecclesiological impasse?

In her collection of essays titled *Powers and Submissions*, Sarah Coakley challenges many of the scholarly *obiter dicta* about the "Cappadocian" trinitarian model. Coakley sets out to explore a number of sophisticated analytic defenses of the "social" notion of Trinity, showing in the process the impact that this notion has had even outside the boundaries of conventional academic theology.[11] At the same time, she also attempts to chart the gradual emergence of the concept of "person," which she links to the fourth century debates about divine agency, unity, and plurality, and whose trinitarian pedigree continues to be evident even in the world of the Enlightenment and postmodernity. As the Baroque additions of some Roman basilicas cannot conceal the antique foundations that still carry the weight of the building, in the same way the mask of the Cartesian *cogito* cannot suppress the trinitarian lineaments of the Western notion of subjectivity. And yet, despite this noble ancestry, the contemporary notion of "person" is quite different from the notion of hypo-

---

2010; both conferences were devoted to the role of the bishop of Rome in the undivided church of the first millennium.

10. The full text of the Ravenna agreement in English is available on the Vatican website at http://www.vatican.va/roman_curia/pontifical_councils/chrstuni/ch_orthodox_docs/rc_pc _chrstuni_doc_20071013_documento-ravenna_en.html.

11. Sarah Coakley, "'Persons' in the Social Doctrine of the Trinity: Current Analytic Discussion and 'Cappadocian Theology,'" in *Powers and Submissions: Spirituality, Philosophy, and Gender* (Oxford: Blackwell, 2002), 109–29.

stasis deployed by a Gregory or a Basil.[12] When Peter van Inwagen suggests the contrary, and argues that ultimately there is no substantial difference between the Cappadocian notion of subjectivity and its contemporary Cartesian rendition, Coakley cannot but disagree. How could a trinitarian hypostasis be an independent center of subjectivity without turning the Christian God into a community of separate individuals? Surely, van Inwagen's sleight of hand carries the mark of theological irresponsibility, and a different reading of "person" ought to be deployed.[13]

Coakley's criticism is also quite pungent when she turns to Richard Swinburne's overt—apparently too overt—acceptance of a "classical" trinitarian model, a model that closely resembles the traditional "Eastern" approach.[14] Like a number of Orthodox theologians with whom he would otherwise have little in common, Swinburne appears particularly allergic to the Thomist conflation of the trinitarian persons into relationships.[15] But if the notion that *personae sunt ipsae relationes* appears to veer too closely in the direction of modalism, the alternative is no less dangerous, and turning the Godhead into "a closely meshed community of divine individuals" makes the scent of tritheism virtually unbearable. Coakley suggests that the reason for this impasse is that even Swinburne's model of subjectivity is ultimately Cartesian, turning intratrinitarian relations into the relationship of three distinct consciousnesses. Perhaps, she concludes, the unqualified or insufficiently critical adoption by trinitarian theology of contemporary notions of subjectivity and agency (with the attendant preoccupation for autonomy and reflective consciousness) can only have as its upshot a tenuously monotheistic tritheism.

Swinburne elaborates a sophisticated notion of the logical inseparability of the three divine persons, who in good scholastic fashion cooperate in every operation toward the created order: *omnis Trinitatis operatio ad extra indivisa est*. Yet Swinburne's account of divine life is no more capable than van Inwagen's of addressing the thorny question of the conflict of divine wills. While Coakley does not raise this point, some readers will remember the protracted monothelite controversies of the seventh century and the vexed question of

12. Sarah Coakley, "Divine Unity and the Divided Self: Gregory of Nyssa's Trinitarian Theology in Its Psychological Context," in *Rethinking Gregory of Nyssa*, 45–66.

13. Coakley, *Powers and Submissions*, 113. See also Peter van Inwagen, "And Yet They Are Not Three Gods but One God," in *Philosophy and the Christian Faith*, ed. Thomas Morris (Notre Dame, IN: University of Notre Dame Press, 1988).

14. Ibid., 115–16. See also Richard Swinburne, *The Christian God* (Oxford: Oxford University Press, 1994), 25–31.

15. For an interesting article on post–Vatican II Catholic theologians joining Orthodox polemicists in their excoriation of Aquinas, see Bruce Marshall, "*Ex Occidente Lux*? Aquinas and Eastern Orthodox Theology," *Modern Theology* 20, no. 1 (2004): 23–50.

the location of Christ's volitional activity. If the three persons of the Trinity share the same nature, but every person of the Trinity has a distinct will, that would imply that the same nature can carry more than one will, or that God has more than one will, opening the way to the possibility—albeit a highly theoretical one—of an intratrinitarian conflict of volitions. When in his *Disputatio cum Pyrrho* Maximus the Confessor defended the dyothelite position and argued that each of Christ's natures was invested with its own volitional activity, he intended also to safeguard the oneness and uniqueness of the divine will, shared by the Trinity of Father, Son, and Holy Spirit in virtue of their shared divine nature. Locating the seat of volition in the hypostasis, some supporters of monothelitism unwittingly anticipated the Cartesian *cogito*.[16]

For all their conceptual skill and sophistication, van Inwagen and Swinburne would do no better than some of François Lethel's "vulgar monothelites," turning their notion of trinitarian subjectivity into some sort of Trojan horse, reintroducing tritheism into the fortress of the classical doctrine of God.[17] For Coakley, this danger can be averted only by disavowing the multiplication of centers of consciousness within the Godhead and by clarifying that self-consciousness, or self-awareness, is not, and *ought not* to be, the defining characteristic of divine hypostasis. Even David Brown's model, whose distancing from "modern" notions of subjectivity Coakley does not fail to appreciate, ultimately falls short of drawing a satisfactory conceptual boundary between the sui generis notion of divine personhood and its conventional human counterpart.[18] Within each trinitarian person, Brown is willing to countenance self-consciousness as well as consciousness of the other persons, and he turns to Gregory of Nyssa as the first full-fledged instantiation of a "social model" of the Trinity. In this perspective, our human experience of distinct hypostases within the Godhead antedates the intuition of a shared divinity: while the presence of a threefold plurality in God is ontologically indistinct from the reality of a unity, from the cognitive-epistemological point of view there is a distinction, as we may have an inkling of the presence of the Holy Spirit in a charismatic experience, an intimation of the presence

16. See Maximus the Confessor, *Disputatio cum Pyrrho* (PG 91:287–353); according to some monothelites, for whom Christ's only will resided in the divine hypostasis, volition was a characteristic of a particular subjectivity rather than of a nature.

17. François Lethel, *Théologie de l'agonie du Christ: La liberté humaine du fils de Dieu et son importance sotériologique mises en lumière par saint Maxime le Confesseur*, Théologie Historique 52 (Paris: Beauchesne, 1979), 37–46, 86–96.

18. Coakley, *Powers and Submissions*, 115–16. See also David Brown, "Trinitarian Person and Individuality," in *Trinity, Incarnation, and Atonement: Philosophical and Theological Essays*, ed. Ronald J. Feenstra and Cornelius Plantinga (Notre Dame, IN: University of Notre Dame Press, 1989), 48–78.

of the Son as we receive the Eucharist, and an appreciation of the presence of the Father as we contemplate the harmony and purposefulness of the natural order.

While the distinction between the order of knowledge and the order of being may be foreign to Gregory's intention, Coakley's misgivings are not with Brown's genealogical reconstruction of trinitarian theology. Her concerns are more fundamental: Is it not the case perhaps that the very search for a patristic patent for "social" models of the Trinity is ultimately—fundamentally—misguided? Can we really assert that in the theology of Gregory of Nyssa the notion of "person" is the ultimate starting point for any subsequent account of trinitarian plurality? If we turn to Gregory's *Ad Ablabium*, we will be at a loss trying to fit this work into Brown's interpretive categories, which appear to match de Régnon's simplified schema better than the actual text under our eyes. In fact, the goal of this treatise is quite different, and a close parsing of its argument will deliver unexpected insights. What is Gregory trying to achieve in this text, which is only a few pages long and was most likely a part of a longer epistolary exchange?[19]

The Ablabius to whom this letter is addressed appears to be different from the fictional straw-man adversary to whom readers of early Christian literature are accustomed; most likely, he was a real acquaintance of Gregory, someone whose Christian faith did not stray from the bounds of "orthodoxy," but who nonetheless lacked rhetorical and theological training. As a result, he agreed—at least implicitly—with Gregory's understanding of the Trinity, but he was unable to offer an articulate rejoinder to those for whom the notion of three distinct divine persons was incompatible with the assertion of divine uniqueness. In writing this letter, Gregory comes to the aid of Ablabius and indirectly responds to the "adversaries" of the latter—"opponents of the truth," who question the construal of personhood within the Trinity as veering dangerously toward polytheism.[20] Indeed, one of the most controversial aspects of Christian theology is its tendency to resort to analogies drawn from the order of creation and everyday human experience. Is it appropriate, Gregory asks, to ground theological discourse about the Trinity within such a mundane frame of reference? It goes without saying that such analogies always fall short of the reality they describe: the mysteries of divine life and of redemption cannot be captured by the limited resources of human reason. Yet such analogies would at least *make sense* to the majority of the readers, and letting go of them would deprive Christian theology of an important propaedeutic tool.

19. See Gregory of Nyssa, *Ad Ablabium: Quod Non Sint Tres Dei* (*GNO* III.1; *NPNF*[2], vol. 5).
20. Ibid. (*GNO* III.1, 42; *NPNF*[2] 5:331).

Gregory's defense—and his simultaneous critique—of analogical discourse about God rests on the distinction that ordinary speech de facto legitimizes linguistic usages that a more careful consideration would reject as incorrect, or at best misleading. To address Ablabius's concerns, Gregory sets out to explain the relationship between the three trinitarian persons as the relationship between "three men."[21] For some of his critics, any attempt to explain intratrinitarian relationships in this manner is fundamentally misguided, because talk of "three men" refers to three distinct subjects and also because it gives the misleading impression that divine nature could also be divided in the same way as human nature, in this case, gives at least *the impression* of being divided. Gregory responds that one should not confuse the ordinary use of the term "nature" (*physis*) and its strict (technical) use: according to the latter, "natures" (*physeis*) are by definition indivisible, so that human nature, despite appearances to the contrary, is not truly divided among the three different individuals.[22] The strict (technical) use ensures that the analogy of three men may offer an entrée into the divine mystery, where the same divine nature is perichoretically exchanged among the hypostases without any ontological break.

As pointed out by Lewis Ayres in *Nicaea and Its Legacy*, commentators such as G. Christopher Stead insist to this day that Gregory of Nyssa's argument is flawed. However, this claim is ultimately inaccurate, because they fail to appreciate Gregory's distinction between specific linguistic usages.[23] It is true that an analogy based on "common usage" would suggest a tritheist notion of the Godhead; Ablabius's interlocutors would have been fully justified in rejecting it. An analogy based on "strict usage," on the contrary, gestures toward the undivided nature of the Godhead that dwells indistinctly in the Father, the Son, and the Holy Spirit. For the purposes of our argument, however, what matters is that this terminological fine-tuning delivers a severe blow to any naive reading of Gregory as a "social" trinitarian. Gregory does not begin from three persons to ascend to a unity of nature; rather, the unity of nature is presumed all along, and—most interesting of all—the question of divine subjectivity or divine agency in the created order is not even addressed directly. For Gregory, the spectacle of the six days of creation, which is the joint work

21. Ibid. (*GNO* III.1, 42; *NPNF*[2] 5:331–32).
22. Gregory uses the term *physis* for nature, as the Chalcedonian definition would do in 451; later theology would substitute this term with *ousia*. On this terminological and conceptual shift, see Lars Thunberg, *Microcosm and Mediator: The Theological Anthropology of Maximus the Confessor* (Chicago and La Salle, IL: Open Court, 1995), 21–43.
23. Ayres, *Nicaea and Its Legacy*, 349; G. Christopher Stead, "Why Not Three Gods? The Logic of Gregory of Nyssa's Trinitarian Doctrine," in *Studien zu Gregor of Nyssa und die Christlichen Spätantike*, ed. Hubertus R. Drobner and Cristoph Klock (Leiden: Brill, 1990), 149–63.

of the three persons of the Trinity, indicates that one does not even need to resort to hypostatic differentiation to account for the diversity displayed by different instantiations of the same nature.[24] Much as Athanasius's teaching of the *logoi spermatikoi* enabled the bishop of Alexandria to affirm creation's dependency on God and its simultaneous autonomy,[25] Gregory insists that the creative power of the Godhead grounds a plurality of different *physeis* within the natural order, while "the power of their being" (*hē tou einai dynamis*) ensures that these *physeis* blossom into a kaleidoscope of diverse manifestations. If *dynamis*, as opposed to *hypostasis*, is the individuating principle setting a bulldog apart from a cocker spaniel, and if *dynamis* is inscribed within the very structure of being, the source of ontological difference is actually located in the one, undivided *physis*, which observers experience in different forms. For Gregory, the "strict" linguistic usage enables human discourse to reflect God's rooting of plurality in a set of unchanging natures: what applies to the "three men" according to the "strict" usage can safely be applied to the three divine *hypostaseis*.[26]

Gregory's emphasis on the unity of the divine nature against the background of a plurality of manifestations will come as a disappointment to the devotees of "Eastern" social trinitarianism, but the goal of *Ad Ablabium* is more ambitious than a mere rejoinder to the critics of early trinitarian theology. While Gregory emphasizes that the "ordinary" use of language is inadequate to convey the mystery of the Godhead, he is not at all claiming that a "strict" use of particular terms will capture the depths of the divine reality. Rather, what he is suggesting is that a "strict" usage can *at least* hint at, or point to, or gesture toward the living mystery of the Trinity, whose inexhaustible reality no metaphor or analogy can fully convey.

Gregory and his contemporaries were quite familiar with speculative experiments that attributed far too much explanatory power to theological concepts, sometimes even claiming that reasonableness and comprehensibility were the ultimate yardsticks of orthodoxy. For instance, in his treatise *Contra Eunomium*, Basil of Caesarea tells us how Eunomius of Cyzicus (335–93) had effectively attempted to reintroduce Arian subordinationism by suggesting that reason could not possibly countenance any other ontological relationship between the Father and the Son.[27] Similarly, in his

---

24. Indeed, as Ayres points out, Gregory also applies this principle to created natures in his *Apologia in Haexaemeron* (PG 44:92): while different cows or different horses are different instances of the same *physis*, the latter remains one and undivided and does not undergo change.

25. Athanasius of Alexandria, *De Incarnatione* (PG 25b:95–197).

26. Gregory of Nyssa, *Ad Ablabium* (GNO III.1, 42; NPNF[2] 5:331).

27. Basil of Caesarea, *Contra Eunomium* 1.17 (SC 299: 232).

own treatise against Eunomius, Gregory tells us how Eunomius sought to bring the Son to the same level of creation, so as to develop an appropriate theological vocabulary and knowledge "having nothing incomprehensible" about them.[28] The only way to accomplish this goal, however, was to drive an ontological wedge between the Father and the Son: in the words of Eunomius's profession of faith, "There is the supreme and absolute being [the Father] and there is another being existing by reason of the first, but after it, though before all others [the Son]."[29] This was tantamount to a rejection of the Council of Nicaea, and Gregory goes on to state quite clearly that, on the contrary, "there is no kinship between the created order and everything which orthodox doctrine asserts about the Father and Son."[30] The goal of theology is not to turn language into a benchmark for theological truth, but rather to explore the ontological character of the divine mystery and, in the words of Jaroslav Pelikan, acknowledge the extent to which this mystery transcends "not only the rational and philosophical constructs of Classical natural theology, but [also] the revealed and orthodox truth of the church's dogmatic theology."[31]

The radical apophaticism of Gregory guarantees a margin of freedom from the strictures of grammar and rhetoric that might apply to other areas of philosophical speculation. In a move that echoes the fascination with language of his brother Basil,[32] Gregory writes that the Greek term *theos* comes from the verb *theaomai*, "to behold."[33] Gregory sees an intimation of this link in the fact that God oversees the cosmic panoply of heaven and earth, and all of humanity witnesses the joint intervention of the three persons of the Trinity in the unfolding of the divine plan for the cosmos. From a contemporary point of view, this argument could be dismissed as fanciful, but Gregory's argument is theological rather than etymological: while human beings cannot see the one divine nature of the Godhead, they can discern the energies whereby this nature is manifest in the cosmos, energies that take different forms despite their underlying unity. Indeed, according to Gregory, all divine attributes—such as omnipotence or omniscience—ought to be talked about in the singular, as they inhere in the one undivided nature.

---

28. Gregory of Nyssa, *Contra Eunomium* 3.2, 8 (*GNO* II.54).

29. Ibid., 1.151 (*GNO* I.72).

30. Ibid., 3.6, 63 (*GNO* II.208).

31. Jaroslav Pelikan, *Christianity and Classical Culture: The Metamorphosis of Natural Theology in the Christian Encounter with Hellenism* (New Haven: Yale University Press, 1993), 234.

32. See, for instance, Basil of Caesarea, *De Spiritu Sancto* 2.4 (PG 32:68–71, 77–86) about the potential advantages, as well as the dangers, of linguistic analysis for theological reflection.

33. Gregory of Nyssa, *Ad Ablabium* (*GNO* III.1, 43–44; *NPNF*[2] 5:332–33).

Therefore, it would be quite inaccurate to read *Ad Ablabium*—or indeed any other work from the first centuries of the Christian era—through contemporary hermeneutic lenses, hoping to find in it a conceptual and linguistic normativity that it never sought to provide. In a different, but no less remarkable, piece that explores the merits and the limits of the Chalcedonian definition, Sarah Coakley argues that the christological claims of Chalcedon inhabit a dimension that is neither that of naive literalism nor that of pure metaphor or linguistic regulation.[34] For example, the claim that Christ is endowed with two *ousiai* and one *hypostasis* does not offer an exhaustive explanation of what these terms indicate, but merely sets a boundary to what theological reflection may do: rather than demanding a purely intellectual assent, they delineate a space for discussion. In this perspective, the example of the three men at the core of *Ad Ablabium* is a trinitarian ancestor of Chalcedon's later claim; both of them are apophatic markers, pointing toward a divine reality whose epistemological inexhaustibility legitimizes, and effectively invites, further theological discussion.[35] In Gregory's trinitarian analogy, our human experience of the joint operation of the three divine persons may reveal God's ultimate unity no less than it reveals his threefold reality, but as Gregory himself warns us in *Contra Eunomium*, "if one searches the whole of revelation, nowhere shall one find a doctrine of the divine nature."[36] The analogy of the three men does not warrant the assertion of three distinct Cartesian individualities and even chooses to be silent about the nature of the divine *ousia* or the constitutive features of the hypostases.

One may echo Gregory's sentiments by noting that if one searches the whole of Scripture and tradition, one will not find a doctrine of the church—or perhaps one will find an overwhelming number of such doctrines, leaving us at a loss for a common starting point. The Ravenna document notes that "in his divine economy, God wills that His church should have a structure oriented towards salvation" (16) and that the dialectic of conciliarity and authority is actualized in a threefold manner: at the local level, where the church of God is gathered together in the Eucharist (17); at the regional level, where catholicity "manifests itself in communion with the other Churches which confess the same apostolic faith and share the same basic ecclesial structure" (22); and finally,

34. Sarah Coakley, "What Does Chalcedon Solve and What Does It Not? Some Reflections on the Status and Meaning of the Chalcedonian 'Definition,'" in *The Incarnation: An Interdisciplinary Symposium on the Incarnation of the Son of God*, ed. Stephen T. Davis, Daniel Kendall, SJ, and Gerald O'Collins, SJ (Oxford: Oxford University Press, 2002), 143–63.

35. Whether Gregory's approach dovetails with the Palamite teaching on the utter cognitive inaccessibility of the divine essence is a question that goes beyond the purview of this essay.

36. Gregory of Nyssa, *Contra Eunomium* 2.106 (*GNO* I, 257–58).

at the universal level, where the catholicity of the church "embraces not only the diversity of human communities but also their fundamental unity" (32). Authority must be considered "in the context of conciliarity," and conciliarity in the context of authority (or primacy) (43). In this perspective, it appears that the different regional churches would embrace and order the endless variety of the local churches, and in turn they would constitute the universal church, thereby functioning like the three different trinitarian persons, in whom the one undivided *ousia* incessantly flows. The acceptance on the part of Roman Catholic, as well as Orthodox, representatives of this conceptual presentation of the church—a multilayered coinherence of unity and diversity—signals the extent to which oppositional ecclesiologies, rather like their trinitarian counterparts, are being increasingly consigned to the past. The different churches are not independent (Cartesian?) subjects; they are distinct manifestations of the one *ekklēsia*. The question remains, however, as to the ordering principle that will ground the different churches within a perichoretically enriching *taxis*. As with "social" theologies of the Trinity, the tendency to interpret the Orthodox understanding of the church in "social" terms turns the one church into a plurality of distinct entities without an explicit center of unity. And if the alleged "social trinitarianism" of the Cappadocians has been weighed and found wanting, where should one look for a new structural paradigm?[37]

We mentioned earlier how Gregory of Nyssa presented *dynamis*, as opposed to the three hypostases, as the ontological springboard that made the mystery of the Trinity cognitively accessible to humanity. The construal of inner-trinitarian causality within the Godhead that is outlined in *Ad Ablabium* insists that the divine nature is inherently diffusive: as in the *Enneads* of Plotinus the One is an ultimately dynamic power without which nothing could exist,[38] and as every nature will be accompanied by an energy in the theology of Maximus the Confessor,[39] according to Gregory God's very nature permeates the cosmos through its incessant activity *ad extra*.[40] Could one find an analogous ecclesiological principle, whereby the church expresses its salvific activity in the world? One possible answer is given by Nicholas Afanassieff in his celebrated essay "The Church Which Presides in Love," where he points out that "the *concors*

---

37. See again Coakley's critique of van Inwagen in *Powers and Submissions*, 113; also John Gresham, "The Social Model of the Trinity and Its Critics," *Scottish Journal of Theology* 46 (1993): 325–43.

38. See Plotinus, *Ennead* 3.8, in *The Enneads: Abridged Edition*, ed. John Dillon, trans. Stephen MacKenna (Oxford and New York: Penguin, 1991), 233–51.

39. See, for instance, Maximus the Confessor, *Ambigua* 26 (PG 91:1268ab). This theme in the theology of Maximus is the subject of Vasilios Karayiannis, *Maxime le Confesseur: Essence et energies de Dieu*, Théologie historique 63 (Paris: Beauchesne, 1993).

40. Gregory of Nyssa, *Ad Ablabium* (GNO III.1, 44; NPNF² 5:333).

numerositas of the bishops is naturally manifested in the councils, where their concord should find means of expression." According to the Russian theologian, only in the councils does the plurality of the different churches come together in articulating the common faith of the one church—that faith that alone opens the way to eternal life.[41] The Ravenna agreement, for its part, notes that "synods" are governed by the principle of concord (*homonoia*) and that this principle is signified by eucharistic celebration (26). To echo Gregory's notion of the shared activity of the three divine persons, one could argue that the joint celebration of the liturgy by the different churches constitutes the primary *dynamis*, or power, whereby the unity of the church is manifested. In the same way as certain events in the history of salvation appear to be primarily associated with one of the divine persons even as all three hypostases are involved in the economy of salvation, so will a particular church be directly involved in spreading the gospel in a particular region at a particular moment in history, even if the faith that it professes is the faith of the universal church. The deeper mystery of the church may forever escape our understanding, but the salvific power of the Eucharist will be available even to the least and most humble members of the Christian community.

An Orthodox ecclesiological treatise mirroring the epistle *Ad Ablabium* could thus be titled *Why There Are Not Fourteen Churches* and could distinguish a "strict" from a "common" usage of the term "church."[42] The former usage would underscore the fundamental ontological unity of this reality, whereas the latter usage would refer to the local manifestations of this unity, which in common parlance could even be said to be distinct, like the three men of Gregory's analogy. Yet, theologically, it is the strict sense that comes closer to capturing the mystery of the church: local ecclesial communities are not independent, ontologically distinct institutions; rather, they express the one, undivided *ekklēsia*, whose goal is the ultimate salvation of humanity. The Ravenna agreement emphasizes the unity of the church in paragraphs 32–33, where the text states that "the same unique Eucharist is celebrated everywhere," and that "no local church can celebrate the Eucharist in willful separation from other local Churches without seriously affecting ecclesial community." Indeed, it is because of the salvific power of the Eucharist and of the other sacraments that the churches (34) are called to issue precise directives concerning their celebration: "canonical rules and disciplinary norms" are absolutely necessary.

41. See Nicholas Afanassieff, "The Church Which Presides in Love," in *The Primacy of Peter*, ed. John Meyendorff (Crestwood, NY: St. Vladimir's Seminary Press, 1992), 100–101.
42. There are presently fourteen autocephalous Orthodox churches, though disagreements exist as to whether more churches should be included. See Ware, *Orthodox Church*, 5–7.

Considering this need for an explicit exercise of authority, Afanassieff distinguishes a church that "presides in love" within the *homonoia* of the different ecclesial communities—a church whose primacy does not rest on a legal notion of jurisdiction, but rather on an organic understanding of universal ecclesiology.[43] In the words of the Ravenna agreement, the universal church is a body in which different members possess different charismas, but since the church with all its members participates in the *exousia* of the crucified Lord (14), it is possible to say that each individual church demands and expects obedience from all other churches. How is this going to play out in practice? The exercise of ecclesial authority must clearly be different from the exercise of political power: it is "a gift of the Holy Spirit destined for the service [*diakonia*] of the community" (13), and "this authority cannot subsist in the church except in the love between the one who exercises it and those subject to it" (14). Yet if one scours the document for any further suggestion, one is left with the anodyne claim that "while the fact of primacy at the universal level is accepted by both East and West, there are differences of understanding with regard to the manner in which it is to be exercised, and also with regard to its scriptural and theological foundation" (43.2). And of course, while the Roman see occupied the first place in the *taxis* of the undivided church, considerable disagreements remain as to the prerogatives as *prōtos* of the bishop of Rome.

Once more, Gregory can offer a way out of this impasse. If one turns to the letter *Ad Ablabius*, Gregory's reflections on the role of the Father may serve as model for an understanding of church primacy that does not wound the ontological equality of the different ecclesial communities or their equal eucharistic dignity in the world. As they analyze Gregory's trinitarian theology, both Michel Barnes and Lewis Ayres observe that transcendental divine causality *ad extra* affects the three divine hypostases indistinctly: we know by now that there is only one divine power that is intrinsic to the divine nature, even if sometimes the Son is called the *dynamis* of the Father by way of appropriation.[44] The centrifugal dynamics of the economic Trinity, however, do not necessarily mirror the inner dynamics of the immanent Trinity. Within the latter, the power or action of God "issues from the Father as from a spring, is brought into operation by the Son, and finally perfects its grace by the Spirit."

---

43. See Afanassieff, "Church Which Presides in Love," 126–27. In the same piece, Afanassieff claims that "universal ecclesiology, so prevalent in modern theology, is not really primitive. It came to replace Eucharistic ecclesiology, which was the only one known in early days" (140–41).

44. See Barnes, *Power of God*, chap. 7 ("Gregory of Nyssa on the Unity of Nature and Power"), 260–78; Ayres, *Nicaea and Its Legacy*, 354–55 (where Ayres notes that Gregory's vocabulary includes the terms *physis* and *dynamis*, but also *energeia*, which would become more common in post-Chalcedonian theology).

This hierarchical *taxis* indicates that the distinction between hypostases is not erased but is actually a necessary presupposition of the joint activity of the Trinity toward creation.[45]

This distinction is analogous to the dual order of causality found in Gregory of Nazianzus's trinitarian orations: the Godhead as a whole is the *aitia* (cause or source) of divine agency toward the world, but the hypostasis of the Father is also the intratrinitarian *aitia*, the source of the Trinity that forever coexists with the Son and the Holy Spirit.[46] If this concept were applied to the "church that presides in love," this church would be ontologically equal to all other churches in eucharistic dignity, but it would also be the foundation of the inner-ecclesial order. While all churches would enjoy equal dignity in their interaction with the outside world, the first see would order the relations between the different ecclesial communities forming the universal church, with the deification of humanity as the overarching goal. Of course, as the Latin Scholastics would say, *dissimilitudo semper maior*: if there is the analogy between the intratrinitarian subordination of Son and Spirit to the Father and the intraecclesial subordination of all local churches to the presiding see, there is no perfect symmetry in the two sets of relationships. While the Father is the source whence the Son and the Spirit proceed, the "church that presides in love"—perhaps providentially so!—is not the ontological source of local and regional churches. Yet, despite this fundamental difference, this intratrinitarian model of causality could translate into an ecclesiological paradigm (or perhaps an ecclesiological *horos*, to use a Chalcedonian term),[47] within which old ecumenical concerns could be reevaluated and rethought.

The Ravenna agreement of 2007 between the Catholic and the Orthodox churches testified to the remarkable progress of ecumenical dialogue in the decades following the Second Vatican Council, while also encapsulating the enduring difficulties that thwart its progress. A reading of Gregory of Nyssa's *Ad Ablabium* in light of the recent conceptual shifts in trinitarian theology may actually offer some constructive suggestions to help Catholic-Orthodox dialogue move beyond the current ecclesiological impasse. Gregory of Nyssa's emphasis on the Trinity's activity *ad extra* by way of an undivided *dynamis* can encourage a new approach to ecclesiology whose starting point would no longer be the vexed dialectic between local and universal forms, but rather

---

45. Gregory of Nyssa, *Ad Ablabium* (GNO III.1, 55–57; NPNF[2] 5:334–36).

46. See, for instance, Gregory of Nazianzus, *Oration* 31.33 (PG 36:172); Richard Cross, "Divine Monarchy in Gregory of Nazianzos," *JEastCS* 14, no. 1 (2006): 105–16.

47. Playing on the etymological connection between *horos* and horizon, Sarah Coakley reminds us in "What Does Chalcedon Solve and What Does It Not?" (162–63) that a doctrinal definition determines the horizon of our understanding but cannot capture the mystery to which it refers.

the church's sanctifying activity that is manifested in the celebration of the Eucharist. At the same time, Gregory's understanding of the Father as ontologically equal to the Son and the Spirit and as simultaneously the inner cause of the Trinity can model a notion of church where catholicity is shared by all the churches in a perichoretic exchange of love, even as the church that "presides in love" is invested with authority over all other ecclesial communities. Perhaps the demise of the oppositional trinitarian paradigm rightly—or wrongly—ascribed to de Régnon will help bring about a turning point in ecclesiological reflection, whose lynchpin will no longer be the tiresome contrast between Eastern autocephaly and Roman centralism, but the ordered unity of all churches grounded in the sanctifying power of the Eucharist.

12

SYRIAC CHRISTIAN TRADITION AND GENDER IN TRINITARIAN THEOLOGY

KATHLEEN McVEY

In this essay I address some rather large questions about gender with re-spect to trinitarian theology and the role of the Syriac tradition in that discourse. I do so in part by closer examination of the trinitarian language and theology of the fourth-century Syriac theologian Ephrem the Syrian. I hope my remarks will be helpful to a wide audience of persons of faith engaged in questions about trinitarian theology and liturgical invocation, including those who consider the Trinity under the names Father, Son, and Holy Spirit and those who—so erroneously from the fourth-century patristic view as well as for many of their modern defenders, yet so engagingly from the viewpoint of some feminist Christians—consider the persons under the names Creator, Redeemer, and Sustainer. Indeed, those who treat the question under yet other formulations that deliberately avoid male metaphors may find that Ephrem's thought advances their understanding of the Trinity.[1] I propose that the retrieval

---

1. The rationale for reformulating trinitarian language in liturgical contexts, major proposals, their shortcomings, and the general feminist consensus for using a multiplicity of names and metaphors are succinctly discussed in Marjorie Procter-Smith, *In Her Own Rite: Constructing Feminist Liturgical Tradition* (Nashville: Abingdon, 1990), 85–115. For the impact of feminism

of female metaphors for God that appear in Ephrem's hymns can both enrich our understanding of the Trinity and provide further resources for liturgical use. My essay has five unequal parts. It begins with a brief synopsis of feminist engagement with trinitarian theology—a complex historical process from which I will lift up a few key moments.[2] Part 2 sketches the way in which this larger discussion has engaged Syriac tradition in general and its foremost fourth-century representative, Ephrem. Part 3 situates Ephrem's trinitarian theology within the larger trinitarian discussion, noting especially Lewis Ayres's treatment of Ephrem among the "pro-Nicene" theologians of the fourth century. Part 4 surveys Ephrem's use of female theological metaphor and observes a few specific points of contact with Gregory of Nazianzus and Gregory of Nyssa. The essay ends with some remarks about the significance of these points of convergence.

1. The Place of Gender in Recent Discussions of Early Christian Trinitarian Doctrine

Mid-twentieth-century American feminist critiques of trinitarian language began with Mary Daly's *Beyond God the Father*.[3] In that book she contended that the religious affirmation that God is more appropriately described in male rather than female terms—however subtle or nuanced it may be—denigrates

on liturgy, see Procter-Smith, "Feminist Ritual Strategies: The *Ekklēsia Gynaikōn* at Work," in *Toward a New Heaven and New Earth: Essays in Honor of Elisabeth Schüssler Fiorenza*, ed. Fernando F. Segovia (Maryknoll, NY: Orbis, 2003), 498–515; for ongoing issues, see Procter-Smith, "Feminist Interpretation and Liturgical Proclamation," in *Searching the Scriptures*, vol. 1, *A Feminist Introduction*, ed. Elisabeth Schüssler Fiorenza (New York: Crossroad, 1993), 313–25; Satoko Yamaguchi, "Father Image of G*d and Inclusive Language: A Reflection in Japan," in Segovia, ed., *Toward a New Heaven*, 199–224; Christie Cozad Neuger, "Image and Imagination: Why Inclusive Language Matters," in *Engaging the Bible in a Gendered World: An Introduction to Feminist Biblical Interpretation in Honor of Katharine Doob Sakenfeld*, ed. Linda Day and Carolyn Pressler (Louisville: Westminster John Knox, 2006), 153–65; for critique from the perspective of narrative theology, cf. Kathryn Greene-McCreight, *Feminist Reconstructions of Christian Doctrine: Narrative Analysis and Appraisal* (New York: Oxford University Press, 2000), 111–27; for an argument for a different theological method, see Francis Schüssler Fiorenza, "From Interpretation to Rhetoric: The Feminist Challenge to Systematic Theology," in *Walk in the Ways of Wisdom: Essays in Honor of Elisabeth Schüssler Fiorenza*, ed. Shelly Matthews et al. (Harrisburg, PA: Trinity Press International, 2013), 17–45.

2. For a brief narrative of the general development of feminist theology, see Rosemary Ruether, "The Emergence of Christian Feminist Theology," in *The Cambridge Companion to Feminist Theology*, ed. Susan Frank Parsons (Cambridge: Cambridge University Press, 2002), 3–22; more fully, Ruether, *Women and Redemption: A Theological History*, 2nd ed. (Minneapolis: Fortress, 2012). On feminist engagement with trinitarian doctrine per se, see n. 22 below.

3. Mary Daly, *Beyond God the Father: Toward a Philosophy of Women's Liberation* (Boston: Beacon Press, 1973).

women. She encapsulated this fundamental argument in her declaration, "If God is male, then the male is God."[4] In her subsequent book, *Gyn/Ecology*, she harshly parodied accepted trinitarian doctrine, alluding to the Augustinian emphasis on the mutual love of the three persons: "It is 'sublime' (and therefore disguised) erotic male homosexual *mythos*, the perfect all-male marriage, the ideal all-male family, the best boys' club, the model monastery, the supreme Men's Association, the mold for all varieties of male monogender mating."[5] Thus she disposed of one of the classic treatments of trinitarian theology with a characteristic, cutting witticism—now a very politically *in*correct remark—how time flies!

Daly's essential point was far from trivial. She raised the question whether there is some sense in which the three "persons" of the Christian Trinity are best conceptualized as male rather than female. Their traditional naming as Father, Son, and Holy Spirit suggests an affirmative answer, at least for the first two. That, in turn, raises implications for women's status as fully human, the topic of theological anthropology, correlated with the presence of the *imago dei* in all human beings, male and female.[6] In the years since Daly's opening

---

4. Ibid., 19.

5. Daly, *Gyn/Ecology: The Metaethics of Radical Feminism, with a New Intergalactic Introduction by the Author* (Boston: Beacon Press, 1990; originally published 1978), 38. Daly's analysis stands out for its directness and clarity, with the result that she is consistently cited not only in feminist studies of religion but also in feminist theory, feminist philosophy, and feminist literary studies. Unsympathetic accounts also recognize Daly's leadership. For example, Manfred Hauke (*God or Goddess? Feminist Theology: What Is It? Where Does It Lead?*, trans. David Kipp [San Francisco: Ignatius Press, 1995], 52–53, 78–86) follows the equally hostile observer Ingeborg Hauschildt in dubbing Daly "the 'foster mother' of feminist theology." Of course, these views may be motivated by the ancient convention of tracing heresy to one wicked leader who falls away from the truth!

6. This has become a central theme of feminist theology; see, for example, Rosemary R. Ruether, *Sexism and God-Talk: Toward a Feminist Theology*, 2nd ed. (Boston: Beacon, 1993), 18–20, 93–115, and passim; Elisabeth Schüssler Fiorenza, *Jesus: Miriam's Child, Sophia's Prophet; Critical Issues in Feminist Christology* (New York: Continuum, 1995), 43–49; Rosemary R. Ruether, *Women and Redemption*, 6, 19–24, and passim (see index s.v. "Image of God, in humans"). A recent broad treatment of this theme is Michelle A. Gonzalez, *Created in God's Image: An Introduction to Feminist Theological Anthropology* (Maryknoll, NY: Orbis, 2007). On *imago dei* in patristic sources, see Kari Elisabeth Børresen, *Subordination and Equivalence: The Nature and Role of Women in Augustine and Thomas Aquinas*, trans. Charles H. Talbot (Washington, DC: University Press of America, 1981; trans. from rev. ed. of *Subordination et Équivalence: Nature et rôle de la femme d'après Augustin et Thomas d'Aquin* [Oslo and Paris: Universitetsforlaget, 1968]); Verna E. F. Harrison, "Male and Female in Cappadocian Theology," *JTS* 41 (1990): 441–71; Kari Elisabeth Børresen, "God's Image, Man's Image? Patristic Interpretation of Gen. 1,27 and 1 Cor. 11,7," in *The Image of God: Gender Models in Judaeo-Christian Tradition*, ed. Kari Elisabeth Børresen (Oslo: Solum Forlag, 1991), 188–207; Børresen, "In Defence of Augustine: How *femina* Is *homo*," "Artistic 'Feminism' in the Case of Augustine," "Gender and Exegesis in the Latin Fathers," and "La féminologie d'Augustin," in *From Patristics to*

salvo against the male bias of Christian theological discourse, feminist Christian theologians have pursued various paths toward solving the dilemma she posed. Here I will consider a few forks in those paths where early Christian literature beyond the New Testament—in other words, patristic literature—comes into play.

First, Elaine Pagels argued for the greater openness of Valentinian and other so-called gnostic Christians to understanding divine persons under female gender categories.[7] In vivid descriptions drawn from the Nag Hammadi texts, she painted a memorable picture of female powers asserting themselves over their male underlings. Who can forget her portrayal of the scenario from the basic gnostic myth? When Ialdabaoth, a thinly disguised alter ego for Yahweh, asserts, "I am father, and God, and above me there is no one," he is brusquely reproached by his mother, the erstwhile fallen Sophia, "Do not lie, Ialdabaoth!"[8] In Pagels's view it was not Christianity but the orthodox suppression of diversity that produced the exclusively male company of the Trinity. Despite critiques, this view has been embraced and repeated often, so that the role and power of Sophia in the basic Valentinian myth has become a staple of the feminist strand of the study of religion.[9]

Second, responses from scholars in the fields of biblical studies and early Christian history and literature were not long in coming. They observed that the figure of Sophia, the personified divine Wisdom, appears in the Wisdom

---

Matristics: Selected Articles on Christian Gender Models (Rome: Herder, 2002), 15–89; E. Ann Matter, "Christ, God, and Women in the Thought of St. Augustine," in *Augustine and His Critics: Essays in Honor of Gerald Bonner*, ed. Robert Dodaro and George Lawless (New York: Routledge, 2000), 164–75; Nonna Verna Harrison, "Women, Human Identity, and the Image of God: Antiochene Interpretations," *JECS* 9 (2001): 206–49.

7. Elaine H. Pagels, "God the Father/God the Mother," in *The Gnostic Gospels* (New York: Random House, 1979), 48–69.

8. Pagels, *Gnostic Gospels*, 58, quoting from Irenaeus, *Against Heresies* 1.30.6, perhaps Irenaeus's rhetorical expansion of the account in *Apocryphon of John* 13.8–14.

9. For example, Ruether, *Sexism and God-Talk*, 34–35; Elizabeth A. Johnson, *She Who Is: The Mystery of God in Feminist Theological Discourse* (New York: Crossroad, 1992), 102, 173; for brief critiques see Kathleen McVey, "Gnosticism, Feminism, and Elaine Pagels," in *Theology Today* 37 (1981): 498–501; Greene-McCreight, *Feminist Reconstructions*, 89–91; see full exposition of the issues in Karen L. King, ed., *Images of the Feminine in Gnosticism* (Philadelphia: Fortress, 1988); more recently, Anne McGuire, "Thunder, Perfect Mind"; Ingvild Sælid Gilhus, "Trimorphic Protennoia"; Karen L. King, "The Book of Norea, Daughter of Eve"; Pheme Perkins, "The Gospel of Thomas"; Karen L. King, "The Gospel of Mary Magdalene"; and Deirdre Good, "Pistis Sophia," in *Searching the Scriptures*, vol. 2, *A Feminist Commentary*, ed. Elisabeth Schüssler Fiorenza (New York: Crossroad, 1994), 39–85, 535–60, 601–34, 678–707. As the ordering of materials in *Searching the Scriptures* reflects, the category "gnostic" has increasingly been challenged and dismissed; see, for example, Michael A. Williams, *Rethinking "Gnosticism": An Argument for Dismantling a Dubious Category* (Princeton: Princeton University Press, 1996).

literature of the Hebrew Bible.[10] They claimed, and emphasized, that she was more important than a mere rhetorical construct—that she was, indeed, the "female *Gestalt*" of the God of Israel.[11] These scholars have then gone on to trace, and defend the importance of, her role in the background of the Gospels and in the imagination of Jesus, showing as well that the figure of Wisdom was significant for Paul, especially as he delineated his Christology.[12]

This has led modern scholars, as it did their second- and third-century patristic counterparts, to the role of Sophia in emergent trinitarian thought as the counterpart, on the one hand, to Logos and, on the other hand, to the Spirit. Portrayals of Jesus as nursing mother have also been recognized as assimilations of Jesus to the Wisdom figure in all her metaphoric richness. Clement of Alexandria's famous hymn and *Odes of Solomon* 19 have most often been cited.[13] A narrow but clearly defined thread of patristic scriptural

10. Athalya Brenner and Carol Fontaine, eds., *Wisdom and Psalms: A Feminist Companion to the Bible*, Second Series (Sheffield: Sheffield Academic Press, 1998); Silvia Schroer, "The Book of Sophia," in Schüssler Fiorenza, *Searching the Scriptures*, 2:17–38; Carole R. Fontaine, "Proverbs," and Sarah J. Tanzer, "Wisdom of Solomon," in *The Women's Bible Commentary*, expanded edition, ed. Carol Ann Newsom and Sharon Ringe (Louisville: Westminster John Knox, 1998), 151–60, 293–97; Linda Day, "Wisdom and the Feminine in the Hebrew Bible," in Day and Pressler, *Engaging the Bible*, 114–27. The canonicity of some of this literature is subject to the Protestant-Catholic divide, resting ultimately on differences between the Masoretic text and the Septuagint.

11. The use of terms and notions drawn from psychological theory was initiated by Joan Chamberlain Engelsman, who introduced a Jungian framework for her tracing of Sophia from the wisdom literature, through Philo, into early patristic literature in *The Feminine Dimension of the Divine* (Philadelphia: Westminster, 1979; rev. eds. Wilmette, IL: Chiron, 1987, 1994). Susan Cole, Marian Ronan, and Hal Taussig, *Wisdom's Feast: Sophia in Study and Celebration*, rev. ed. (Kansas City, MO: Sheed and Ward, 1996; based on the same authors' *Sophia: The Future of Feminist Spirituality* [San Francisco: Harper & Row, 1986]) link the biblical materials to feminist theology and worship. Adopting the term *gestalt* without the Jungian framework, and integrating Sophia into feminist New Testament scholarship, are Elisabeth Schüssler Fiorenza, *In Memory of Her: A Feminist Theological Reconstruction of Christian Origins*, 2nd ed. (London: SCM, 1995; originally New York: Crossroad, 1983), 130–40, and Elizabeth Johnson, *She Who Is*.

12. See, for example, Schüssler Fiorenza, *Jesus: Miriam's Child*, 131–62; M. Jack Suggs, *Wisdom, Christology, and Law in Matthew's Gospel* (Cambridge, MA: Harvard University Press, 1970); Gordon D. Fee, *Pauline Christology: An Exegetical-Theological Study* (Peabody, MA: Hendrickson, 2007); but cf. Luise Schottroff, "The Sayings Source Q," in Schüssler Fiorenza, ed., *Searching the Scriptures*, 2:510–34, esp. 525–34.

13. On Clement, see Ritamary Bradley, "Patristic Background of the Motherhood Similitude in Julian of Norwich," *CSR* (1978): 101–13; Børresen, "L'usage de metaphors féminines dans le discours sur Dieu," in Børresen, *From Patristics to Matristics*, 93–108; on these texts and Isis, see Gail Paterson Corrington, "The Milk of Salvation: Redemption by the Mother in Late Antiquity and Early Christianity," *HTR* 82 (1989): 393–420; on Clement of Alexandria's joining of Logos and Sophia, see Kathleen E. McVey, "In Praise of Sophia: The Witness of Tradition," in *Women, Gender, and Christian Community*, ed. Jane Dempsey Douglass and James F. Kay (Louisville: Westminster John Knox, 1997), 34–45; Johnson, *She Who Is*, 94–100, 194, alludes to

interpretation leads from these toward the now familiar Western medieval piety of Jesus as mother.[14] A similar strand in the East leads eventually also to Sophia as the immanence of God in creation.[15]

Third, theologians have explored female dimensions of the Holy Spirit.[16] One *logion* from the *Gospel according to the Hebrews* in which Jesus calls the Holy Spirit his mother was quoted with some deference by both Origen and Jerome. Origen remarks: "But if someone accepts the Gospel according to the Hebrews, where the Savior himself says, 'My mother the Holy Spirit took me just now by one of my hairs and carried me off to the great mountain Thabor,' he will question how the 'mother' of Christ can be 'the Holy Spirit' which was made through the Word."[17] In his *Commentary on Isaiah*, Jerome cites the same saying in slightly truncated form: "The Lord says, 'Just now my mother, the Holy Spirit, carried me.'"[18] Both writers puzzle over the epithet, and

this process more generally. On the *Odes of Solomon*, see Susan Ashbrook Harvey, "The Odes of Solomon," in Schüssler Fiorenza, *Searching the Scriptures*, 2:86–98.

14. Bradley's concise but groundbreaking article ("Patristic Background") is remarkably comprehensive, yet it has been infrequently cited; see esp. 103–9. Much better known and more fully developed for the medieval period is the work of Caroline Bynum, "Jesus as Mother and Abbot as Mother: Some Themes in Twelfth-Century Cistercian Writing," in *Jesus as Mother: Studies in the Spirituality of the High Middle Ages* (Berkeley: University of California Press, 1982), 110–69.

15. John Meyendorff, "Wisdom-Sophia: Contrasting Approaches to a Complex Theme," in *Studies on Art and Archeology in Honor of Ernst Kitzinger on His Seventy-Fifth Birthday*, ed. William Tronzo and Irving Lavin, Dumbarton Oaks Papers 41 (Washington, DC: Dumbarton Oaks Research Library, 1987), 391–401.

16. For example, Johnson, *She Who Is*, 124–49; Robert Murray, *Symbols of Church and Kingdom: A Study in Early Syriac Tradition* (London: T&T Clark, 2006), 312–20; P. J. Jacob, "The Motherhood of the Holy Spirit," *Journal of Dharma* 5 (1980): 160–74; Sebastian Brock, "The Holy Spirit as Feminine in Early Syriac Literature," in *After Eve: Women, Theology, and the Christian Tradition*, ed. Janet Martin Soskice (London: Marshall Pickering, 1990), 73–88; and Susan Ashbrook Harvey, "Feminine Imagery for the Divine: The Holy Spirit, the Odes of Solomon, and Early Syriac Tradition," *SVTQ* 37 (1993): 111–39.

17. Origen, *Commentary on John* 2.12 (E. Preuschen, ed., *Der Johanneskommentar*, *Origenes Werke* 4, GCS [Leipzig: Hinrichs'sche Buchhandlung, 1903], 67:19–23; trans. Ronald E. Heine, *Origen: Commentary on the Gospel according to John Books 1–10*, FC 80 [Washington, DC: Catholic University of America Press, 1989], 116).

18. *In Isaiam* 11.24.77–78: *Sed et in euangelio quod iuxta Hebraeos scriptum Nazarei lectitant, dominus loquitur: <<Modo me tulit mater mea, spiritus sanctus>>*. Roger Gryson and P.-A. Deproost, eds., *Commentaires de Jérôme sur le Prophete Isaie*, Aus der Geschichte der lateinischen Bibel 30 (Freiburg: Herder, 1996), 2:1246. On the other citations by Origen and Jerome of this saying, on further fragments of Jewish-Christian gospels, and on unresolved issues in the scholarship, see Philipp Vielhauer and Georg Strecker, "The Gospel of the Hebrews," in *New Testament Apocrypha*, vol. 1, *Gospels and Related Writings*, ed. Wilhelm Schneemelcher, trans. R. McL. Wilson (Louisville: Westminster John Knox, 1991), 134–78, esp. 172–78, and Bart D. Ehrman and Zlatko Pleše, eds., "The Gospel according to the Hebrews," in *The Apocryphal Gospels: Texts and Translations* (New York: Oxford University Press, 2011), 196–221, 197–200, 216–21.

each finds a solution that avoids embracing the maternal Holy Spirit without entirely dismissing the witness of this gospel. Origen opines that

> it is not difficult to interpret these words also as follows. If he who does "the will of the Father in heaven is" his "brother and sister and mother," and the expression "brother of Christ" is applicable, not only to the human race, but also to beings which are more divine than the human race, it will not be strange at all for the Holy Spirit to be his "mother," since every woman is called the "mother of Christ" because she does the will of the Father in heaven.[19]

Jerome quotes this *logion* in the midst of a complicated typological exegesis that involves the application of birthing metaphors to Christ and his apostles as well as the feminine gender of "Holy Spirit" in Hebrew. He chooses a grammatical argument to extricate himself. The fact that the word "spirit" is feminine in Hebrew, but masculine in Latin and neuter in Greek, he observed, should remind us that God has no gender—*in divinitate enim nullus est sexus*.[20] He does not go on to muse on its Syriac cognate *ruha*, nor does he consider how the idea of the Holy Spirit as Mother might transform theological discourse! Modern scholars have remedied this deficit, pointing out the image of the Holy Spirit as Mother especially in early Syriac Christianity. We will look more closely at this in a moment.

Fourth, one response to the problem of the absence of female theological imagery in Christian trinitarian theology is the insistence that God has no gender. Jerome has already been mentioned in this regard, but it is the Cappadocians to whom we must turn for a more consistent and thorough enunciation of this principle. Basil of Caesarea, Gregory of Nazianzus, and Gregory of Nyssa all assert that God is neither male nor female. All three link this observation to exegesis of the crucial passages regarding *imago dei* and the equality of men and women in Christ (esp. Gen. 1:27; Col. 3:11; Gal. 3:28), as Verna Harrison has shown.[21]

A few feminist theologians have undertaken comprehensive treatments of trinitarian development.[22] Catherine LaCugna, for example, drew on some of

---

19. Origen, *Comm. John* 2.12 (Preuschen, 67:22–29), trans. Heine, 117.

20. Jerome, *In Isaiam* 11.24.77–81 (Gryson-Deproost 1246). In Jerome's Latin the Hebrew for Holy Spirit is *ruha codsa*. Whether or not he considers the *Gospel according to the Hebrews* to be authentic, he appears, like Origen, to "treat it with respect"; for this assessment regarding Origen, see Ronald E. Heine, *Origen: Scholarship in the Service of the Church* (Oxford: Oxford University Press, 2010), 36–37. This passage is also cited and discussed by Murray, *Symbols of Church and Kingdom*, 313–14; by Børresen, "L'usage de metaphors féminines," 104–5; by Brock, "Holy Spirit as Feminine," 73; and by Harvey, "Feminine Imagery for the Divine," 121.

21. Harrison, "Male and Female in Cappadocian Theology," esp. 441–42, 456–57, 467.

22. Short surveys of feminist theologies in relation to trinitarian doctrine include Marjorie H. Suchocki, "Trinity," in *Dictionary of Feminist Theologies*, ed. Letty M. Russell and J. Shannon

the ante-Nicene writers, the Cappadocians, Augustine, Thomas Aquinas, and Gregory Palamas to engage contemporary theologians such as Karl Rahner and John Zizioulas and to bring forth a trinitarian theology of God's tripersonal and living presence in Christian life.[23] Elizabeth Johnson also addresses classic trinitarian theologies to construct her liberationist, Sophia-centered, compassionate understanding of God; her main traditional Western interlocutors are Augustine, Anselm, and Aquinas, but also Hildegard of Bingen and Julian of Norwich.[24] Further, weaving together strands from the Cappadocians, Augustine, and Thomas Aquinas, Johnson contends that "the classical themes of the incomprehensibility of God, the analogical nature of religious language, and the necessity of many names for God are a heritage most useful to women's desire to emancipate speech about God."[25]

Verna Harrison, Denise Buell, Virginia Burrus, Sarah Coakley, and others have explored theological metaphor in relation to the rhetorical construction of gender in late antiquity.[26] The intersection of eroticism with mystical experience forms part of the subject matter for Coakley's discussion of the "paradox of power and vulnerability."[27] This relatively new strand is both rich and intriguing and has addressed Greek patristic literature ranging from Clement of Alexandria to Athanasius and to the Cappadocians, especially Gregory of Nyssa, and Pseudo-Dionysius. Although the contemporary authors represent a wide variety of stances vis-à-vis both the church and feminism, their work is closely related to issues raised in the feminist conversation.

Clarkson (Louisville: Westminster John Knox, 1996), 304–5; Janet M. Soskice, "Trinity and Feminism," in Parsons, *Cambridge Companion to Feminist Theology*, 135–50; Ann Loades, "Trinity," in *An A to Z of Feminist Theology*, ed. Lisa Isherwood and Dorothea McEwan (Sheffield: Sheffield Academic Press, 2006), 227–28; Patricia A. Fox, "Feminist Theologies and the Trinity," in *The Cambridge Companion to the Trinity*, ed. Peter C. Phan (Cambridge: Cambridge University Press, 2011), 274–87.

23. Catherine LaCugna, *God for Us: The Trinity and Christian Life* (San Francisco: Harper, 1991).

24. Johnson, *She Who Is*.

25. Ibid., 120. Patricia Fox has argued, in turn, that in her trinitarian theology Johnson shares many themes and concerns with Zizioulas (*God as Communion: John Zizioulas, Elizabeth Johnson, and the Retrieval of the Symbol of the Triune God* [Collegeville, MN: Liturgical Press, 2001]).

26. See, for example, Verna E. F. Harrison, "A Gender Reversal in Gregory of Nyssa's First Homily on the Song of Songs," *Studia Patristica* 27 (1993): 34–38; Harrison, "Gender, Generation, and Virginity in Cappadocian Theology," *JTS* 47 (1996): 38–50; Denise Kimber Buell, *Making Christians: Clement of Alexandria and the Rhetoric of Legitimacy* (Princeton: Princeton University Press, 1999); Virginia Burrus, *"Begotten, Not Made": Conceiving Manhood in Late Antiquity* (Stanford, CA: Stanford University Press, 2000); Sarah Coakley, ed., *Rethinking Gregory of Nyssa* (Oxford: Blackwell, 2003).

27. Sarah Coakley, *Powers and Submissions: Spirituality, Philosophy, and Gender* (Oxford: Blackwell, 2002).

2. The Role of Syriac Tradition in the Feminist Discussion of Trinitarian Theology

Syriac tradition has most often been invoked to champion the role of the Holy Spirit as Mother. The *Odes of Solomon*, the Bardaisanite fragments, the *Acts of Thomas*, and the fourth-century writers Aphrahat and Ephrem have all been brought into the discussion as early witnesses to this notion.[28] This tradition is built upon the simple fact that the word for spirit in Syriac (as in Hebrew) is grammatically feminine. Yet it is significant that female metaphors were elaborated upon that foundation. Especially in liturgical texts even beyond the fifth century, the Holy Spirit continued to hover like a mother bird over baptismal waters and eucharistic elements. Likewise, in the contemporary discussion of female theological language, references to the Holy Spirit as feminine have found a place.[29]

But this is not the only context in which Syriac theological literature is relevant to feminist trinitarian discussion. The *Odes of Solomon* provide a wealth of female imagery not only for the Holy Spirit but also for Father and Son.[30] Both the *Odes of Solomon* and Bardaisan are pertinent to the question whether so-called heretical movements, especially (so-called!) Valentinian gnosticism, found female theological language more congenial than their proto-orthodox counterparts did. Unfortunately, here we find ourselves in a series of circular debates. To wit, are these sources themselves gnostic or Jewish-Christian, or are they simply regional variants, the indigenous versions of second-century Christian teaching in the Syriac environment?[31] Depending on the answers to these questions, the Syriac evidence either supports or contradicts the view that heresy and female theological imagery are naturally compatible.

Ephrem's use of metaphorical language has gained attention not only because of the rich abundance of his poetry but also because his poetry includes

28. See Murray, *Symbols of Church and Kingdom*, 312–20; Jacob, "Motherhood of the Holy Spirit"; Brock, "Holy Spirit as Feminine"; Harvey, "Feminine Imagery for the Divine"; and Harvey's "Odes of Solomon."

29. For example, Johnson, *She Who Is*, 82–86, 124–49; Nicola Slee, "The Holy Spirit and Spirituality," in Parsons, *Cambridge Companion to Feminist Theology*, 171–89.

30. Especially in the enigmatic Ode 19; see Harvey, "Feminine Imagery for the Divine," 125–32; Harvey, "Odes of Solomon," 89–95; but cf. H. J. W. Drijvers, "The 19th Ode of Solomon: Its Interpretation and Place in Syrian Christianity," *JTS* n.s. 31 (1980): 337–55, esp. 352–55; Majella Franzmann, *The Odes of Solomon: An Analysis of the Poetical Structure and Form* (Göttingen: Vandenhoeck & Ruprecht, 1991), 146–52.

31. For a balanced view of these questions in the case of Bardaisan, see Alberto Camplani, "Rivisitando Bardesane: Note sulle fonti siriache del bardesanismo e sulla sua collocazione storico-religiosa," *Cristianesimo nella storia* 19 (1998): 519–96.

reflection on the limits of discursive theological language. His hymns constitute a symbolic mode of doing theology, a choice of genre based not merely
on personal preference but rather on the profound conviction that poetry is
a more suitable form for speech about the mystery of God.[32] As Sebastian
Brock has shown, for Ephrem a chasm (*peḥtā*) separates the Creator from the
creation. That chasm has been bridged by God in three ways.[33] First, God,
who is Being (*itutā*), bridged the gap between Godself and nothingness by
creating the world; further, in creating, God placed signs (*rāzā*, pl. *rāzē*) of
himself in the creation for those who are able to see through the development
of the "luminous eye."[34] Second, God communicated through Scripture, stoop-
ing down to adopt human language, but still speaking in signs or mysteries.
Finally, and most definitively, God bridged the chasm between himself and
the creation by the incarnation. His incarnate Son provides the key to all the
mysteries of nature and Scripture. Despite all these modes of reaching across
the vastness between himself and his creation—or perhaps it is better to say
because of the reality of that reach—God remains hidden and mysterious.
It is precisely for forgetting the hiddenness of God that Ephrem reproaches
the Arians. They "pry" into God's nature and "investigate" God when they
should meditate on the mysteries of revelation.

Yet Ephrem is hardly reduced to silence; he overflows with metaphors just
as he sees the natural world and Scripture overflowing with signs. Although
he loves paradox, he does not simply assert antinomies.[35] Ephrem proposes
that God adopted our language "to explain the incomprehensible through the
comprehensible."[36] Putting on human language like a garment, God took on
names for himself. Some of those names are "borrowed and transient" (*š'ilē
w-'abōrē*), but others are "perfect and holy" (*gmirē w-qaddišē*). The "perfect
and holy" names of God are "exact" or "correct names" or "proper names"
(*šmahē ḥattitē*). They include "Being," "Creator," "the Good," "the Just,"
and "Father." There is no prohibition from using other images for God—we

---

32. Sebastian Brock, *The Luminous Eye: The Spiritual World Vision of Saint Ephrem the
Syrian* (Kalamazoo, MI: Cistercian Publications, 1992), 13–14 and passim.

33. Brock, *Luminous Eye*, 24–27, 40–46, 62–71, and passim; also see Thomas Koonammakkal, "Divine Names and Theological Language in Ephrem," *Studia Patristica* 25 (1993): 318–23;
fully expounded in Koonammakkal, "The Theology of Divine Names in the Genuine Works of
Ephrem" (PhD diss., Oxford University, 1991).

34. Brock, *Luminous Eye*, 71–79 and passim.

35. On the central role of paradox and antinomy in Ephrem's theology, see Kees den Biesen,
Simple and Bold: Ephrem's Art of Symbolic Thought (Piscataway, NJ: Gorgias Press, 2006).

36. Ephrem, *Hymns on Faith* (= HdF) 76:12 (Edmund Beck, ed., *Des Heiligen Ephraem des
Syrers Hymnen de Fide*, CSCO 154, Scriptores Syri [= Scr. Syr.] 73 [Louvain: Durbecq, 1955],
233; English trans. Koonammakkal, "Divine Names," 321).

need only be wary of confusing the "borrowed" and transient names with the "perfect and holy" names.[37]

In light of his dual concern, on the one hand, to recognize the iconic nature of creation alongside revelation in Scripture and, on the other hand, to cultivate an awareness of the hiddenness of God, Ephrem's use of female theological metaphor is arresting. He marks the point of transition from an ante-Nicene Syriac tradition that includes female theological metaphor spontaneously, apparently without a second thought, to a more careful theology engaged with fourth-century Greek debates about the nature of God and the relations of Father, Son, and Holy Spirit.

This brings us to the third segment of my essay and to the question, What do we learn by comparing Ephrem's trinitarian doctrine with the better-known Greek representatives of "pro-Nicene" theology?[38]

3. Ephrem the Syrian's "Pro-Nicene" Trinitarian Doctrine

Ephrem was appointed by Bishop Jacob of Nisibis, a signatory to the Council of Nicaea, to be the "interpreter" (*mpašqānā*)—a post that modern scholars assume combined his skills as hymnographer and scriptural interpreter and put them at the service of the community.[39] His compositions were intended to persuade Syriac Christians that Nicene Orthodoxy was the best statement of Christian truth.[40] For the first time, in Lewis Ayres's *Nicaea and Its Legacy*, Ephrem was included in an overview of fourth-century trinitarian theology.[41] Ayres situated Ephrem as "another major pro-Nicene figure writing in the mid-360s and early 370s" whose opponents were more probably "the Ho-

---

37. Ephrem, *HdF* 44:1–3 (Beck, 141); see Brock, *Luminous Eye*, 60–66; Koonammakkal, "Divine Names," 320–21; Koonammakkal, "Theology of Divine Names," 84–182; Ute Possekel, "Ephrem's Doctrine of God," in *God in Early Christian Thought: Essays in Memory of Lloyd G. Patterson*, ed. Andrew B. McGowan, Brian E. Daley, and Timothy J. Gaden (Leiden: Brill, 2009), 195–237, esp. 212–23.

38. Adopting here the terminology of Lewis Ayres, *Nicaea and Its Legacy: An Approach to Fourth-Century Trinitarian Theology* (New York: Oxford University Press, 2004), 236–40.

39. Kathleen E. McVey, "Introduction," in *Ephrem the Syrian: Hymns*, Classics of Western Spirituality (Mahwah, NJ: Paulist Press, 1989), 3–48, esp. 10.

40. See Sidney Griffith, "The Marks of the 'True Church' according to Ephraem's *Hymns against Heresies*," in *After Bardaisan: Studies in Continuity and Change in Syriac Christianity*, ed. G. J. Reinink and A. E. Klugkist (Leuven: Peeters, 1999), 125–40, esp. 135–36; and Griffith, "Setting Right the Church of Syria: Saint Ephrem's *Hymns against Heresies*," in *The Limits of Ancient Christianity: Essays on Late Antique Thought and Culture in Honor of R. A. Markus*, ed. William E. Klingshirn and Mark Vessey (Ann Arbor: University of Michigan Press, 1999), 97–114, esp. 102–5.

41. Ayres, *Nicaea and Its Legacy*, 229–40.

moian theology promoted by Valens" and, to some degree, Aetius, but not the Heterousian theology of Eunomius.[42]

As Ayres noted, little has been done to define precisely how Ephrem used trinitarian language in his writings as a whole.[43] Essential landmarks were put in place by Edmund Beck's publication of critical texts with German translations of all Ephrem's works; most important among these for Ephrem's understanding of the Trinity are the *Sermons on Faith* and *Hymns on Faith* and Beck's studies of those works.[44] Although Ute Possekel has demonstrated that Ephrem had a working knowledge of some Greek philosophical concepts,[45] Ephrem's manner of argumentation, especially in his hymns and sermons, makes it difficult to present his ideas systematically and to compare him with contemporaneous Greek and Latin theologians; his use of the essential theological terminology does not correspond precisely to theirs.[46] Even his manner of alluding to "Arians" and other nonorthodox Christians has puzzled scholars.[47]

Likewise fairly rudimentary is our knowledge of the way in which he may have adopted and adapted the ideas and images of his Syriac and Greek predecessors and his Greek contemporaries. Again, Beck drew attention to the importance for Ephrem of the metaphor of sun, light, and warmth—a significant variation on the light metaphors used by Greek and Latin writers. Original to Ephrem is the analogy of the Holy Spirit with warmth rather than exclusively with fire or light—images shared with Father and Son.[48] Warmth (or fire) is linked especially with the maternal hovering of the Spirit not only throughout his theology but also in later Syriac liturgical tradition.[49] Paul Russell adduced and explored significant parallels between the trinitarian theologies of Ephrem and Gregory of Nazianzus, notably on the limitations

42. Ibid., 229–31.

43. Ibid., 235.

44. Edmund Beck, ed., *Des Heiligen Ephraem des Syrers Sermones de Fide*, CSCO 212, Scr. Syr. 88 (Louvain: Secrétariat du CorpusSCO, 1961); Beck, *HdF*; Beck, *Die Theologie des Hl. Ephraem in seinem Hymnen über den Glauben*, SA 21 (Città del Vaticano: Libreria Vaticana, 1949); Beck, *Ephraems Reden über den Glauben: Ihr Theologischer Lehrgehalt und ihr Geschichtlicher Rahmen* (Rome: Herder, 1953); Beck, *Ephräms Trinitätslehre im Bild von Sonne/Feuer, Licht und Wärme*, CSCO Subsidia 62 (Louvain: Peeters, 1981).

45. See Ute Possekel, *Evidence of Greek Philosophical Concepts in the Writings of Ephrem the Syrian*, CSCO 580, Subsidia 102 (Louvain: Peeters, 1999).

46. See, for example, Beck, *Ephraems Reden*, 1–20.

47. Griffith, "Setting Right," esp. 101–7.

48. Beck, *Ephräms Trinitätslehre*, 86–116.

49. Sebastian Brock, "Fire from Heaven: From Abel's Sacrifice to the Eucharist. A Theme in Syriac Christianity," *Studia Patristica* 25 (1993): 229–43; Brock, "'Come, Compassionate Mother . . . , Come Holy Spirit': A Forgotten Aspect of Early Eastern Christian Imagery," *Aram* 3 (1991): 249–57; both reprinted in Brock, *Fire from Heaven: Studies in Syriac Theology and Liturgy* (Burlington, VT: Ashgate Variorum, 2006).

of theological language.[50] Rhetorical and theological analysis of Ephrem's work brought Kies den Biesen to assert that Ephrem's theological language is neither antirational nor agnostic nor apophatic but is instead anagogical.[51] This leads the conversation toward spirituality and theosis. A kind of reciprocity between incarnation and theosis, as in Athanasius, has been noted in Ephrem, and it is closely related to his female metaphors of God.[52] Recently Possekel has advanced this discussion with a subtle treatment of Ephrem's doctrine of God, giving particular attention to his engagement with both "Arian" and "Neo-Arian" theological concerns. Especially significant for our subject is her observation that "in addition to the perfect names of God, Ephrem employs a vast number of other metaphors for God. Although these would be considered among God's borrowed names, they do convey important insights into God's nature, and they provide useful vehicles for theological explanations."[53]

4. Female Imagery for God in Ephrem's Theology

The hovering Holy Spirit is not the only feminine presence in Ephrem's trinitarian doctrine. His poetry is rich in maternal symbolism—much of it centered on the womb ('ubā or karsā) and birth-giving (yaldā).[54] For example, he sets in parallel the birth from the womb of Mary and the hidden birth from the Father's womb:

> Christ, You have given life to the creation by Your birth
> that took place openly from a womb of flesh ['ubā d-besrā].
> Christ, You dazzled understanding by Your birth
> that shone forth from eternity from the hidden womb ['ubā gnizā].[55]

50. Paul S. Russell, *St. Ephraem the Syrian and St. Gregory the Theologian Confront the Arians* (Kerala, India: SEERI, 1994); also see Brock, *Luminous Eye*, 145–47; and Biesen, *Simple and Bold*, 293–307.

51. Biesen, *Simple and Bold*, esp. 77–90, 279–319.

52. Brock, *Luminous Eye*, 148–54; McVey, *Ephrem the Syrian*, 74n66; Sebastian Brock, "Introduction," *Hymns on Paradise* (Crestwood, NY: St. Vladimir's Seminary Press, 1990), 72–74; for relevance to female metaphors, see Kathleen McVey, "Ephrem the Syrian's Use of Female Metaphors to Describe the Deity," *ZAC* 5 (2001): 283–84.

53. Possekel, "Ephrem's Doctrine of God," 223.

54. For a more detailed account, see McVey, "Female Metaphors," 261–88; further, McVey, "Images of Joy in Ephrem's Hymns on Paradise: Returning to the Womb and the Breast," *Journal of the Canadian Society of Syriac Studies* 3 (2003): 1–19; see also Brock, *Luminous Eye*, 171–72; Brock, "Holy Spirit as Feminine," 83–84; Harvey, "Feminine Imagery for the Divine," 133–39; Possekel, "Ephrem's Doctrine of God," 227–30.

55. Edmund Beck, ed., *Des Heiligen Ephraem des Syrers Hymnen de Virginitate* (=*Virg.*), CSCO 223 Scr. Syr. 94 (Louvain: Secrétariat du CorpusSCO, 1962), 64; translation, McVey, *Ephrem the Syrian*, 398; for further examples, see McVey, "Female Metaphors," 262–64.

He uses this device of the "twofold birth" to compare and contrast the human and divine in Christ by playing off his human birth and his mother, Mary, against his divine birth/generation and God his Father. Although Ephrem does not call God Mother, he seems also to avoid the name Father when he is speaking of the hidden womb and hidden birth; instead he refers to the Deity/Divinity (f. *alahutā*) or the Parent (m. *yaludā*), the Great One (m. *haw rabā*), or the Great Being (f. *itutā rabtā*).[56] But in one exception to this pattern when he does choose to couple the name of Father with the womb, he also selects the title Word [*meltā*, which is feminine in Syriac] to refer to the Son and develops the image using feminine verb forms:

> The Word [*meltā*] of the Father came from His womb [*'ubeh*]
> and clothed herself in a body in another womb [*b-'ubā*].
> She went forth from womb to womb [*men 'ubā l-'ubā*].
> Filled by Her are chaste wombs [*'ubē*].
> Blessed is the One Who [m.] dwells in us![57]

It appears that he deliberately mixes the gendered language—never restricting any of the persons of the Trinity—or all of them together—to male or female. Instead he allows the gendered images to jostle and confront one another, finally signifying G*d who both incorporates and transcends gender categories.[58]

Ephrem's womb imagery permeates all aspects of his theology from trinitarian doctrine, soteriology, and Mariology to eschatology, sacramental theology, and spirituality.[59] Wombs are to be found everywhere; they are often warm and vital, but they may be cold and dead. So the cosmos, the earth, and the sea

56. Examples culled from Edmund Beck, ed., *Des Heiligen Ephraem des Syrers Hymnen de Nativitate* (=Nat.), CSCO 186, Scr. Syr. 82 (Louvain: Secrétariat du Corpus SCO, 1959): *Nat.* 13.7.3 (Beck 74); *Nat.* 21.5.2; 21.6.3; 21.7.6; 21.8.4 (Beck 105–6); *Virg.* 52.6.8; 52.7.7; 52.7.8 (Beck 167–68); for variations and exceptions, see McVey, "Female Metaphors," 265–66.

57. *Res.* 1.7 (Edmund Beck, ed., *Des Heiligen Ephraem des Syrers Paschahymnen: De azymis, De Crucifixione, De Resurrectione* [= *Res.*], CSCO 248, Scr. Syr. 108 [Louvain: Secrétariat du Corpus SCO, 1964], 79); on gendering the translation in this verse, see McVey, "Female Metaphors," 266n20; cf. Brock, "Invocations to the Holy Spirit," 74, 83.

58. Citing Harvey's remarks on a similar phenomenon in the *Odes of Solomon* ("Feminine Imagery for the Divine," 127), Soskice aptly terms it "rhetorical excess" wherein "God is not lacking gender, but more than gender—that to which our human experience of gender and physicality feebly but none the less really points" ("Trinity and Feminism," 144). On the use of "G*d" in place of "God," its origin and justification of its continued use, see J. Severino Croatto, "Recovering the Goddess: Reflections on God-Talk," in Segovia, *Toward a New Heaven*, 33–53, esp. 47; also Yamaguchi, "Father Image of G*d," in Segovia, *Toward a New Heaven*, 199–224.

59. McVey, "Female Metaphors," 262–76; see also Simon Jones, "The Womb and the Spirit in the Baptismal Writings of Ephrem the Syrian," *Studia Liturgica* 33 (2003): 175–93.

are wombs. Mary's sealed womb anticipates the sealed tomb of Jesus, which, like the cold womb of Sheol, must yield its power to the fiery Firstborn. The womb of baptism gives birth "with three labor pangs . . . the three glorious names of Father, Son, and Holy Spirit."[60] The mind is a receptive womb in which Christ may come to dwell.[61]

Images of the breast and suckling are also prominent in Ephrem's theology. He portrays God (or Deity) as "attuned to us like a nursing woman to her infant."[62] Christ himself as an infant was suckled by Mary, yet as our Redeemer and as Logos/Sophia he brings the milk of life to all the creation:

> He is the Living Breast of living breath.
> By His life the dead were suckled and they revived.
> Without the breath of air no one can live;
> without the power of the Son no one can rise.
> Upon the living breath of the One Who gives life to all
> depend breathing beings above and below.
> As indeed He was suckled with Mary's milk,
> He has suckled—given life to—the universe.[63]

With this sampling of Ephrem's use of womb, birth, and suckling imagery in mind, let us turn to the Cappadocians. Verna Harrison has identified some themes especially in Gregory of Nyssa that bear significant similarities to some of the motifs culled here from Ephrem.[64] For example, she observes that Gregory's *Commentary on the Song of Songs*

> contains texts that speak of *each* member of the Trinity in feminine language. . . . Moreover, it is essential to note that in all the cases where the divine persons are called "mother," "wisdom," or "dove," this feminine language is taken from biblical texts that are read allegorically. The words are givens of sacred Scripture, and Gregory interprets them as referring to a God who is actually neither male nor female. That is, he transforms already existing gender concepts so they can name realities which transcend gender.[65]

60. Ephrem, *Virg.* 7.5.5–6 (Beck 26).
61. Ephrem, *Res.* 2.1; further see Brock, *Luminous Eye*, 129–30, 157, 171; McVey, "Female Metaphors," 275–76; McVey, "Ephrem the Syrian's Theology of Divine Indwelling and Aelia Pulcheria Augusta," *Studia Patristica* 35 (2001): 458–65, esp. 460–65.
62. Ephrem, *Eccl.* 25.18.1 (Edmund Beck, ed., *Des Heiligen Ephraem des Syrers Hymnen de Ecclesia* [= *Eccl.*], CSCO 198, Scr. Syr. 84 [Louvain: Secrétariat du Corpus SCO, 1960], 57).
63. Ephrem, *Nat.* 4.150–53 (Beck 39); translation mine.
64. Verna E. F. Harrison, "Gender, Generation and Virginity in Cappadocian Theology," *JTS* 47 (1996): 38–68.
65. Ibid., 40.

Arguing against Eunomius, Gregory, too, distinguishes between certain names, "Father, Son, and Holy Spirit," that have an essential claim to being true names of God and other names that may be used in a lesser, human sense.[66]

Again, in a manner similar to Ephrem's "twofold birth" theme, yet different in emphasis, Gregory elucidates the generation of the Son from the Father as free from passion and hence "virginal"; thus in his treatise *On Virginity* he draws a parallel with the miraculous impregnation of the Virgin Mary:

> Indeed, it is a paradox to find virginity in a Father who has a Son whom He has begotten without passion, and virginity is comprehended together with the only-begotten God who is the giver of incorruptibility, since it shone forth with the purity and absence of passion in His begetting. And, again, the Son, conceived through virginity, is an equal paradox.[67]

Again, in his *Refutation of Eunomius's "Confession of Faith,"* Gregory links the divine and human virginal parents: "When appearing in the flesh God did not allow the passion of human nature in the constitution of his own body, but rather a Child was generated for us by the power of the Holy Spirit and neither did the Virgin suffer passion nor was the Spirit diminished nor was the Power of the Most High divided up."[68] Harrison has found similar language and imagery in Gregory of Nazianzus's poem *In Praise of Virginity*, where he asserts:

> The original virgin is the Holy Trinity. From the unoriginate Father came Christ the Lord, not having an external origin (for he himself is the Way and the Root and the Beginning of all things), nor again being born in the way that mortals are, but as Light coming forth from Light. From the Child then there is no other beloved child who makes similar boast; so that the one remains the sole Parent, while the other is the sole Son, the most Unique from the Unique; these come together with the great Spirit who comes likewise from the Father, one God opening up in threefold lights. Such is the Trinity's pure nature.[69]

In his *Homily on the Nativity*, Gregory of Nazianzus succinctly hits a similar note: "He that was without Mother becomes without Father (without Mother

---

66. Ibid., 40–41.

67. Gregory of Nyssa, *GNO* 8.1.253.11–16; English translation in *Saint Gregory of Nyssa, Ascetical Works*, trans. Virginia Woods Callahan, FC 58 (Washington, DC: Catholic University of America Press, 1967), 10; cf. Harrison, "Gender, Generation," 46–47.

68. *GNO* 2.335.12–17; English trans. Harrison, "Gender, Generation," 47.

69. PG 37:523.20–524.30; English as quoted in Peter Gilbert's unpublished translation by Harrison, "Gender, Generation," 51.

of His former state, without Father of His second)."[70] But both these Cappadocian writers' stress on the passionless engendering of the Son/Child differs significantly in emphasis from Ephrem's "double birth" theme. Their imagery is more ascetic and centered on the moment of conception or engendering even when it serves as shorthand for the economy of salvation; Ephrem's imagery focuses instead on birth and does not shy away from naming the "wombs" of both God and Mary.

Finally, Harrison notes that in Gregory of Nyssa's treatise *On Virginity*, Mary is put forth as the paradigm of a spiritual birth-giving that may take place in the soul of every Christian, but especially in the virgin: "For what happened corporeally in the case of the immaculate Mary, when the fullness of the divinity shone forth in Christ through her virginity, takes place also in every soul through a virginal existence, although the Lord no longer effects a bodily presence."[71] Similarly, we observe that, again in his *Homily on the Nativity*, Gregory of Nazianzus exhorts, "O women, live as virgins so that you may become mothers of Christ!"[72]

5. Conclusions

What can we conclude from this? First, regarding Ephrem's use of female imagery, Ephrem

not only provides a rich treasury of female metaphors which offset the usual preponderance of male imagery. He also integrates this profusion of images with a sophisticated awareness of the limitations of all human language and experience, and, consequently, of all symbols—whether based in sight, hearing, sound or abstract thought. He formulates this tension, in part, in terms of the theological categories of transcendence and immanence. But he adds new dimensions to this tension by applying notions of compassion and mutuality to God, especially in the context of the Divine love for humankind realized in the incarnation. His use of the feminine theological metaphors is germane to the expression of those insights.[73]

70. Gregory of Nazianzus, *Homily on the Nativity*, PG 36:313.4–16; English trans. C. G. Browne and J. E. Swallow, *NPNF²* 7:345.
71. Gregory of Nyssa, *On Virginity*, GNO 8.1.254.24–28; trans. Callahan, *Ascetical Works*, 11, quoted by Harrison, "Gender, Generation," 56; again, for Gregory of Nyssa the emphasis is on virginity more than on motherhood, though, of course, the latter is implied. On this theme more broadly, see McVey, "Ephrem the Syrian's Theology of Divine Indwelling," and, most fully, Judith M. Foster, "Giving Birth to God: The Virgin Empress Pulcheria and Imitation of Mary in Early Christian Greek and Syriac Traditions" (Master's thesis, Concordia University, Montreal, 2008).
72. PG 36:313.3–4; trans. Brown and Swallow, *NPNF²* 7:345.
73. McVey, "Female Metaphors," 262.

Here I have sketched Ephrem's principal theological motifs, based in metaphors of the female body, and noted their resemblance to the imagery of the two Cappadocian Gregorys. While the one differs from the other two somewhat in the themes of "double birth" versus parallel virginal conception/generation, they share the notion of spiritual birth-giving in the believer. Further similarities, particularly in the concern for theological language, suggest that considerable common ground remains to be explored.

This "gold standard" endorsement of some, although certainly not all, of the Syriac theologian's central motifs emboldens me to ask, Should we not, like Ephrem, search out the symbols of God strewn in nature and Scripture—even those that clearly invite comparison of female bodies with God? When such images are paired with deep awareness of the limits of human thought, language, and experience, why not search them out and, indeed, revel in them, as a form of gratitude for the gracious condescension of the Creator? In his argument for the pertinence of the image of Christ the Physician for contemporary pastoral theology, Vigen Guroian observes, "St Ephrem understood that none of these metaphors and images can stand alone or completely illumine the meaning of salvation. Yet, at a particular moment in civilization, one of these metaphors or images may enjoy special power to reach and touch human hearts and minds."[74] I propose that, likewise, when hearts and minds cry out in prayer, openness to diverse metaphorical language is appropriate. Ephrem himself is an advocate for this approach since his hymns, composed for liturgical use, include many vivid metaphors of God; his use of female metaphors has particular resonance for many in our time. Hence I end with my version of a doxology that is both traditional and radical:

> Glory to the Father from whose womb came forth the eternal Son!
> Praise to Mary from whose womb came forth the Incarnate One!
> Glory to the Son, the Living Breast of Living Breath!
> With His life the dead are suckled and live!
> Glory to the Holy Spirit, our Mother,
> Who brought us forth to true life from the
> watery womb of baptism!

---

74. Vigen Guroian, "Salvation: Divine Therapy," *Theology Today* 61 (2004): 309–21, esp. 310; again, see Possekel, who focuses especially on "God the physician" and on "female metaphors of God" within her discussion of Ephrem's trinitarian language and his understanding of the names of God ("Ephrem's Doctrine of God," 223–26, 227–30).

CONCLUSION

A God in Whom We Live:
Ministering the Trinitarian God

BRIAN E. DALEY, SJ

Eight weeks after Easter, the Catholic Church celebrates the Feast of the Most Holy Trinity, and I suspect that many preachers scratch their heads in desperation at the prospect. In a fairly obvious way, of course, the feast forms an appropriate and solemn conclusion to what we have been celebrating at length and in depth during the whole Easter season: the revelation of the full mystery of the saving God in Jesus Christ. Easter begins with the proclamation of the news that Jesus, who offered up his life in obedience to his Father's will, has been raised from the tomb in glory, has moved among his disciples freely and spoken with them; and it ends with the great feast of Pentecost, fifty days later, when this same Jesus, now in the glory of his Father's right hand, sends the Spirit of holiness—the Spirit who had descended upon him at his baptism—onto those who knew him and saw him risen, to enable them to continue his work and his witness in the world. The season of Easter is the time when the church realizes anew, year after year, that its long tradition of experience following Jesus has led it to a wholly new, paradoxical, endlessly challenging way of conceiving of the ultimate mystery of reality itself, which we call God: that God *is*, as Saint Augustine often reminds us, Father, Son, and Holy Spirit, a "triad" of distinct yet inseparably united figures whom we call—for lack of a better term—"persons." Since the early fourteenth century, the whole Catholic Church has taken this Sunday, at the end of Pentecost week and the beginning of what we now call "ordinary time," as an occasion to meditate on that mind-bending mystery of God and to confess what we have come to know of God only through the resurrection of Jesus and the sending of his Spirit; many of our Western Protestant sister-communities since the Reformation have continued the practice. It is, in a sense, the liturgical year's most general celebration of *God*!

Preachers, of course, and most of us responsible for communicating the church's sense of the good news in an understandable and attractive way, tend to blanch a bit when confronted with the task of talking about God's reality as radically one and irreducibly three. The annals of the Cistercian order, for instance, record a decision reached by a General Chapter in 1230 to observe the new feast of the Holy Trinity—a liturgical celebration just getting started in monastic circles at the turn of the thirteenth century—with high solemnity in all its houses. Feasts of this magnitude were usually designated in the calendar as "feasts with sermon," because the abbot was expected to preach about the day's theme, after Mass, in the chapter house; but on this particular Sunday, the Chapter decided that "a sermon in the chapter house need not be given, because of the difficulty of the subject"! This attitude remains with us. A few years ago, a colleague of mine and I attended a theological conference in Chicago, which ran through a weekend. On the Sunday morning, my colleague went to an early Mass at a local parish and heard from the presider, as probably more than a few of us have heard in our own churches, something like this: "Today we celebrate the feast of the Holy Trinity, which means our belief, as Catholics, that God is one single substance or reality, but is three persons—Father, Son and Holy Spirit. None of us can understand or explain how this can be, and it really isn't worth breaking our heads over it. So let's live good Christian lives and love one another, and we'll probably find out all about the Trinity in heaven!"

Attitudes like this probably come from the Scholastic thinkers' habit, in the late Middle Ages, of thinking and talking about the persons and the reality of God, active in history, in largely analytical and abstract terms: of trying to identify with conceptual clarity what is one in God and what is three. In the old Tridentine rite, for instance, the preface for Trinity Sunday (which was used on all subsequent Sundays from then until the end of the liturgical year) expressed this same desire for conceptual precision in tones of contemplative, devotional awe:

> It is truly right and just [the celebrant would pray] . . . always and everywhere
> to give thanks to you, holy Lord, Father almighty, eternal God, who—with your

only Son and the Holy Spirit—are one God, one Lord: not in the singularity of one person, but in the threeness of one substance. What we believe, then, about your glory, because you have revealed it, this we also hold of your Son and of the Holy Spirit, without any difference or distinction; so that in the confession of the true, eternal Godhead, specific characteristics are adored in the persons, and oneness in the essence, and equality in their majesty. And this the angels also praise with us, as we say, "Holy, holy, holy."

There is grandeur here and wonder at the unfathomable reality of God; but there are also signs of a certain unwillingness, it seems, to go further—to probe the actual implications of this central dogma of faith for the life and prayer of the church. The mystery of God has become a puzzle rather than an invitation.

This theological hesitancy, this reluctance to speak of God as we know him "because of the difficulty of the subject," stands out even more clearly—if only by contrast—when we look at some of the writings of the church fathers, who were directly engaged in the linguistic and conceptual battles over articulating the Christian faith that led, by the end of the fourth century, to our formulation of the doctrine of God's "threeness," as we have come to affirm it. St. Irenaeus, for instance, writing against various forms of gnostic Christianity about 185, emphasizes above all the continuity of God's work in creating the world, in revealing his own nearness and love, and in reaching into history to save the humanity that has largely turned away from him—chiefly in Israel, in Christ, and in the church. In Irenaeus's view, that revelation and growing involvement of God with us is precisely our grounds for thinking and speaking of God as Father, Son, and Holy Spirit, and for enacting our entry into his community of faith by baptism into those names. So he writes, in book 4 of his great work *Against the Heresies*:

> The human person does not see God by his or her own powers, but when God pleases he is seen by men and women—by whom God wills, and when he wills, and as he wills. For God is powerful in all things, having been seen in that [earlier] time indeed, prophetically, through the Spirit, and seen, too, adoptively through the Son; and he shall also be seen paternally in the kingdom of heaven, the Spirit truly preparing us in the Son of God, and the Son leading us to the Father, while the Father, too, confers [upon us] incorruption for eternal life, which comes to everyone from the fact of our seeing God. For as those who see the light are within the light, and partake of its brilliance, even so those who see God are in God, and receive of his splendor. But his splendor vivifies them. Those therefore who see God receive life. (*AH* 4.20.5–6 [*ANF* 1:489, modified])

Later on in the patristic period, as further questions were raised about just how the church is to understand the relationship of Jesus, God's Son, to the one he calls "Father," and how the Holy Spirit Jesus breathed upon his apostles is related to them both, theologians and bishops laboriously worked their way to the coordinated, densely summarized formulation of our understanding of God's reality that we so take for granted. After the challenges of the so-called Arian position in its various forms—all of which agreed in conceiving the Son of God as in some way the first of creatures, the instrument by whom the eternal, unknowable God brought the rest of reality into being—and after a somewhat briefer discussion with those who were reluctant to see the Spirit of prophecy as a distinct divine agent or "person," it was chiefly Greek theologians of the last quarter of the fourth century who convinced the church that its traditional baptismal faith, its sense for God's reality in our midst, can best be summed up in the terse intellectual emblem of a single, indivisible reality or substance that is constituted by the mutual giving and taking of three irreducible, concrete personal agents or hypostases, all working and living as one. So St. Gregory of Nazianzus, the powerfully eloquent preacher and humanist who was, for a little less than two years, the pro-Nicene Patriarch of Constantinople at the beginning of the 380s, speaks repeatedly of the heart of his own pastoral ministry as proclaiming the Trinity that is the Bible's one God; teaching the complex yet simple reality of the biblical God as Father, Son, and Spirit was for him the quintessence of the message all ministry is appointed to give. In his *Second Oration on the Peace*, for instance (*Or.* 23 of his collected sermons), a plea for a doctrinal unity that is able to live within a variety of theological and liturgical formulations, he writes:

> As for me, I will pronounce one formula: always the same, always concise. The Trinity is really a trinity, my brothers and sisters! A Trinity—not a way of listing unequal things together. . . . This trinity, instead, is a combination of things that are equal, of the same value; the word unites things that are naturally one, and does not allow things that cannot be broken apart to be scattered by divisible numbers. . . .
>
> Here [Gregory continues a paragraph later] is what the great mystery means for us. This is what we mean by our baptismal faith in—and our regeneration in—a Father and a Son and a Holy Spirit, and their common name: a rejection of atheism, a confession of divinity. For this is what their common name means. So that to fail to honor one of the three, or to separate them, is to dishonor our baptismal confession: our rebirth, the reality of God, our own share in his divinity, and our hope. (*Or.* 23.10, 12)

In another address, given to his faithful congregation in Constantinople, as he prepared to retire, in the summer of 381—during the Council of

Constantinople, in fact, that gave us the classical summary of faith we profess every Sunday at Mass—Gregory returns to the subject, insisting that preaching about God in the appropriate trinitarian terms has been the core of his pastoral work and is enshrined in the lives and the prayer, the concrete unity in faith and love, of his local congregation:

> There is one concise, public expression of our teaching, a kind of inscription available for all to read: this people! They are authentic worshippers of the Trinity, so much so that any one of them would sooner be separated from this present life than separate one of the three from the Godhead. They think as one, praise as one, are ruled by one doctrine in their relationships to each other, to us, and to the Trinity.
>
> To recount the details [of what we confess] briefly: the One without beginning and the Beginning and the One who is with the Beginning are one God. . . . The name of the one without beginning is "Father," of the Beginning "Son," of the One with the Beginning "Holy Spirit." There is one nature for all three: God. The unity [among them] is the Father, from whom and towards whom everything else is referred, not so as to be mixed together in confusion, but so as to be contained, without time or will or power intervening to divide them. These three have caused *us* to exist in multiplicity, each of us being in constant tension with ourselves and with everything else. But for them, whose nature is simple and whose existence is the same, the principal characteristic is unity. (*Or.* 42.15)

For Gregory of Nazianzus, confessing God as radically one, radically beyond our knowing, radically simple in all that God is, yet always—as that One—Father and Son and Holy Spirit working to create and to save us, is what the Christian community, at heart, is all about. It is how we pray, how we are called to act, how we are able to become one in love with each other.

Gregory's younger, Latin-speaking contemporary, Augustine of Hippo, also devoted a great deal of effort—including one of his most elaborate and challenging treatises—to showing that thinking of the one God of the Hebrew and Christian Bible in relentlessly trinitarian terms is the inescapable linguistic structure of the Catholic faith. The God who is the source and heart of all things is, Christians profess, Father and Son and Holy Spirit. The root of their unity of being and action lies in the Father himself, the infinite and essentially unknowable source who generates the Word or Son eternally from within himself and bestows on the Son the Spirit, whom the Son bestows upon him in return. It is the Spirit's characteristic role—within the life of God and in the history of creation—to be "God-given-away," God as the expression and spiritual embodiment of love. Augustine begins his work with the insistence that this understanding of God is an inescapable summary of what we find in the Scriptures. So he writes near the start of book 1 of the work:

> The purpose of all the Catholic commentators I have been able to read on the divine books of both testaments, who have written before me on the Trinity which God is, has been to teach that according to the Scriptures Father and Son and Holy Spirit in the inseparable equality of one substance present a divine unity and therefore there are not three gods but one God. . . . It was not however this same three (their teaching continues) that was born of the Virgin Mary, crucified and buried under Pontius Pilate, rose again on the third day and ascended into heaven, but the Son alone. Nor was it this same three that came down upon Jesus in the form of a dove at his baptism, or came down on the day of Pentecost . . . , but the Holy Spirit alone. Nor was it this same three that spoke from heaven "You are my Son" at his baptism by John . . . but it was the Father's voice alone addressing the Son; although just as Father and Son and Holy Spirit are inseparable, so do they work inseparably. This is my faith, inasmuch as it is the Catholic faith. (*The Trinity* 1.7)

Much of Augustine's effort in this elaborate meditation on the life and activity of God is to seek for some workable analogy within the created world that we know for this baffling mystery: a spiritual being, radically one in itself, which exists always in something like this threefold structure of activity— something that exists as spirit, present to itself, and generates spiritually, and gives itself spiritually away. His argument, in the course of books 8 through 14 of the work, is essentially to invite us to look within our own spiritual selves, to see in our own existence as unique and conscious persons—in our inalienable capacity to generate concepts and ideas and to love what we are and what we know—at least a dim reminder, "an image in a glass, darkly," of what God is in infinite fullness. It is only the fully redeemed mind, Augustine eventually contends—the mind saved from its own destructive patterns of false knowing and false loving by the incarnation and death of God's Son and by the gift of the Spirit—that can love truly. So only in the bliss of eternity can the created mind become at least a dim parallel, a restored "image" and thus also a "likeness," of its creator.

So in book 14 of the treatise, Augustine recalls Paul's phrase in the twelfth chapter of Romans, "Do not be conformed to this world, but be transformed by the renewal of your mind" (Rom. 12:2 RSV), and suggests that it is this ultimately transformed mind, knowing God and sharing in his life in the activity the Bible refers to as "wisdom," that will at least reflect something of what God is. He writes:

> Although the human mind is not of the same nature as God, still the image of that nature, than which no nature is better, is to be sought and found in that part of us than which our nature also has nothing better [i.e., our conscious self]. . . . This trinity of the mind is not really the image of God because the mind remembers and understands and loves itself, but because it is also able to remember and understand and love him by whom it was made. And when it does this it becomes wise. . . . But when the mind loves God, and consequently as has been said remembers and understands him, it can rightly be commanded to love its neighbor as itself. For now it loves itself with a straight, not a twisted love, now that it loves God; for sharing in him results not merely in its being that image, but in its being made new and fresh and happy after being old and worn and miserable. (*The Trinity* 14.11, 15)

Knowing how God is at once three and one, Augustine seems to be saying, is not simply a challenge to our categories of knowing, but an invitation to us, on the basis of what we know of ourselves and each other, to see all of this human life as an icon of the inner reality of God, in the hope of someday sharing fully in that life as the community of the redeemed. To do this is to be wise.

One could easily multiply the examples. My point is that for these early Christian theologians, speaking of God as three persons composing one unique and ultimate substance, three faces of one transcendent, infinite reality, was anything but airy speculation. It was a summary statement of the whole central message of biblical faith, a way of affirming that the one encountered in creation, in salvation from sin, and in the ongoing life of the church really is God, yet not simply a vague and inarticulated divine principle; rather, the God of the biblical narrative is a God in whose activity the apparently distinct agents of the drama are inextricably related with one another and work our ultimate salvation precisely by drawing us into those relationships.

As religious people, we believe that everything that is, the entire world of our experience, is rooted and grounded in an ineffable mystery of self-revealing, generative love whom we call our God. With ancient Israel, we believe that this God has made our world with the purpose of involving it, and especially the human society that lives and works in it, with himself: that he is near us and has acted continually in history to bless us, to reveal himself to us, and to call us, through chosen human representatives, to belong to him. As disciples of Jesus, who believe that he has risen from the dead and reigns among us as Lord and Christ, we have come to understand God's transcendent presence in a new way, unparalleled in any other religious tradition. We recognize in Jesus a second "face," a second "agent," within the same divine mystery: one who calls the God of Israel his "Father" and who invites us to join him in that same relationship as his brothers and sisters, God's adopted sons and daughters (see Matt. 11:27; John 20:17; Gal. 4:4–7). And thanks to St. Paul (1 Cor. 12:3; Rom. 8:14–17), we are aware, too, that our power to know Jesus and the God of Israel this way—to call Jesus "Lord" and to cry out with him "Abba! Father!"—is possible only because he has given us his Spirit, poured forth within us that incomprehensible, dynamic power who is himself, as Augustine reminds us, "God the Gift."

So to confess Father, Son, and Holy Spirit—the three actors in this drama of creation and salvation—as parallel and coordinate in honor and power, as sharing a single divine name, is to proclaim in a brief, emblematic formula that all three of these "persons" we have encountered and observed in biblical history are, taken together, what Christians mean by "God"; that *each* of them is God, fully; that each of them is irreducibly *distinct* from, and inseparably *one* with, the other two; that what distinguishes them from each other is really only the relationships they have with each other, as sender and sent, giver and given; and that they work *collaboratively*, reciprocally, in human history to reveal to us what God really is and (more wonderful still) to involve us in God's inner life. To speak of God as Father, Son, and Holy Spirit is possible only from the perspective of the *church*'s faith: faith that it has become the heir of Israel, God's unique and special people, in bringing a consciousness of God's reality to the wider world and that it does this on the basis of its own experience of Easter and Pentecost. It is to say that we believe Israel's God—the God of Sinai—has entered the world in a new and final way by sending his own eternally generated Son to be human with us, to take our vulnerability on himself—the results of our sinfulness—and to bear it through death to new and glorious life. And it is to say that we believe the risen Son of God has sent the Holy Spirit, whom he and the Father eternally share with each other, into each of our lives and all of our lives together as a church: to be permanently present in us, sharing God's life with us in the sacraments of the church, guiding and forming the church's faith, enabling us to cry out with Jesus, "Abba! Father!"

To confess God as Father, Son, and Holy Spirit, then, is not simply to confess God as uncaused cause, unmoved mover, source and goal of all that is, but to confess our faith that he has caught us up into his very mystery: that the Father of Jesus calls all of us to be sons and daughters with his own Son, to walk toward him on the way of Jesus, and that he has poured his own Spirit into our hearts and our church to give us the foretaste of our fulfillment, our participation in God's eternal living relationships—what the church fathers call our divinization. And to begin our prayers and our liturgy with this confession, while tracing a cross on ourselves, is to confess that this all-inclusive, saving reality of God has been revealed to us first of all in the paschal mystery of Jesus's death and resurrection. The formulated doctrine of the Trinity of God, which we make in the sign of the cross, is really the shortest profession of faith that we have as Christians; it says it all!

What does all this rather heady reflection imply for our life and our ministry as Christians? One thing, pointed out by a number of theologians in recent years, has been the undeniable fact that our understanding of God is primarily *personal*, and that the way God is personal—by being three eternal, active realities living out constant, uniquely formed relationships to each other—helps us to realize that personhood is always constituted by free, selfless, disinterested relationships of knowledge and love: in us, who are made in God's image, as well as in God's own being. We are persons, in other words, because in our freedom and in our loving relationships with others we come to be more than simply units within the species *homo sapiens*; we are persons because we relate to each other. Our modern, individualized assumptions about human life, which lay so much stress on the autonomy of individuals, on the one hand, and which are so driven by scientific notions of human behavior, on the other, tend to lead us toward an understanding of the person as a natural monad, programmed to perform in certain ways by heredity and conditioned by our environment, but only marginally influenced by our reactions to others. If we are, however, created as persons in the image of God, then the fact that God *is* eternally personal only in the relationships by which Father and Son and Spirit give and receive from one another reveals something crucial about human personhood as well, even if it is only by distant analogy. Our personhood, too, is realized and even constituted by our relationships with each other.

The main proponent of this understanding of the relationship of all personal existence to the trinitarian life of God, in recent decades, has been the Greek Orthodox theologian John Zizioulas, now serving as chief theological advisor to Patriarch Bartholomew of Constantinople under the "curial" title of Metropolitan John of Pergamon. In a collection of studies first published in 1985 under the title *Being as Communion*, Metropolitan John makes his point this way:

> The ontological "principle" of God [i.e., the way God *exists* at all] is traced back . . . to the person. Thus when we say that God "is," we do not bind the personal freedom of God—the being of God is not an ontological "necessity" or a simple "reality" for God—but we ascribe the being of God to his personal freedom. In a more analytical way this means that God, as Father and not as substance, perpetually confirms through "being" his *free* will to exist. And it is precisely his Trinitarian existence that constitutes this confirmation: the Father out of love—that is, freely—begets the Son and brings forth the Spirit.

If God exists, he exists because the Father exists, that is, he who out of love freely begets the Son and brings forth the Spirit. Thus God as person—as the hypostasis [concrete reality] of the Father—makes the one divine substance to be that which it is: the one God.[1]

In response to criticism from a variety of quarters, mainly to the effect that his understanding of personal existence owes more to modern European philosophy than to the thought of the church fathers who first developed our understanding of God as Trinity, Metropolitan John has published a number of further articles refining and developing his "personalist" conception of God, many of which are gathered in a volume called *Communion and Otherness*. Here he reaffirms his earlier position in perhaps still clearer terms:

> The Cappadocian Fathers [Gregory of Nazianzus, Gregory of Nyssa, Basil of Caesarea, in the late fourth century] gave to the world the most precious concept it possesses: *the concept of the person, as an ontological concept in the ultimate sense.* . . . The person cannot exist in isolation. God is not alone; he is *communion.* Love is not a feeling, a sentiment springing from nature like a flower from a tree. Love is a *relationship*; it is the free coming out of one's self, the breaking of one's will, a *free* submission to the will of another. It is the other, and our relationship with him, that gives us our identity, our otherness, making us "who we are"—that is, persons; for by being an inseparable part of a relationship that matters ontologically we emerge as *unique* and *irreplaceable* entities. This, therefore, is what accounts for our being, and our being ourselves and not someone else: our personhood. It is in this that the "reason," the *logos* of our being lies: in the relationship of love that makes us unique and irreplaceable *for another*.[2]

One must bear in mind, of course, that in referring to Father, Son, and Holy Spirit as "three persons" who constitute God, we must be careful not to think of them as "persons" in the same sense each of us is a person: the Holy Trinity is not made up of three *people*, three individuals belonging to the same general species, as would be the case in a small human family; the Holy Trinity is not a committee, or even a community, of three persons with three consciousnesses, three minds, and three wills. As Augustine commented, when outlining the Cappadocian fathers' approach to God:

> In truth, because the Father is not the Son and the Son is not the Father, and the Holy Spirit, who is also called "the gift of God" (Acts 8.20; John 4.10), is

1. *Being as Communion* (Crestwood, NY: St. Vladimir's Seminary Press, 1985), 41.
2. *Communion and Otherness* (Edinburgh: T&T Clark, 2006), 166–67.

neither the Father nor the Son, they are certainly three. . . . Yet when you ask, "Three what?" human speech labors under a great dearth of words. So we say three persons, not in order to say that precisely, but in order not to be reduced to silence. (*The Trinity* 5.10)

Even so, if we are to take seriously—as Christian theology has always done— the Bible's assertion that God created the human being in his own image and likeness, it seems especially appropriate to assume that the way each of us is most centrally and authentically human reflects the way God is most centrally and authentically God: not in the range of our powers, presumably, or in the extent of our knowledge, but in the fact that we exist as persons in relationship to other persons—in the fact that freedom and love, and mutual recognition and communication, lie at the very heart of who and what we are, and that the freely affirmed unity of human persons is central to what we are called, as a species, to become in Christ. To be fully human is to be a person in the fullest sense, because God is infinitely personal.

A second implication of the church's trinitarian conception of God, closely related to what we have just said about human and divine personhood, is the realization that being a person made in God's image involves being sent on a mission. It involves not simply being related to other human and divine persons, in other words, but having the vocation to transform and sanctify the historical human community, to redeem God's creation, as a personal responsibility, by sharing in the historical roles of God's Son and God's Holy Spirit—the very roles that reveal them, in the first instance, as distinct persons within the one divine mystery (see, for instance, Augustine, *The Trinity* 4.29). To be human is to share in some limited yet real way in the triune God's responsibility for the world.

The Second Vatican Council makes this point strikingly in a famous passage in its Constitution on the Church in the Modern World, *Gaudium et Spes*—a passage often cited by Pope John Paul II in his encyclicals:

In fact, it is only in the mystery of the Word incarnate that light is shed on the mystery of humankind. For Adam, the first human being, was a representation of the future, namely of Christ the Lord. It is Christ, the last Adam, who fully discloses humankind to itself and unfolds its noble calling by revealing the Mystery of the Father and the Father's love. . . . He who is "the image of the invisible God" (Col 1.15) is the perfect human being who has restored to the offspring of Adam the divine likeness which had been deformed since the first sin. Since the human nature which was assumed in him was not thereby destroyed, it was by that fact raised to a surpassing dignity in us also. For by his incarnation the Son of God united himself in some sense with every human being. . . .

Christians conformed to the image of the Son, who is the first-born of many brothers and sisters, receive "the first fruits of the Spirit" (Rom 8.23), which enable them to fulfill the new law of love. Through the Spirit who is the "guarantee of our inheritance" (Eph 1.14), the whole person is renewed within. . . . Christians are certainly subject to the need and the duty to struggle against evil through many tribulations and to suffer death; but they share in the paschal mystery and are configured to the death of Christ, and so are strengthened in the hope of attaining to the resurrection.

This applies not only to Christians but to all people of good will, in whose hearts grace is secretly at work. Since Christ died for everyone, and since the ultimate calling of each of us comes from God and is therefore a universal one, we are obliged to hold that the Holy Spirit offers everyone the possibility of sharing in this paschal mystery in a manner known to God. Such is the great Mystery of humankind, which is illuminated for believers through the Christian revelation. (*Gaudium et Spes* 22)

The calling of every human being is identified here, in other words, as being an invitation to share in the way of Jesus, by the power of the Holy Spirit: to love as Christ has loved us, to hope for life in the midst of death, to recognize God not simply as a metaphysical possibility but as our common Father. Understood in these terms, our very humanity sets us a distinct set of tasks: to resist the culture of death and the tyranny of individualism and self-promotion, to build the human family as a community of collaboration toward shared goals, to labor for a peace based on justice and mutual esteem. And our Christian vocation becomes the explicit call to bear a clear witness to this common human destiny, in our life and teaching as a church.

I am a Jesuit: one working at Notre Dame, I hasten to add (and you can form your own judgments about whether this amounts to espionage or simple lack of focus), but a Jesuit all the same—one who has been consistently and most generously welcomed by his friends and brothers in the Congregation of the Holy Cross! So let me bring these reflections to a close with a bit of unashamedly Jesuit lore about our society's founder, St. Ignatius of Loyola. Ignatius, as you may know, like a number of his sixteenth-century Spanish contemporaries, was fascinated by the mystery of God's triune being and meditated on it a great deal in the course of his life—so much so that it became, in a way, the overarching context that shaped his prayer and his understanding of his mission, the "composition of place," as he might have put it, for his growing sense of vocation.

Early in his mature journey of faith, as he was struggling to identify more deeply the call of Christ and to distance himself from his own past sinfulness, while living in the small town of Manresa, near Barcelona, in 1522, Ignatius was privileged to receive a number of mystical experiences of the inner life of the triune God, which seem to have shaped his relationship with God for the rest of his life. His companion Jerónimo de Nadal, one of the most important contemporary interpreters of Ignatius's spirituality and mission, later wrote about that year at Manresa:

> There the illuminations of his understanding were multiplied, his ease in prayer and contemplation was increased, a higher intelligence of spiritual and heavenly things was infused into him. There he received a penetrating knowledge of the Persons of the Trinity and of the divine essence. Even more, he received not only a clear intelligence but an interior vision of how God created the world, of how the Word became flesh. (*Dialogues* 8: *Fontes Narrativi* 2.239)

So fifteen years later, for instance—after having traveled to Jerusalem as a pilgrim, studied in several Spanish universities and at Paris, and assembled around him the group of priest-companions who were to be the core of what would become known as the *Compañía de Jesus* or the Society of Jesus— Ignatius stopped at a church a few miles outside of Rome, in a place called La Storta, while he was on his way to offer the work of his newly formed company to the pope. He tells us in his *Autobiography* that he had been praying for some time to Our Lady that she would "place him with her Son," and in the church of La Storta he "experienced such a change in his soul and saw so clearly that God the Father had placed him with his Son Christ that his mind could not doubt that God the Father had indeed placed him with his Son."[3]

This experience seems to have given him simply a deeper confirmation that the central objective of his own *Spiritual Exercises* had actually been ratified, for him and his companions, by God himself: identification with the mind and heart of Christ, assimilation into Christ's ministry and Christ's plans for the world. And in his own later deliberations about the actual form of life that he and his companions in the Society of Jesus would take upon themselves—as we know from the fascinating fragment of a spiritual diary he kept during 1544 and 1545, while he was discerning God's will for the level of religious poverty the Society should observe—it becomes obvious that prayer for him, even the very practically oriented prayer in which he sought the concrete will of God to guide his own organizational decisions, was almost constantly situated within a consciousness of God's trinitarian being.

> Feeling spiritual intelligences [he writes, for instance, for February 21, 1545], so much so that I seemed to understand that there was practically nothing more

---

3. Ignatius of Loyola, *Autobiography* 96, in *Ignatius of Loyola: Spiritual Writings and Selected Works*, ed. George E. Ganss (New York: Paulist Press, 1991), 109.

to know in this matter of the Most Holy Trinity. . . . I knew or felt—only God knows—that in speaking to the Father, in seeing that he was a person of the Most Blessed Trinity, I was moved to love the entire Trinity, especially since the other Persons were in him essentially. I had the same experience in the prayer to the Son. The same too in that to the Holy Spirit, rejoicing in one after the other as I felt consolations, attributing this to—and rejoicing that it came from—all three.[4]

This emphasis on being so frequently aware of God's being as Father, Son, and Holy Spirit might be taken to reveal nothing more than the particular orientation of one man's quest for God: the very personal spiritual habits of a very practical saint and founder who was also (like many Spaniards of his century) a mystic and visionary. I am convinced, though, that there is more to it than that: that for Ignatius, at least, and for those who share his apostolic vision and urgency in various ways, to share in the work of Christ in the world is always to be drawn into the very life and plan of the Father who sent him, by the power of God's Spirit poured forth within us and in the life of the church. To do the work of Christ, after all—whether in campus ministry or academic teaching or parish work, in ministry to the poor and the marginalized, in service to the sick, or in any other way that the life of the church is extended outward in and to the world—is first of all to speak of God, to bear witness to God's infinitely concrete reality in creation and human history. If we take Christ and the church seriously, this witness is necessarily to point, in some way or other, to a Trinity of persons who form a single, active, dynamically related, ever-present God: the God of the sacraments, the God of human origins, the God of the world's future. If the Trinity is, put simply, what God is, then all Christian ministry is in some way or other to give voice to that mystery, to think and pray within it, to live from it. To do the work of Christ in the world, for all of us, is to be "placed with the Son" in God's plan of salvation.

Father Pedro Arrupe, one of the recent Superiors General of the Jesuits, wrote a remarkable extended essay on this aspect of Ignatius's inner life in 1980, for the instruction of the whole Society, which he published under the title "The Trinitarian Inspiration of the Ignatian Charism." It was a subject that had engaged Fr. Arrupe for some time; his essay was something he had written entirely on his own, as the expression of his own deep convictions about what Jesuit ministry in the world today ought to be. Toward the end, he makes a connection between the existence of every human person and the tripersonal existence of God in terms not all that distant from the approach of John Zizioulas, which we have already mentioned:

4. Ignatius of Loyola, *Spiritual Diary* 62–63 (see Ganss, ibid., 247).

The consummate perfection of the divine personality in its otherness is the exemplar of what a human personality should be: it should not close in on itself, but perfect itself in its relationships and otherness, renouncing all ego-centeredness. In the Divine Persons is found the ultimate model of the "man [or woman] for others." . . . Feeling myself in the other, feeling the other in myself, accepting the other and being accepted, is an ideal of supreme perfection, especially since I know that the other is God's dwelling, that Christ is in him, suffers and loves in him, is waiting for me in him. An apostolate conceived that way is of a purity without limit, of an absolute generosity. (*Five Recent Documents* 96–97)[5]

A few pages further on, near the end of the essay, Fr. Arrupe applies this understanding of our personal union with the persons in God to the ministerial work each Jesuit—and by extension, each of us engaged in the church's work—is called to do in the world:

Just as being "inserted" in the world invigorates our apostolic zeal by enabling us to know at first hand the realities and needs in which the redemption and sanctification of our brothers and sisters is worked out, so knowing the place of the Trinity in the gestation of our charism gives us a living participation in that divine life which is knowledge and love, and directs our apostolic zeal along the right road. Even more: practical experience strengthens and deepens our knowledge down on the level of earthly realities; but at the level of spiritual contemplation, a living knowledge of God is already a sharing and a bliss, a *via ad illum* . . . ; it is the way to the Trinity. That is the road the Society [and surely all of us] must travel; a long road that will end only when we arrive at the plenitude of Christ's Kingdom. But the road has been traced out for us and we must travel it, following the footsteps of Christ as he returns to his Father, illumined and strengthened by the Spirit who dwells in us. (Ibid., 101)[6]

To have even a distant, sketchy conception of what God really is, of how God really acts and really loves, is to share in the mission of Jesus to transform the world and to experience the power of his Spirit as it reshapes our hearts to be like his.

---

5. Pedro Arrupe, *The Trinitarian Inspiration of the Ignatian Charism* (St. Louis: Seminar on Jesuit Spirituality, 2001), 50–51.
6. Ibid., 56.

ABBREVIATIONS

AC	*Apostolic Constitutions*
ANF	*Ante-Nicene Fathers*
AsSeign	*Assemblées du Seigneur*
AT	*Apostolic Tradition*
AugStud	*Augustinian Studies*
Bib	*Biblica*
BZ	*Biblische Zeitschrift*
ca.	circa
CCSG	Corpus Christianorum: Series graeca. Turnhout, 1977–
chap./chaps.	chapter/chapters
CSCO	Corpus scriptorum christianorum orientalium. Edited by I. B. Chabot et al. Paris, 1903–
CSR	*Christian Scholar's Review*
d.	died
Dial.	*Dialogue with Trypho*
Did.	*Didache*
ECR	*Eastern Churches Review*
ET	English translation
EvT	*Evangelische Theologie*
FC	Fathers of the Church. Washington, DC, 1947–
1 Apol.	*1 Apology*
1 Clem.	*1 Clement*
GCS	Die griechische christliche Schriftsteller der ersten [drei] Jahrhunderte
GNO	*Gregorii Nysseni Opera*
HTR	*Harvard Theological Review*
HvTSt	*Hervormde teologiese studies*
IBC	Interpretation: A Bible Commentary for Teaching and Preaching
ICC	International Critical Commentary
Ign. *Smyrn.*	Ignatius, *To the Smyrnaeans*
JEastCS	*Journal of Eastern Christian Studies*

JECS	*Journal of Early Christian Studies*
JEH	*Journal of Ecclesiastical History*
JTS	*Journal of Theological Studies*
KAV	Kommentar zu den Apostolischen Vätern
LCL	Loeb Classical Library
Mart. Pol.	*Martyrdom of Polycarp*
MS	*Mediaeval Studies*
NCBC	New Century Bible Commentary
NPNF²	*Nicene and Post-Nicene Fathers*, Series 2
NRTh	*La nouvelle revue théologique*
NTS	*New Testament Studies*
PG	Patrologia graeca [= Patrologiae cursus completus: Series graeca]. Edited by J.-P. Migne. 162 vols. Paris, 1857–86
PNTC	Pillar New Testament Commentary
Pol. *Phil.*	Polycarp, *To the Philippians*
ProEccl	*Pro ecclesia*
RB	*Revue biblique*
RevScRel	*Revue des sciences religieuses*
RHE	*Revue d'histoire ecclésiastique*
RSR	*Recherches de science religieuse*
RThom	*Revue thomiste*
RTL	*Revue théologique de Louvain*
SA	Studia anselmiana
SC	Sources chrétiennes
ScEs	*Science et esprit*
StPatr	Studia patristica
SVTQ	*St. Vladimir's Theological Quarterly*
TD	*Theology Digest*
TJ	*Trinity Journal*
TS	*Theological Studies*
VC	*Vigiliae christianae*
VCSup	Supplements to *Vigiliae christianae*
Vulg.	Latin Vulgate
WA	Weimar Ausgabe, i.e., *D. Martin Luthers Werke, Kritische Gesamtausgabe.* Weimar, 1883–
WBC	Word Biblical Commentary
WUNT	Wissenschaftliche Untersuchungen zum Neuen Testament
ZAC	*Zeitschrift für Antikes Christentum*
ZKT	*Zeitschrift für katholische Theologie*
ZNW	*Zeitschrift für die neutestamentliche Wissenschaft und die Kunde der älteren Kirche*
ZWT	*Zeitschrift für wissenschaftliche Theologie*

List of Contributors

Khaled Anatolios is professor of historical theology at Boston College. He is the author of *Retrieving Nicaea: The Development and Meaning of Trinitarian Doctrine* and *Athanasius: The Coherence of His Thought*, as well as of the Athanasius volume of the Routledge Early Church Fathers series. He is presently preparing a monograph on soteriology from an Eastern Christian perspective.

John Behr is the dean of St. Vladimir's Orthodox Theological Seminary in New York. He has published numerous books, most recently an edition and translation of the fragments of Diodore of Tarsus and Theodore of Mopsuestia and a monograph on Irenaeus.

Thomas Cattoi (PhD, Boston College) is currently associate professor of Christology and cultures at the Jesuit School of Theology at Santa Clara University. He recently published *Theodore the Studite: Writings on Iconoclasm* (Paulist Press, 2014) and is currently working on a volume on the relationship between patristic and comparative theology.

Brian E. Daley, SJ (DPhil, University of Oxford), is the Catherine F. Huisking Professor of Theology at the University of Notre Dame in Notre Dame, Indiana, and the author of many articles and translations. His books include *Gregory of Nazianzus* and *The Hope of the Early Church: A Handbook of Patristic Eschatology*.

Robert J. Daly, SJ (DrTheol, Würzburg, Germany), is professor emeritus at Boston College. Specializing in liturgical theology and in the Christian understanding of sacrifice, he is the author of *Sacrifice Unveiled* (T&T Clark/ Continuum, 2009).

Matthew Drever (PhD, University of Chicago) is an associate professor of religion at the University of Tulsa. His book *Image, Identity, and the Forming of the Augustinian Soul* was published by Oxford University Press in 2013. Currently he is engaged in a new book project on the theology of human and divine personhood.

Nonna Verna Harrison (PhD, Graduate Theological Union), an experienced patristics scholar interested in the Trinity and theological anthropology, is the author of *God's Many-Splendored Image* (Baker Academic, 2010) and numerous articles and translations.

Paul A. Hartog (PhD, Loyola University Chicago) is an associate professor of New Testament and early Christian studies at Faith Baptist Seminary. His primary interest is second-century Christianity; his books include *Polycarp and the New Testament* (Mohr Siebeck, 2002) and *Polycarp's Epistle to the Philippians and the Martyrdom of Polycarp* (Oxford University Press, 2013).

Joseph T. Lienhard, SJ (Dr. theol. habil., Freiburg, Germany), is professor of theology at Fordham University. He is the author of *Contra Marcellum: Marcellus of Ancyra and Fourth-Century Theology*, among other works. His translation of several of Saint Augustine's writings on the Old Testament is in press.

Bruce D. Marshall is Lehman Professor of Christian Doctrine in the Perkins School of Theology at Southern Methodist University. He is the author of *Trinity and Truth* and *Christology in Conflict* and is presently at work on a book on the Trinity, faith, and reason.

Kathleen McVey (PhD, Harvard University) is J. Ross Stevenson Professor of Church History at Princeton Theological Seminary. Her interests are in patristics and the Orthodox traditions of Christianity. Her publications include *Ephrem the Syrian: Hymns*, and her current project is a book on female theological metaphors in early Christian literature.

John Anthony McGuckin, DD, Archpriest of the Romanian Orthodox Church, holds the Nielsen Chair at Union Theological Seminary and is professor of Byzantine Christianity at Columbia University. He has written extensively on patristics, the New Testament, and Eastern Orthodoxy; his books include *The Orthodox Church: An Introduction* and *St. Gregory of Nazianzus: An Intellectual Biography*. He is currently working on a translation of the *Hymns of Divine Eros* of Saint Symeon the New Theologian and a history of the church in the first millennium for InterVarsity Press.

SUBJECT INDEX

Ablabius, 56, 189–90
Abraham, 90, 123, 169
Adam, 92, 108n32, 128, 169, 227
agency, 34, 154–60, 187
Ammonius Hermeiou, 80
analogy, 163, 189, 190, 191, 222, 225
anaphora, 17–19, 28–29, 30–31
angels, 60–61, 69, 108n32
anthropology, 134, 201
antinomies, 208
Antioch, 35
apophaticism, 192
apostles, 170–71
apostolic authority, 178
apostolic tradition, 8, 30–31, 176
Arianism, 4n2, 27, 31, 32–34, 68, 72, 97, 191, 208, 210, 220
Aristotle, 80, 83, 120, 131
asceticism, 91, 98, 215
assurance, 124–25, 129
Athanasius, 10, 72, 75, 118, 160–61, 170, 191, 211
Augustine of Hippo, 16, 73, 81, 184, 217, 221–24, 226–27
authority, 8–12, 193–94, 196
autocephaly, 185, 198
autonomy, 187, 225

baptism, 3–4, 88, 139
    Augustine on, 111
    as authoritative, 8–12

and the church, 176–81
formulae of, 4–8, 12–14, 47
grace of, 131
Basil of Caesarea, 10–11, 33, 76, 155–57, 161–62, 205
beatific vision, 104n14, 105–6
beauty, 107–8
benediction, 49
berekah, 20, 49
Bernard of Clairvaux, 120
binitarianism, 24, 28, 29, 37
bishop, 170, 179
blasphemy, 127
body of Christ, 16, 167–68
branch theory, of the church, 180

Caesarea, 4n3, 156
Cappadocians, 72, 83, 89, 94, 148, 155, 168, 184, 205, 226
catechesis, 8, 68
catholicity, 193, 198
causality, 58, 184, 194, 197
Chalcedonian Christology, 86, 88
characteristics, of members of Trinity, 66
charity, 142
Christology
    of Athanasius, 170
    of Augustine, 104n13
    of Chalcedon, 86, 88
    of the *Didache*, 22, 43
    formulation of, 79
    in New Testament, 72

of Paul, 203
vs. pneumatology, 167, 173
Chrysostom, John, 28, 33, 34–37
church
    as body of Christ, 167–68
    boundaries of, 176–81
    calling of, 174–76
    confession of, 68–69
    and Eucharist, 19
    as mother, 181–82
    and Trinity, 165–74
    as universal, 43
Clement of Alexandria, 203
Codex Mosquensis, 45
Codex Parisinus, 45
coequality, 66
communion, 150, 160–62, 166.
    See also *koinōnia*
compassion, 57, 70, 215–16
comprehension, 71, 87, 206
conciliarity, 186, 193–94
confession, 68–69
conglorification, 52
consubstantiation, 38
contemplation, 90–91
conversion, 83, 174, 179n30
Cosmas (Alexandrian deacon), 89n21
Council of Chalcedon (451), 79–82, 193
Council of Constantinople (381), 27, 30, 162, 220–21
Council of Constantinople II (553), 80, 81–82, 84

239

Modern Authors Index

Afanassieff, Nicholas, 194–95, 195n41, 196, 196n43
Anatolios, Khaled, xi n3, 157n29, 160n35
Arrupe, Pedro, 230–31, 231nn5–6
Ayres, Lewis, 102n4, 167n7, 184n5, 190, 190n23, 196, 196n44, 209n38, 209n41, 210nn42–43

Balthasar, Hans Urs von, 84, 84nn9–10
Barkhuizen, Jan Harm, 49n65
Barnard, Leslie, 40n6, 43n27, 51n86
Barnes, Michel René, 102, 102n5, 149, 149n9, 183n1, 184, 184n3, 196, 196n44
Barth, Karl, 150, 150nn10–11
Beck, Edmund, 210n44, 210n46, 210n48, 211n55, 212n56
Beeley, Christopher, 74n8
Behr, John, 149n9, 171n12, 176n24
Berding, Kenneth, 48n62
Best, Ernest, 49nn67–68
Biesen, Kees den, 208n35, 211, 211n51
Bonner, Gerald, 103n11, 106n22
Børresen, Kari Elisabeth, 201n6, 203n13, 205n20

Bourke, Vernon, 103n7
Bradley, Ritamary, 203n13, 204n14
Bradshaw, Paul F., 22n13, 23n15, 25, 25n22, 26, 26n26, 26n28, 27n30, 29n35, 30, 30n40, 52n90
Brock, Sebastian, 204n16, 205n20, 207n28, 208n32, 208n34, 209n33, 209n37, 210n49, 211n52, 211n54
Brown, David, 188, 189
Buckley, Michael, 185n7
Buell, Denise, 206, 206n26
Burrus, Virginia, 206, 206n26
Buschmann, Gerd, 40n6, 49n63
Bynum, Caroline, 204n14

Cabrol, Fernand, 47, 47n56
Cadoux, Cecil John, 52n87
Cambier, Jules, 50, 50n78
Cameron, Michael, 110n41
Camplani, Alberto, 207n31
Carpenter, Mark, 40n7
Casiday, A., 104n12
Cavadini, John, 102n4, 105n20
Chadwick, Henry, 104n12
Chilton, Bruce, 19n8, 20nn9–10
Coakley, Sarah, 186–87, 187nn12–14, 188n18, 189, 193, 193n34, 194n37, 197n47, 206, 206n27

Cole, Susan, 203n11
Connolly, R. H., 41n10, 47n54
Constas, N., 181n36
Coppieters, Honoré, 49n66
Corrington, Gail Paterson, 203n13
Courcelle, Pierre, 104n14
Coutts, J., 49n68
Croatto, J. Severino, 212n58
Cuming, George J., 23n14, 28n31, 28n34, 29n36, 30n41, 31nn42–43, 32n45, 33n46, 33n49, 34nn50–52, 37n55, 45n39

Daley, Brian E., 80n2, 81n4, 83n7, 92n30, 94n37
Daly, Mary, 200–202, 200n3, 201nn4–5
Daly, Robert J., 16nn2–3, 18n5, 20n11, 32n44
Day, Linda, 203n10
de Halleux, André, 148, 148n6
Deichgräber, Reinhard, 49n66
Delehaye, Hippolyte, 52n87
Denzinger, Henrici, 19n7
de Régon, Théodore, 184, 184n4
Donaldson, James, 44n36
Dreyfus, François, 50n77
Drijvers, H. J. W., 207n30
Du Roy, Olivier, 102n4

245

Ancient Sources Index

Ambiguum ad Thomam

1 95n40, 96n44

Chapters on Theology and the Economy

2.1 86n14

Epistle

15 89n21

To John the Cubucularius

Letter 2 99n50

Mystagogy

23 85

Opuscula

4 93n33
8 96n45
17 96n45

Quaestiones ad Thalassium

60 90n24, 94
136 90n23

Quaestiones et Dubia

39 90n25

Origen

Commentary on John

2.12 204n17, 205n19

On First Principles

1.2.1 155n21
1.2.12 155n23
1.3.5–7 155n22

Sharar

in toto: 27–30

Tertullian

Against Praxeas

2 152n15
11 153n16, 153n18
23 153nn17–18

On Baptism

6 6n8
13 6n10

Other Ancient Works

Plotinus

Ennead

3.8 194n38

Printed and bound by CPI Group (UK) Ltd, Croydon, CR0 4YY

13/04/2025

14656456-0001